PREFACE

UNIX™* is an elegant and powerful computer "operating system" developed at AT&T's Bell Labs. It is one of the world's most successful operating systems; over 80% of the American universities use UNIX! Now it is becoming available on microcomputer systems, and its use there is expected to grow vigorously, perhaps even astoundingly. Market researchers expect over 100,000 UNIX-based computer systems will be sold in 1985; many of them will be priced well under $10,000. Thus, if you are going to use a computer, the chances are increasing daily that you will use a UNIX system.

An operating system is the software that breathes life into a computer. It gives the computer a personality, it manages the resources of the system, it runs programs, and it handles the interaction between you and the computer. Compared to other operating systems, particularly microcomputer operating systems such as CP/M®†, UNIX offers much greater freedom of action and much more comprehensive services. And, UNIX's sophisticated modular structure lets you expand its abilities even further. UNIX's features spoil its users and make them reluctant to use other systems.

What are these powerful, alluring features? First, UNIX is a "multiuser" OS (operating system)—meaning it allows many users to share the resources of one powerful computer system. Second, UNIX is "multitasking"—meaning it allows any one user to perform several processes simultaneously. Thus you can edit a file, print out another file, and check the spelling of a third file, all at the same time. But what is most important is that UNIX is comprehensive; a low performance operating system like CP/M has 7 built-in commands, but UNIX recognizes over 200 commands! And while you can purchase dozens of utilities and software tools to enhance CP/M (such as spelling correctors, languages, text editors, graphics routines, pattern scanners, etc.), with UNIX these and other tools are already built in and come as standard files! Furthermore, UNIX is an open system. You can customize it to meet your needs, and you are not locked into an inflexible system.

---

*UNIX is a trademark of Bell Laboratories.
†CP/M is the registered trademark of Digital Research, Inc.

UNIX is thriving and growing, and this means that there is a need for good introductory texts. We have tried to meet that need with this book. Our primary aim is to present the basic features of this fascinating operating system and yet not overwhelm you with *all* the ramifications. (That's why we call the book a primer.) But we also introduce you to some of UNIX's most interesting advanced features. (That's where the "plus" in the title comes in.) Throughout, we have used plain language, and we have used examples and figures freely to make the important points clear. We began learning UNIX through a trial-and-error approach that brought us a lot of surprises, some of them pleasant. Then we tried to pass on the benefit of our labors by teaching others to use the system. These experiences have helped us identify with the problems of a new user and we think we can steer you around the pitfalls that await an unwary beginner. We find using UNIX a joy and we have tried to infuse our writing with that pleasure.

We hope this book helps you fully appreciate and enjoy the powers of the wonderful UNIX operating system.

MITCHELL WAITE
DONALD MARTIN
STEPHEN PRATA

UNIX™ PRIMER PLUS

by

**Mitchell Waite, Donald Martin,
and Stephen Prata**

Howard W. Sams & Co., Inc.
4300 WEST 62ND ST. INDIANAPOLIS, INDIANA 46268 USA

International Standard Book Number: 0-672-22028-8
Library of Congress Catalog Card Number: 83-60162

Edited by: *Frank N. Speights*
Illustrated by: *Kevin Caddell*

Printed in the United States of America.

How To Use This Book

Whether you are new to computers or an experienced programmer, this book will give you a good introduction to the UNIX operating system and to many of its important application programs. Here are a few suggestions on how you might use this book.

The best way to learn UNIX is to use it. When you start reading the book in earnest, sit down at a terminal and duplicate our examples. Improvise your own examples. You may be surprised occasionally, but you won't hurt the system.

Glance through the first seven chapters. These chapters contain the *basic* ideas and commands that you will need. We furnish analogies, pictures, and stories to provide mental hooks on which you can hang these concepts. If you are a casual UNIX user, you may not need to read beyond these chapters.

Read the beginning of Chapter 5. It discusses the two editors we cover, and you can decide which one better suits your needs. To a large degree, the presentation of the editors is independent from the rest of the book, so you can switch back and forth between studying an editor and reading the other chapters.

Try the Questions and the Exercises at the end of each chapter. They should give you more confidence in your new skills and they may clarify a point or two for you.

The later chapters explore a variety of the more interesting and powerful UNIX commands and features. You may wish to just browse through them, picking up on those commands and uses that most interest you.

Use this book as a reference book. Our summaries document a large number of UNIX commands. You also can use this book as a lead-in to the official UNIX manual. The manual is rather terse and it is written for knowledgeable users; the summaries and examples that we provide can help you to understand the manual.

Leave the book lying in a prominent place. Your friends and other visitors will be very impressed.

Have fun!

This book is dedicated

To Jim Copening
... who opened a door
M.W.

To Kathleen
... for your love and support
S.P.

To Katie, Jenny, Theresa, Susan, and Greg
... for your love and understanding
D.M.

ACKNOWLEDGEMENTS

Any book attempting to teach the use of a computer operating system to beginners would surely be useless without copious amounts of human feedback and testing of the manuscript. This is especially true for the UNIX system because of its large number of built-in facilities and commands. Further, since UNIX is becoming so popular (as an excellent 16-bit operating system for micros), it is even more critical that the teaching of its operation be carefully explained and completely tested. We have been lucky enough to have several people contribute to the testing and critiquing of our original manuscript and we would like to pay tribute to them here.

First, we would like to thank Jon Foreman, Dan Putterman, and Steve Saunders at College of Marin for the many technical discussions we held regarding UNIX. David Fox of Lucasfilms (author of *Pascal Primer* and *Computer Animation Primer*), Scot Kamins of Technology Translated (author of *Apple Backpack* and the *Apple IIe User Manual*), and Logo/UNIX expert, Brian Harvey of Atari, read the first draft and made invaluable suggestions to improve its readability and accuracy. We are particularly indepted to Brian Harvey, who made numerous technical contributions to the second draft.

The good people at Howards W. Sams gave us the strong support necessary to make this book a real visual treasure, and we would like to give them our sincere regards: Janice Pascoe, Don Herrington, Bill Oliphant, John Obst, and Frank Speights.

We also wish to thank our colleagues at the College of Marin for their help and support: Bob Petersen, Dick Rodgers, Bernd Enders, and Fred Schmitt. Thanks too, to Anne Petersen, Kathleen Prata, Theresa Martin, and Jennifer Martin for their expert proofreading and typing. And, of course, our sincere appreciation to the numerous students who struggled through our earliest efforts at creating a user-friendly introduction to UNIX, especially Jody Evers, Mark Tillinghast, and Judith Griesgraber.

Finally, thanks to Bob Johnson for his fantastic cartoons.

Even with this wonderful support, we may have allowed an error or two to creep into this book. For them, we are responsible; such is the authors' burden.

CONTENTS

1

Introduction to UNIX

In this chapter, you will find:

1   INTRODUCTION TO UNIX

Introduction

Did you know that there are more than 8,000 UNIX installations around the country that are supporting over 200,000 users. Furthermore, the recent introduction of dozens of relatively inexpensive ($8,000–$25,000) computer systems capable of running UNIX means that in the next few years many more of us will become members of the New Information Age.

This book will help you take that step. It is designed to introduce newcomers to the powerful magic of one of the world's most successful operating systems.

An Overview of UNIX

A computer needs special programming called "software" to make it work. UNIX systems have two kinds of software: (1) the operating system software, and (2) the "application" or "utility" software. The operating system software is what breathes "life" into the computer. It behaves somewhat like our subconscious, taking care of a myriad of everyday "housekeeping" details. If the operating system is doing its job, you can do your tasks without ever needing to worry about the computer's inner workings.

The other kind of software, the utilities or application software, does *our* work. This software might include an "editor" (a program that lets you write, change, and store text and data), electronic mail programs, business applications, languages for programming (such as Pascal), and so forth.

UNIX consists of both kinds of software. The term UNIX, then, refers to both the operating system and to a host of useful application programs. In this book, we will just briefly describe the operating system part of UNIX and will spend the majority of our time on how to use the powerful UNIX utilities.

What Is an Operating System?

Those who have suddenly found themselves caught up in computers, and in computing, will find terms, such as "operating system," "utilities," "multiuser," and the like, to be confusing when they are first encountered. We will

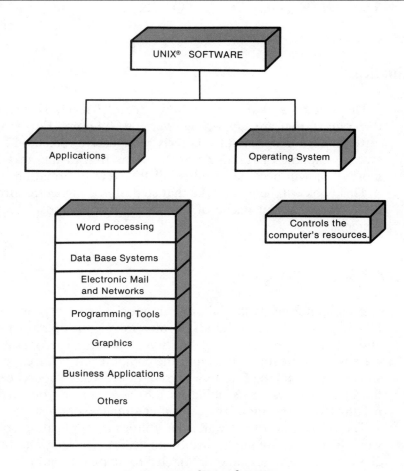

An overview of UNIX.

make a small digression at this point to explain exactly what an operating system is, why it is necessary, and what it does. Those of you who are already familiar with operating systems may want to skip ahead to the next section.

In a very rough way, an operating system is like a teacher in a classroom. The teacher gives out assignments, schedules use of equipment, and, in general, coordinates student activities.

In a much more restrictive way, the operating system coordinates the inner workings of the computer. The operating system relies on an internal clock within the computer to help make simple scheduling decisions, such as when to send information to the printer or when to load and execute user programs. Operating systems, themselves, are just programs created to reduce

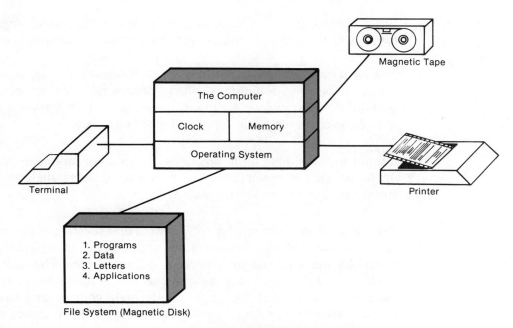

The operating system.

the amount of programming required of you and me, especially the programming that is required to take care of routine and repeated tasks.

An operating system can also be defined as the *link* between the computer and the computer user. Its purpose is to provide the user with a flexible and manageable means of control over the resources of the computer. The three primary functions fulfilled by all operating systems are:

1. *Set up a file system.* A "file" is a block of information stored in the computer. Files can hold letters, programs, budgets, schedules, and anything else that you can type on a typewriter. In UNIX, we can write new files, add to old files, copy files, rename them, or move them elsewhere, all by giving rather simple commands. The UNIX file management system keeps all unnecessary details "hidden" from the computer operator, making it very easy to use, unlike some other systems.
2. *Provide for the loading and execution of user programs.* "Loading" a program consists of placing the program instructions into the proper locations; "executing" a program means to run the program. In providing this service, the operating system lets you run programs that might be written in a high-level language, such as Pascal or BASIC, as well as

17

run programs already written and stored in the file system. Again, the purpose of the operating system is to make this task as simple as possible.

3. *Provide a communication link between the computer and its accessories.* These accessories, sometimes called "peripheral" devices, or "input-output" devices, include terminals, printers, and information storage devices, such as magnetic tapes and magnetic discs.

In addition to these three basic functions, a variety of more elaborate features are found on the newer or larger operating systems such as UNIX. Some additional features in UNIX include:

1. *Provide multiuser time sharing.* This means that several people at different terminals can use the computer at the same time. This process resembles the workings of a kitchen in a restaurant. The staff in the kitchen divides its time preparing and serving several customers simultaneously, sending out the soups, salads, main courses, and so on. An efficient staff will give each patron the feeling of being waited on as if he or she were the only customer. An efficient time-sharing computer will give you the same sensation.

2. *Provide multitasking.* This feature allows one user to run several computing jobs simultaneously, allowing the user to set different priorities for each job as appropriate.

Along with these basic housekeeping operations, UNIX has a library of application and utility software that has grown over the years to provide an essential service to thousands of users. We will take a brief look at how UNIX has evolved into what it is today.

The History of UNIX

During the early 1960s, computers were expensive and had small memories. For example, one middle-priced work horse of that day, the IBM-1620, had only 24K of memory, and was capable of storing about 40,000 numbers. The primary design criteria for all software—languages, programs, and operating systems—was to use memory efficiently and to make programs simple for the computer. This was usually at the cost of being unwieldy for the programmer and other users.

UNIX grew out of the frustrations that programmers faced when working with this early time-consuming software. UNIX was born in 1969 at Bell Laboratories, the prestigious research arm of the American Telephone and Telegraph Company. Surprisingly, it began when one man, Ken Thompson, decided to try to create a less expensive and more hospitable programming environment.

Ken Thompson was working on a program called *Space Travel* that simulated the motion of the planets in the solar system. The program was being run on a large computer made by General Electric, the GE645, which was using an operating system called Multics. Multics was developed at MIT and was one of the first operating systems designed to handle several users simultaneously. However, its use on the GE computer was expensive and awkward. Each run of the *Space Travel* program cost over $70.00. Thompson found a little-used smaller computer made by Digital Equipment Corporation called the PDP-7. He began the burden of transferring his *Space Travel* program to run on the smaller computer. In order to use the PDP-7 conveniently, Thompson created a new operating system that he christened UNIX, as an offshoot of Multics, since it incorporated the multiple-user feature of that system. Thompson was successful enough in this effort to attract the attention of Dennis Ritchie and others at Bell Labs, where they continued the process of creating a useful environment.

The combined work of Dennis Ritchie and the others quickly progressed to the point where UNIX became operational in the Bell Labs system in 1971. Like most software (and hardware, too), UNIX evolved from the best ideas of its predecessors. During the early 1970s, UNIX ran primarily on computers that were manufactured by Digital Equipment; first on the PDP-7 and, then, on the PDP-11/40, /45, and, finally, blossoming on the PDP-11/70 where it achieved widespread acceptance throughout Bell Labs. During the same time, universities and colleges, many of which were using the PDP-11/70 computers, were given license to run UNIX at minimal cost. This shrewd move by AT&T eventually led to UNIX being run at over 80% of all university computer science departments in the United States. Each year, thousands of computer science students graduate with some experience in running and in modifying UNIX.

UNIX, like most operating systems, was originally written in what is called "assembly language." This is a primitive set of instructions that controls the computer's internal actions. Since each computer model has its own particular set of internal instructions, moving UNIX to another computer would involve a significant programming effort. The solution to this problem, and perhaps the key to UNIX's popularity today, was Ken Thompson's decision

19

to rewrite the operating system in a higher level language—one less primitive than assembly language.

The language was called B. Soon it was modified extensively by Dennis Ritchie and rechristened C (in 1973). As a general-purpose language featuring modern commands, C is much easier to understand and use than assembly language. Although not as efficient as assembly language in terms of the speed with which the computer carries out its manipulations, C is much more convenient. This convenience has encouraged users to modify and improve UNIX, thus creating a tremendous amount of additional UNIX software, especially in the areas of word processing and programming support.

The use of C makes UNIX easily portable to other computer systems. Only a very small fraction of UNIX is still written in assembly language. Today, UNIX can be run on a host of other computers besides the PDP-11 series, including the large IBM, Honeywell, and Amdahl computers.

Probably more important (for us potential computer users) is the fact that C compilers (a compiler translates C into the host computer's internal language) are now available for every major 16-bit "microprocessor" on the market.

Microprocessors form the "brains" of microcomputers. One significant fact about microprocessors is that their sophisticated, complex, electronic circuits are all contained in a single small package called a "chip." The first

CHOCOLATE CHIP

microprocessor was a 4-bit chip made by Intel in 1970. It was followed by the 8-bit chip which launched the microcomputer revolution of the late 1970s. Today, we have 16-bit and 32-bit microprocessors that promise even greater computing power at lower cost.

The net result of these advances in hardware is that UNIX can now run on newer, relatively inexpensive, microprocessor-based computer systems. For example, in the late 1970s, a PDP-11/70 time-sharing system with 15 terminals might cost $150,000. In the 1980s, a microprocessor-based system with 15 terminals can be installed for about $35,000. Single-user UNIX systems can cost as little as $10,000.

Today, there are several dozen companies manufacturing microprocessor-based computer systems that will run UNIX. UNIX has already established itself as one of the major operating systems for these new breeds of computers. In addition to UNIX itself, there are several UNIX "look-a-likes," or enhanced UNIX systems, such as Xenix, Cromix, Onyx, Idris, and Coherent.

There are two major reasons why UNIX has achieved such widespread acceptance. First, and probably the most important, is the fact that UNIX is adaptable. Since UNIX is written in the language C, it is fairly easy to modify and can continue to evolve, incorporating the best ideas that are currently available. This adaptability not only applies to adding new software created by experts, but it also allows casual users, even beginners, the power to modify UNIX commands, using the "alias" feature described in Chapter 11 or the "shell script" feature described in Chapter 12.

Of course, UNIX's flexibility means that there will be numerous versions and offshoots in the marketplace. For example, the current most-popular versions of UNIX are the Bell Labs version 7, the Berkeley version 4, and the new Bell Labs System III. This book is based on the Berkeley version 4.1, but even so, 80%–90% of what we discuss will apply to the other versions. Also, some of the commands listed in this book may work slightly differently on different computers. However, UNIX will continue to grow, primarily by adding new features rather than changing old ones. This is a result of the UNIX philosophy, which is the second major reason why UNIX is so widely accepted.

The UNIX Philosophy

The major design factors behind UNIX were to create an operating system and supporting software that was simple, elegant, and easy to use. Elegant, in this context, generally means using a good programming style and thrifty memory management.

These design characteristics led to the following maxims among UNIX builders.

1. Make each program do one thing well. These simple programs often are called "tools."
2. Expect the output of every program to become the input to another, yet unknown, program. This means simple tools can be connected to do complex jobs.
3. Don't hesitate to build new programs to do a job. The library of tools keeps increasing.

The net result of these maxims is that UNIX systems are sometimes said to embody Schumacher's dictum that "small is beautiful." Each UNIX program is a compact, easily used tool that does its job well.

The verdict on UNIX software is already in. Thousands of students, teachers, programmers, secretaries, managers, and office workers have found that UNIX's friendly environment and quality software have become time-saving tools that improve their productivity and employ their creativity.

The following picture was created to give you a peek into the UNIX toolroom and to sum up some of the ideas presented here.

What Can UNIX Do for You?

As we mentioned earlier, in addition to the UNIX operating system, which manages the internal workings of the computer system, UNIX provides a host of built-in software. An easy way to get a quick overview of these UNIX features is to divide this software into two major categories. These software categories could be called the Electronic Office and the Programming Support areas. Since this book is for beginners, most of the UNIX software we will discuss deals with the services that we describe under the term, "The Electronic Office."

The Electronic Office

The concept of an electronic office is still young and changing. Most discussions of what it involves center around four interrelated functions. These are:

1. Word processing.
2. Electronic filing.
3. Electronic mail and networking.
4. Electronic data bases.

Word Processing

UNIX has dozens of tools to help you do word processing. These tools go by such names as editors, text formatters, spellers, and even syntax checkers that test your sentence structure. With these tools, here's what you can do.

You can throw away the liquid correction fluid, correction tape, scissors, erasers, paper clips, scotch tape, and all the old tools you used for dealing with printed words on paper. You now deal with words inside an electronic memory. They can be moved and changed easily, quickly, and efficiently, allowing you to type in your words without thinking about the appearance of your finished product.

A text "formatting" program permits you to turn a ragged right margin into a beautiful, professional looking, typeset format just by using a few keystrokes. Or, suppose you want to add a new sentence in the middle of your many paged document? No problem. Simply enter the editor "insert" mode and start typing away. Because the editor has an electronic brain, it can instantly shift all the text in its memory forward to make room for new words and do it without losing its paragraph structure. Or, suppose you spelled the same word incorrectly in 157 places? Quick work for your editor . . .; merely enter the "search and replace" command and the computer will automatically change all occurrences of the misspelled word as you sit back comfortably and sip on your cafe mocha. Other things you can do with simple key operations include the moving of paragraphs and blocks of text, doing boldface, underlining, superscripts, and subscripts.

These UNIX tools allow you to do things that would require days of work using a standard typewriter, such as converting a long double-spaced document to a narrow column width, single-spacing a document that is suitable for publication, printing individually addressed copies of the same letter, sorting and merging mailing labels, proofreading and correcting large documents for spelling and syntax errors, and generating an index.

This kind of power will change your writing experience drastically. The ability to change words quickly and easily gives them a new malleability. Words become like wet clay. You rework the same sentence over and over, deleting old words with hardly a care until the words say exactly what you mean. Because of the fluid nature of the work, you become braver. Your creativity tends to flow more freely because you're not concerned with how the typing looks. Neither are you hampered by the fear of putting an idea in the wrong place, for you can easily move the words around later. You create and let the machine manage the words.

Electronic Filing

Supporting the word processing function and providing even more services is the electronic file system. To visualize the file system, imagine that all of the written information you now store in a file cabinet or on shelves were placed in an electronic file cabinet.

A file can contain anywhere from one to several thousand words or numbers. Anything you can type on a typewriter can be placed in a file. Each file has a name that you give it and each file contains whatever information you put in it, as we will discuss in Chapters 4 and 7.

Once you have a file system set up and your information stored there, here's what you can do. Using just simple commands, you can get a listing of the titles of every document or file, or you can read any one file in its entirety, or you can scan (search) the first 10 lines (or the last 10 lines) of a number of files looking for specific information. Better still, suppose you want to find a certain letter that was sent to you about a specific product. No problem. You can let "UNIX do the walking." A simple command will scan one or more files searching for the product name. Phone listings, product listings, bills, and bookkeeping can all be kept on file and scanned in the UNIX file system. And the best part about the UNIX file system is that the files can be organized in exactly the same way that you might arrange them in a cabinet.

You can build categories of files. For example, you might group together all of your travel files in one drawer (called a directory in UNIX), insurance records in another drawer, clients' accounts in a third drawer, and so on. Files can be easily moved from one drawer to another, copies can be placed in several drawers, or files can be cross-referenced. Files can be added together, cut in two, or merged alphabetically. In fact, all of the word processing functions described earlier can be applied to any of your files, even though you may not have originated them.

Electronic Mail and Networking

Another related, necessary, and very useful function of the electronic office is electronic mail and networking. As you might have noticed by our comments at the beginning of this chapter, electronic communication is the glue that holds together the Electronic Office. With electronic mail, you can emerge from the doldrums of paperwork shuffling into the more creative and rewarding task of information processing. For example, in writing letters, you have all the advantages of word processing that were described earlier. And, you can send copies instantly to anyone on the UNIX system.

One extremely valuable use of electronic mail occurs when two or more people collaborate on a letter, book, report, plan, or any typewritten document while using the word processor/mail system. Each person can write his or her portion of the plan, mail it to someone else for changes or additions, and then receive a new copy back again. No paper or postage is involved. These plans, as well as any UNIX file containing any kind of written information, can be mailed (transmitted) easily and simply with just a few keystrokes.

Another useful and related feature of UNIX mail is the "reminder" service. If you keep a diary of your important dates in a file called "calendar," the UNIX operating system will send you mail each day reminding you of your day's schedule.

In addition to sending "local mail" to people connected up to your computer, another feature of the UNIX mail system is its ability to send mail to other UNIX computer systems anywhere in the country. This is done by one

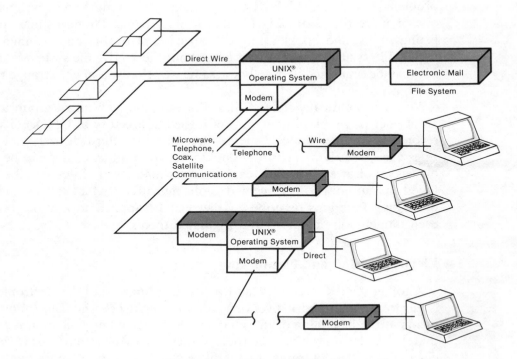

Electronic mail and networking.

UNIX computer automatically telephoning other UNIX computers using a device called a "modem" and, then, sending "mail" over the phone lines. There are several such telephone "networks" that offer this service; some, such as USENET, are devoted exclusively to UNIX computer systems.

Sending electronic signals over telephone wires can be relatively slow (about one page of text per minute). Other types of networks, such as Ethernet, allow several UNIX computers to be connected together, sharing resources at very high speeds. Ethernet is a local network for use in one or more adjacent buildings.

Meanwhile, over the horizon, there are various satellite networking systems.

However, no matter which network or what kind of computer you have, if it's running the UNIX operating system, you can communicate with other UNIX systems using all the resources of the word processing and electronic filing system plus the electronic mail features we have described in this book.

Electronic Data Bases

The electronic data base is essentially an extension of the filing system. In fact, the UNIX file system already has the features of a very simple data base. For example, if you placed all the phone numbers you use (or even a whole telephone book full of numbers) into one or more UNIX files, you can search those files for a particular name and number with just a single command. Or you could pull out all the names beginning with "John" and place them in a new file.

A simple data base is just a collection of information that you can add to or delete from, or can sort in various ways. It can be searched using key words and specific information can be copied and/or printed. The UNIX file system can do all of this easily as we will show you in later chapters.

There are more powerful data base systems, such as "INGRES," available for running under UNIX. These systems have more sophisticated searching and storing techniques. To give you a simple example (using the telephone book again), you might want to find all the phone numbers listed under "John," living on "Beachside Avenue," but *not* those starting with the numbers 454-. The beauty of a data base system like INGRES is that you can pull out specific information and can create a new data base from it extremely fast and easily.

Although UNIX can easily set up both small data bases (using ordinary file commands) and sophisticated data bases (using a specialized program), UNIX is not designed to handle large volumes of high-speed transactions such as a bank or airline might use.

The future of electronic data bases looks especially promising for business firms. Payroll, sales, and employee records, inventories, clients' records, and economic data can all be placed right at your fingertips for easy access.

However, to make the maximum use of data bases, they must be tied into the electronic office. The features of word processing, electronic filing, and electronic mail give the data base user additional powers. For example, you could extract specific information about an inventory, add a few remarks, and mail the result to several other people.

UNIX has all four of these features ready to go.

It should be emphasized again that these four features of the electronic office add together synergistically so that the total is much greater than just the sum of its parts. You can purchase computer systems and software that would do two or three of these functions or provide these services to just a few people. However, when all these services are provided to the majority of the office workers in a company, it can radically change the nature of their work. It has already been demonstrated that these features improve productivity and communications, save money, and improve the general attitude people have towards work. That's why organizations large and small, local and national, such as the National Research Council of England, have adopted UNIX as their software standard.

Another key element in the use of these electronic tools is "user-friendliness." How easy is it to use them? How much time do they save? Is it worth spending the time to learn how to use them? In the case of UNIX and the Electronic Office, we believe the answer is an overwhelming "YES." The thousands of employees at Bell Labs, AT&T, at colleges and universities, and in other businesses and industries have already discovered this fact.

Besides the electronic office features described above, another major service of UNIX is to help programmers solve programming problems, as we will briefly discuss in the next section.

Programmer's Support Tools

UNIX was originally developed to make life easier for the programmer. However, it turned out that programmers wanted the electronic office programs just as much as everyone else. Thus, both types of UNIX software have evolved side by side and are widely used. The programmer's support tools can be classified into four major areas. These are:

1. *Programming Languages and Compilers.* All of the major languages (FORTRAN, BASIC, Pascal, COBOL, etc.) can be run under UNIX. This means that if UNIX has a standardized form of a language (for example, Standard FORTRAN 77), then any FORTRAN 77 programs written anywhere in the country (and there are thousands of these) can be run on your system and vice versa. In addition to the most popular languages, dozens of other languages, such as SPITBOL, APL, LOGO, RPG, RP-1, and so Forth, have been placed on specific UNIX systems.

   Of course, since UNIX is written in C, that language is available and widely used to write programs. A "compiler" translates programs written in the high-level languages into the primitive instructions that the machine can understand.

   In Chapter 6, we show you how to write and run programs that are written in different languages.

2. *Command Line Interpreter* (called the *shell*). The "shell" is the link between most users and the computer. It is a program that accepts

commands that you type into the computer and, then, executes them. The shell contains over 100 built-in commands just ready for your use. Actually, there is more than one version of the shell. The shell provided with the standard Bell Labs version of UNIX is called the *Bourne shell* after its developer. The other widely current shell is called the *C shell* and was developed at the University of California, Berkeley. Most of the features we discuss in this book are common to both shell versions, but some are exclusive to the C shell. In this book, we will explain over 60 commands and what they will do for you.

The shell can be used as a programming language having many of the features of C. The programmability of the shell, which few other systems offer, plus the large number of built-in commands that the shell already knows, gives programmers exceptional flexibility and power. This power is enhanced by the "pipe," a UNIX concept that has since been widely copied. Pipes, as we will discuss later on, allow programs or commands to be coupled together. The output of one program becomes the input to another, etc.

3. *Programmer debugging tools.* The first time a program is written, it rarely runs correctly. Usually, the program has errors or "bugs" that need fixing. UNIX, like most systems, has built-in programs that help locate these errors. However, we will not be discussing these programming aids in this book. If you're interested in reading further, you might look at the articles suggested in Appendix B.

4. *The Programmer's Workbench.* This package of UNIX tools is especially valuable for team-oriented programming projects. These software tools maintain a complete record of all changes made to a program as it is written. They also allow programs to be tested in part as they are developed. The package also simplifies the task of transferring programs to other computer systems. The Programmer's Workbench is available from Bell Labs. We will not discuss it in this book.

All of these support services for programmers, together with the adaptability of the UNIX software in general (written in C), are the main reason that UNIX is so widely used and taught on college campuses.

Who Should Read This Book?

As we mentioned in the preface, the goal of this book is to introduce UNIX's marvelous tools to both the beginning and the experienced computer

user. The tools that we have chosen to present are those most needed for work in an electronic office and those needed to write and run simple programs in various computer languages, such as Pascal, FORTRAN, or C. So if you are a secretary or manager in an office, or just a student in a computer science class or a computer hobbyist, who is interested in UNIX, this book is for you. We hope you will enjoy learning UNIX as much as we have enjoyed writing this book.

2

Getting Started: *login, who,* and *finger*

In this chapter, you will find:

- Getting Started
- Establishing Contact With the Shell
  - The Keyboard
  - Logging In
  - The Prompt Character
  - The Password
  - Setting Up and Changing Passwords
  - Logging Out
- Correcting Typing Errors
- Erasing Characters
- Canceling Lines
- Some Simple Shell Commands
  - The *date* Command
  - The *cal* Command
  - The *who* Command
  - The *finger* Command {BSD}
- Review Questions
- Exercises at the Terminal

2   GETTING STARTED: *login, who,* and *finger*

Frederick Porteous Ramshead III answered the door. Outside stood a small, white-haired woman with rosy-red cheeks, a merry grin, and an avaricious glint in her eyes,

"Freddie Pet, let me in!"

Frederick made way, noting the small suitcase in her hand.

"Grandma! You haven't left Grandpa again! And my name is Frederick, not Freddie Pet."

"Of course I haven't, and of course it is, deary. Now offer your dear Granny a seat and a pitcher of lemonade."

"Yes, yes, please make yourself comfortable. But why . . ., I mean, to what do I owe the honor of this visit?"

"Freddie, I am here to make you a wonderful offer, one that will change your life for the better—and you certainly can use that!"

"That's wonderful, Grandma," beamed Frederick, while inwardly groaning. He recalled the 20 newspaper subscriptions she sold him last year so she could win that trip to Disneyland.

"You have a computer terminal, right?"

"Right, Grandma." She had sold him one last Christmas.

"Well, I'm going to give you access to a UNIX system."

"A UNIX system?"

"You're sure quick on the uptake, Pet. Yes, a UNIX system." Grandma spilled open the suitcase, liberating a mass of documents, brochures, and contracts. She fixed Frederick with a steely gaze. "Now pay attention to what I am going to tell you."

An hour later, a triumphant Grandma left with a nice new check, and a dazed Frederick Porteous Ramshead III sat down at his terminal, wondering what he had gotten into this time. He attached the modem and dialled the number Grandma had given him. Soon the following display appeared on his screen:

```
Grandma's Old-Fashioned UNIX
Login:
```

He typed in the login name Grandma had given him: freddie (someone already had taken frederick). The terminal responded with

```
password:
```

He typed in the password Grandma had given him: pet. The system responded with

```
WELCOME TO GRANDMA'S OLD-FASHIONED UNIX, WHERE
VALUE AND QUALITY ARE NEVER COMPROMISED.
```

```
%
```

What did that "%" mean? Did it indicate that Grandma was getting a percentage of his computer time payment? Oh, now I remember; that was the signal that UNIX was ready for his next command. Grandma called it the UNIX "prompt." The first thing he wanted to do was change the "password" Grandma had given him. He typed in the **passwd** command and changed his password to "hotshot." Ah, that was better.

What next? He tried **date** and the system displayed today's date and time. Frederick set his calendar watch by it. Next, he typed in **cal 11 1912** to find out on what day of the week Grandma was born. The UNIX system showed the month of November, 1912. Then he typed **who** to find out who else was logged in. Hmmm, was "pierre" his brother? He looked at the handy reference card Grandma had left him and found the command **finger**, which gives more detail on users. He typed in **finger pierre** and found that "pierre" was, in fact, his brother, Pierre Robustus Ramshead; yes, Grandma had hit him up, too. Well, he'd better learn some more about the system. He typed in **learn**, a command used to access a built-in UNIX tutorial.

An hour later, much more knowledgeable about the UNIX file system, he sat back, typed in **logout**, and gave a sigh of relief. *This* time, Grandma really had done him a favor. UNIX *was* going to improve the quality of his life.

* * * *

Getting Started

How do you get involved with UNIX (aside from the obvious method of being hustled into it by your grandmother)? For many, it is a matter of circumstances. UNIX is by far the leading computer operating system used on our college and university campuses; large numbers of students learned their first computing knowledge on UNIX systems. Now, college graduates, in increasing numbers, are entering business and industry and are demanding access to UNIX and UNIX-like systems. Computer manufacturers are responding to this demand by offering a wide range of microcomputer and minicomputer systems.

Another possibility is that you might buy time on a UNIX system. Some universities and private companies are now offering this service at very reasonable rates. And recently, we have started to see the introduction of UNIX operating systems on some of the more expensive home personal computers. This last possibility is perhaps the most attractive. With your own computer, you don't have to wait for open terminals or open phone lines, and you don't have to see your work slowed down by heavy demands on a time-sharing system. Yet, if you want, you still can tie into other UNIX systems with your modem and you can share information and programs with other UNIX users.

We'll suppose that by choice or fate, you now are involved with UNIX. So let's begin our study of the nitty-gritty of UNIX. We'll begin by showing you how to get started on a UNIX system. The first sections of this chapter describe the major characteristics of a typical terminal that you might use to communicate with UNIX. Then, we'll discuss the "login" and "password" process in detail. Finally, we'll look at the first of many simple, yet powerful, commands in the UNIX shell.

Establishing Contact With the Shell

Lured on by the wonders of UNIX, you want to unleash its powers. But how do you get in touch with the system? The precise details will vary from system to system, but the following general features will hold:

1. You need a means to communicate with the system; normally the means will be a keyboard and a screen display. That is what we will assume you have.
2. You will have to tell the system who you are by "logging in." (Computers that handle multiple users are usually selective about whom they deal with.)
3. You may have to give the system a password. (Computers are not too good at recognizing faces, so they may need a password to reassure them that you are who you say you are.)
4. When you are done, you need to "logout" to tell the UNIX system you are done. Otherwise the system will just sit there, waiting for your next instructions.

Now we will go over how these features are implemented.

The Keyboard

If you have seen a typewriter, you should find the typical computer terminal keyboard at least vaguely familiar. It will have keys bearing symbols such as D and U; you may recognize them as the English alphabet. The top row of letters on the standard keyboard start with the letters QWERTY. There also are keys bearing the likenesses of the digits—5, 3, and so forth. Then there is an assortment of other symbols—#, *, ~, @, etc. Some of these symbols (or characters, as they are called) are not usually found on a typewriter. Then there are keys bearing words or abbreviations of words—keys such as RETURN (C/R on some keyboards), CTRL (for control), break or BREAK, SHIFT, and ESC (for escape). Many of these keys have been added to the standard keyboard just to make life easier for us computer users. The convention we will use to indicate which keys to push as part of a UNIX command will be to place the key in brackets [ ]. Thus we might say, push the [return] key or the [esc] key. In addition, we will always use lowercase letters to indicate keys even though some keyboards list their letters in uppercase. When we want you to type out the letters in a command, we will place the letters in boldface, as in "type the **who** command."

Other special keys and their meaning to UNIX will be discussed later in this chapter. In the following figure, we present a typical keyboard.

A typical keyboard.

It would be nice if there were a standard keyboard layout, but not all keyboards are identical. Fortunately, there is a standard "character set" that most keyboards carry. It's called the ASCII (pronounced askee and standing for American Standard Code for Information Interchange) character set. You can find a copy of this set of characters in Appendix D. It includes the uppercase and lowercase alphabets, the ten digits (0–9), punctuation marks, and an assortment of symbols including " ", the blank or space that we find between words. Unfortunately, although different terminal manufacturers agree on where to place the alphabet and the numbers, they mostly go their separate ways when it comes to deciding where to physically place the other characters of the ASCII set. So if you learn on one terminal, be alert when you use a different kind of terminal that some keys will be in a different location. Also, be aware that many terminals have special keys not found in the ASCII character set, for example, keys with special editing or graphics uses.

Using the keyboard is a straightforward procedure; you depress a key to send the symbol on it to the computer. To send a 6, depress the [6] key. There are a few additional facts you should know.

1. Some keys bear two symbols. Ordinarily, the lower of the two characters is sent when the key is depressed. To send the upper character, depress one of the [shift] keys at the same time you depress the character key. For example, on the keyboard shown earlier, you must depress a [shift] key, hold it down, and then press the [6] key to send the & character.

2. Standard terminals (there are exceptions) transmit lowercase alphabetic characters unless the [cap lock] key is on or if a [shift] key is used at the same time. Thus, depressing the [a] key transmits an a (lowercase), but depressing the [a] key while pressing the [shift] key transmits an A (uppercase). This combination often is represented by [shift-a]. The [cap lock] key acts like you are permanently holding a [shift] key down, except that it only affects the letters. Thus, if the [cap lock] key is engaged, hitting the [b] key produces a B, but hitting the 6 key produces a 6, not an &. To get an & with the [cap lock] on, you must use the [shift] key as before. *Note:* Often the the actual keys on the terminal are labeled with uppercase letters, but since they nonetheless normally transmit lowercase letters, we will use labels like [a] rather than [A] to stand for the key.

3. Additional characters are produced by depressing a regular key and pressing the [control] key or [ctrl] key. For example, pressing the [control] key and the [d] key together produces a character called "control–d." We will use the notation [control–d] to indicate when this character is to be typed. It sometimes is displayed on the screen as ^d and sometimes it is not displayed at all. It is truly one character although it takes two symbols to represent it on the screen. Such

"control-characters" are often used for special purposes in computer systems.

4. On many typewriters, the lowercase letter "l" and the numeral "1" are interchangeable. This is *not* so for a computer keyboard. If, in your typing, you have used the letter "l" for the number "1," you must break that habit. The same situation holds true for the uppercase letter "O" and the digit "∅" (zero). They are *not* interchangeable.

5. Develop a good touch. Many keyboards will repeat a letter if you hold a key down too long. You may find yourself typing lines like "Myy ssincereest apoloogiees.." if your terminal is sensitive and your fingers are not.

There is one key we wish to spotlight now; this is the [return] or [c/r] (for carriage return) key. On an electric typewriter, depressing this key advances the paper a line and returns the typewriter to the left-hand margin of the page. It performs a similar function on a computer terminal. More importantly, depressing the [return] key tells the system that you have finished that line. For example, we soon will discuss the UNIX command **who**. If you are on the system and type the letters w-h-o and nothing else, nothing will happen. A useless command? No, the problem is that UNIX doesn't know you are finished. You could be a slow typist working on **whoami** or **whoa there, black thunder, i think i see trouble ahead**. What you need to do is press the [return] key! Depressing the [return] key tells the system, "Okay, I'm done; take it from here." Thus, the correct way to use the **who** command is to type

who [return]

where [return] stands for the return key, not for typing the word "return." At first, we will remind you a few times to hit the return key after each new line command, but later we won't bother—we have confidence that you will soon be hitting [return] automatically. (A lot of times people bang the [return] key when the system seems to be "stuck." This usually is harmless and occasionally even helps.)

Logging In

The first step in using a UNIX system is to login. The word "login" comes from the old shipping era when you would fill out the daily "log" with a record of activities. In our context, we are signing into the "log" of the UNIX system. We will assume that you are at a computer terminal that uses a screen display that is turned on and you are rarin' to go. The first key you should push is the [return] key. UNIX should respond with something like

```
Welcome to UNIX VERSION 7.3. Enjoy Your Computing
login: ☐    <──────────────────────────────── (cursor)
```

Immediately after the colon in "login:", there should appear a rectangle of light, or else an underscore mark (blinking on some terminals), called the "cursor." The cursor is nothing less than your guiding light; it shows you where your next letter will be placed on the screen. Now you type in your login name. (What's your login name? It is a name by which you are known to the UNIX system and it usually is assigned to you by the folks running the system. Let's assume your login name is "sneezy.") Each time you type a letter, it appears on the screen and the cursor moves over a space. *Don't* put in a space before or after your name; the space is just another character, so adding a space would make the name different. Login names normally are in lowercase letters only, so type "sneezy," not "Sneezy" or "SNEEZY." Finish up with a [return]. This, then, is the line:

login: **sneezy** [return]

The Prompt Character

If your account has been set up without a password, and if the system recognizes "sneezy" as a valued client, there will be a pause while the system sets up things for you. It may give you some messages, and then it will display a "prompt," which is a special symbol at the left of the screen that tells you UNIX is in operation and waiting for your next command. Each time you give UNIX an instruction, it will give you a new prompt symbol when it has finished and is ready for the next instruction. The standard prompt usually is a "%" or a "$". We will assume the prompt is a %. The [return] and the % serve the same purpose as "over" in CB talk; [return] tells UNIX that you are done and it is its turn, and % tells you that UNIX is done and it is your turn.

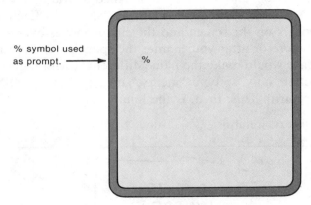

% symbol used as prompt. →   %

The UNIX prompt.

The Password

What if you do have a password or what if the system does not recognize "sneezy" as a login name? In either case, the system responds to the previous line with

```
password:
```

You then type in your password. The letters you type *will not* appear on the screen as you type them. (After all, what good is a password if someone can look over your shoulder and read it off the screen!) Again, follow with [return]. (It may happen that your account will be set up so that you neither have nor need a password to use the system.) If you have no password and still get this message asking for one, then you've blown it. The system doesn't recognize you, but being a bit cagey, it asks you for a password anyway. The login procedure won't continue unless you give some password (anything) at this point, so fake one. This won't get you on the system, but it will cause the system to revert to asking for your login name again. At this point, you may notice that you mistyped your login name. For example, suppose in answer to "password," you (sneezy) type

```
snowwhite
```

for your password. UNIX then compares the password you typed with its record of sneezy's password. If the two agree, you are welcomed to the system and presented with the system prompt. If you typed either your login name or password incorrectly, the system responds with

```
login incorrect
login:
```

and you get to try again. You can repeat this as many times as necessary unless the powers-that-be are worried about CPU thieves and have installed a trap to catch repeated attempts to login.

Setting Up and Changing Passwords

It is a simple matter to give yourself a password if you lack one. Once you are logged in and have the UNIX prompt, you type in the command

```
passwd [return]
```

Notice that the command **passwd** is in lowercase letters. Also note that the command is **passwd** and not **password**. This saves you time in typing a command you may use once a season, if that often. (For some people, these UNIX abbreviations are a minor system foible, since the abbreviations are harder to remember than the full word.) After you type in this line, UNIX will respond with

```
changing password for sneezy
New password:
```

You then type in your choice of password. It will not appear on the screen. Then, hit [return]. UNIX will respond with

```
Retype new password:
```

This is to check to see that both you and UNIX have the same word in mind. Since you don't see what you type, this check is valuable. If the two words you typed in disagree, UNIX responds with

```
Mismatch-password unchanged
%
```

The return of the % prompt means UNIX is finished with the **passwd** command. If you want to continue, you have to start over again by typing **passwd** and [return]. You should get used to the fact that when UNIX does something successfully, it *doesn't* say "good" or "correct." Instead, it just gives the old prompt.

If the words you typed did agree, UNIX will accept the new password and you will have to use it the next time you log in. It is a good practice to write down your password and keep it somewhere handy.

To change your password, you go through the same procedure, except there is one extra step. After you type **passwd** and [return], UNIX will ask

```
old password:
```

You type it in, follow it with [return], and the procedure continues as described above. This step is a precaution to keep your friends from jokingly changing your password when you get called away from the terminal for a moment.

What sort of passwords can you use? Generally, a password should contain at least one nonnumeric character and should be at least 6 characters long if you use only uppercase or only lowercase characters. (You can get away with 4 characters if you use a wide variety of character types.) Thus, some unacceptable passwords are 007007, pip, and doog. Some acceptable examples are cowboy, hog666, TOADLIFE, 747F22, and rPg@2. Oh yes, make sure you remember your password. If you forget it, you will have to deal with whoever administers the system.

Logging Out

The process of signing off when you are done is called "logging out." To log out, you need the UNIX prompt showing. Thus, you can't log out in the middle of the **passwd** process. If the prompt is showing, just type

```
logout [return]
```

This should log you out, and the screen should now show your system's standard welcome message:

```
Welcome to UNIX VERSION 7.3 Enjoy Your Computing
login:
```

You can now walk away feeling that you have said goodbye properly to UNIX and that the terminal is ready for the next user.

There are things you can do that will cause the system to not log you out right away after you give the command. We assume you don't know how to do these things yet. Later, we will give some examples (such as background jobs running) and tell you what to do.

Correcting Typing Errors

Even the most talented fingers sometimes stumble as they sweep across the keyboard, and even the most talented minds sometimes have second thoughts about commands they have typed. One of the major advantages of an interactive system such as UNIX is that it gives you the opportunity to see and correct errors immediately.

The mechanics of making corrections depends on the terminal you use and on how your particular system has been set up, so what we will describe here are just possible examples. You'll have to check out what works on your system.

Erasing Characters

The key most commonly used to "erase" a character (usually moving the cursor back one space and removing the offending character) is the [backspace] key. For example, if you type

```
passqr
```

and, then, press the [backspace] key twice, the cursor will back up (move left) over the last two letters, erasing them at the same time, and leaving the word

```
pass
```

The user then can correctly complete the command by typing a "w" and a "d" to produce

```
passwd
```

Another common choice for erasing characters is [control–h]; this means depressing the "control" key and the "h" key simultaneously. Yet another choice that is widely used on "hard-copy" terminals is the "pound" or "number sign" (#) key. This choice works somewhat differently since a hard-copy terminal cannot erase parts of text on a screen. In this case, using the "#" key erases the character from the computer's memory but not from the screen. Thus, the correction for the last example would appear this way on the screen:

```
passqr# #wd
```

The first # cancels the "r" and the second # cancels the "q." When you hit [return], **passwd** is transmitted to the computer.

For all these examples, you can't erase a letter in the middle of a word without also erasing all the letters after the erroneous one. For example, to correct

```
pusswd
```

you would type, using the #-example,

```
pusswd# # # # #asswd
```

Here you had to erase (from right to left) the d, w, s, and s to reach the u. We then had to retype the letters s, s , w, d after replacing the u with an a. The other less common keys used to erase characters are the [delete] key and the [rub] key.

Canceling Lines

A character that cancels a whole line instead of just one letter is called a "kill" character. For example, on our system, the kill character is [control–u].

(Note that [control–u] is considered a single character even though it involves two keys–[control] and [u]–depressed simultaneously.) Thus, the sequence

```
passwd [control–u]
```

produces a blank line; **passwd** is deleted.

Some systems use "@" as kill character. Usually, in this case, the line is not erased from the screen, just from what is transmitted. For example, the following sequence will transmit **passwd**:

```
osddef@passwd [return]
```

Another special character is the "interrupt" character, which usually is generated by a [control–c]. This causes the system to "interrupt" what it is doing. It will not only erase lines but will halt many procedures after they have started running. This is the common way to stop the computer from doing something and returning to the shell (%).

The [break] key sometimes will do the same thing: "interrupt" a process. However, on some systems, [break] will lock up a terminal, not only interrupting UNIX but, also, the user. We suggest that you *do not* use [break] for any reason.

Some Simple Shell Commands

Suppose you have logged on successfully by answering the login: and password: questions properly. The UNIX prompt appears on the screen, telling you that UNIX is ready to obey your every command. After your first flush of joy and power, you may wonder "What do I tell it do?" There are literally thousands of legitimate possible answers to that question and, in this section, we will look at four of the simplest: the commands **date**, **cal**, **who**, and **finger**. These are examples of "shell commands," which are standard commands recognized by the shell program. We choose these four commands because they are easy to understand and useful.

The Bourne Shell and the C Shell

The shell is that part of the UNIX operating system that acts as an intermediary between you and the computer. It relays your commands to the computer and returns its responses to you. As we write this book, there are two main varieties of shells in widespread use. The first is the Bourne Shell, named after the man who developed it. It is the shell that comes with the standard Bell Labs release. (It may vary slightly from older to newer releases.) The second is the C Shell, developed at the University of California at Berkeley, and included as part of Berkeley Software Distribution (BSD) packages. Most of what we say in this book applies equally well to both shells, but there are differences. We have confined the major differences to Chapter 11, but we do discuss occasional commands and options that belong to the C Shell and which may not be found on other versions. We will mark them {BSD}.

How can you tell which shell you have? You can ask. You can try using a C-Shell-only feature and see if it works. Usually you can tell by the prompt. The Bourne Shell normally uses a **$** as the main prompt, and the C Shell normally uses the **%** as the main prompt.

We've talked about the shell as being the liaison between you and the computer. Let's see how that works in the context of shell commands. First, after you log in, the shell provides you with a prompt (a %, we're assuming). It's now ready for your move. You then give it a command, such as **date**, and hit [return]. The shell then identifies this command as something it knows and causes the command to be executed, usually giving you an output on the screen. Whether it gives you an output or not, you will know when it is finished since the shell sends another prompt to the screen to let you know it is your turn again. If you type in a command it doesn't recognize—**getlost**, for example—the shell lets you know with a response like

```
getlost: Command not found
```

Now, let's try out one of the commands that does work; the **date** command.

The *date* Command

The **date** command displays the current date and the time on the screen. To use it, type **date** after the prompt. (Recall that commands to be typed literally will be given in boldface.) Thus the line will appear as follows:

```
% date
```

UNIX provides the %, you provide the **date**. (Don't forget that you have to hit the [return] key. In a way, the [return] key is *your* prompt to UNIX while

% is its prompt to you.) This line of instruction is known technically as the "command line." The result of giving this command is that UNIX prints out the date. It would look something like this:

```
Tue Jun 1 14:49:19 PST 1983
```

Note that UNIX uses a 24-hour clock and gives the time to the second. The full sequence of command and response would look like this:

```
% date
Tue Jun 1 14:49:19 PST 1983
%
```

You can now give another command after the last prompt.

As we introduce each new command, we generously will supply you with a summary of the command. Here is the summary for **date**.

Summary: `date`—gives date and time		
name	**options**	**argument**
`date`	none	none
Description:	When you type **date**, UNIX returns the date and time of day to you.	

Although **date** has no options or arguments, we will give a brief explanation of what those terms mean now. Some commands perform "operations" such as printing or listing information. These types of commands often need something to operate on. The name of the thing operated on is called the argument. Many commands are not complete without an argument and some commands can have more than one argument. For example, to print two files one after the other, you would use a print command and the names of the two files. These two file names would be two arguments.

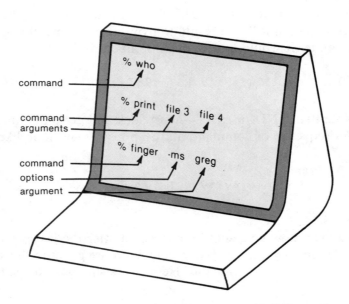

Commands, options, and arguments.

Options generally are variations on the command. For example, a printing command may have an option to double-space the output.

Our next command gives another example of arguments.

The *cal* Command

You might want to use the **cal** command next; this does not give information about California, but rather it prints out a calendar. This command takes you up a level in sophistication for it requires an argument. This argument does not mean to give UNIX any backtalk or disputation; it means, as we mentioned above, to provide additional information. In this particular case, we have to supply the command with the year for which we want the calendar. Thus, the command line to produce a calendar for the year 1776 would look like this:

```
% cal 1776
```

When we push [return], the display shows:

```
                              1776

        Jan                        Feb                        Mar
 S  M  Tu  W  Th  F  S      S  M  Tu  W  Th  F  S      S  M  Tu  W  Th  F  S
    1   2  3   4  5  6                  1  2  3                      1  2
 7  8   9 10  11 12 13      4  5  6  7   8  9 10      3  4  5  6   7  8  9
14 15  16 17  18 19 20     11 12 13 14  15 16 17     10 11 12 13  14 15 16
21 22  23 24  25 26 27     18 19 20 21  22 23 24     17 18 19 20  21 22 23
28 29  30 31               25 26 27 28  29           24 25 26 27  28 29 30
                                                     31
```

(We are only showing the first three months of the twelve-month display here to save space.)

The command is **cal** and the argument is **1776**.

The full calendar may not fit on your screen. You can hit [control–s] to stop the screen display before January rolls up off the screen and, then, hit [control–q] to start it up again.

You also can get just the calendar for one month by typing the number of the month before the year. You can use either a one-digit or a two-digit number for the month; thus May is 05, or 5. Here is the command line to get the calendar for July 1872:

```
% cal 7 1872
```

Summary: cal—provides a calendar		
name	**options**	**arguments**
cal	none	[month] year

Description:	This command provides a calendar for the year typed in after the command; there must be at least one space between the command and the year. The year should be in the range of 0–9999 AD. You can get the calendar for just one month by preceding the year with the number of the month, numbered from 01 to 12.
Example:	To see the calendar for May 1942, type **cal 05 1942**

The month is an "optional argument," meaning it can be omitted. The year is not optional, however, you must give it. We can represent the form of this command by

    cal [month] year

The brackets around "month" tell us "month" is an optional argument. You don't actually type in the brackets when you use the command. In this book, the fact that neither [month] nor year is in boldface tells us that we don't type those words literally but, instead, type in a value for them.

You can use **cal** for future calendars (up to the year 9999) as well as for the present and the past.

The *who* Command

UNIX is a time-sharing system, which means several people can use the system at the same time. In recognition of the inquisitive human nature, UNIX has a **who** command. When you give this command, UNIX responds with the list of people logged into the system at that moment. The command and its results might look something like this:

```
% who
bob         tty04   Aug 23    8:27
nerkie      tty07   Aug 23    8:16
catfish     tty11   Aug 23    8:38
sneezy      tty15   Aug 23    8:52
granny      tty21   Aug 22   23:13
boss1776    tty24   Aug 23    9:01
%
```

The first column gives the login name of the user. The second column identifies the terminal being used. The label "tty" is a throwback to the days when most terminals were Teletype® machines that printed out on paper rather than on a screen. The number of the tty can provide a clue as to where the person is logged in from if you know what room specific terminals are placed in. The remaining columns give the date and the time each user logged in using the 24 hour clock. It looks like granny has been on the system all night, or maybe she forgot to logout again.

Teletype is a registered trademark of the Teletype Corporation.

But who is catfish? Your system may have some commands that tell you more about your comrades in computing. An example is **finger**, which we will discuss after the following **who** command summary.

Summary: who—who's on the system		
name	**options**	**arguments**
who	none	**[am I]**

Description: This command, when typed without an argument, tells you who is currently on the system. It gives you the user's login name, the terminal name, and when he logged on. If you ask **who am I**, it gives you this information just about yourself and it may also tell you which UNIX system you are on.

Example: To find who's on the system, just type **who**.

The *finger* Command {BSD}

This command can be used with or without an argument. Without an argument, it works like **who** but it also gives the users' "full" name, their idle time, and office number. The idle time is the time, in minutes, since they last gave UNIX a command. The **finger** command might give the following display.

```
% finger
Login          Name          TTY  Idle  When        Office
bob       Robert Sniggle     04         Tue  9:27    SC256
nerkie    Nercules Pigrow    07    7    Tue 10:16    BH019
catfish   Kitty Trout        11         Tue  9:38    WD40
sneezy    U. R. R. Reader    15         Tue 10:52    WD38
granny    Henrietta Goose    22   15    Mon 23:13    ZX280
boss1776  V.I. Parsons       26         Tue 11:59    Penthouse
%
```

Ah, Ha! "catfish" is the new person in the next office. To learn more about her, you can use **finger** with an argument. In this case, the argument is her name: login or first or last. For example, use the login name:

```
% finger catfish

Login name: catfish                In Real Life: Kitty
                                      Trout
Directory: /usr/catfish            Shell: /bin/csh
Last login: Tue Aug 23 9:38 on
  tty11
Plan: To utterly master Pascal
%
```

Here we learn her home directory (more about home directories in the next chapter) and that she uses the C-shell (/bin/csh is the C-shell and /bin/sh is the original Bell Labs shell). We also learn her current intentions in using UNIX. This full printout of information is called the "long form." Yes, there is also a "short form"; it is the one line per user form we saw in the first example.

If we had used **finger Kitty** as a command, we would get a similar listing for all persons named "Kitty" who have accounts on the system, whether or not they are currently logged in. The command **finger Kitty Trout** would provide information about all persons named "Kitty" or named "Trout."

The **finger** command is useful if you need to know someone's login name (to send "mail," for example) but you only know his or her real name.

The **finger** command also has what are known as "flag options," or "options," for short. Such options come after the command and before the argument and usually are in the form of a hyphen followed by a letter. Here is an example:

```
finger -s catfish
```

Here the **-s** option stands for short form. Note that there is no space between the - and the **s**, but that there are spaces on either side of the option. The result of giving this command would be

```
catfish  Kitty Trout            11          Tue  9:38  WD40
```

You can use more than one flag option in a command; an example would be **finger -m -s catfish**.

Some commands allow options to be strung together in any order. For example,

```
finger -m-s John
finger -ms John
finger -sm John
```

would all give the same results. However, rearranging option flags is not always possible.

In the following summary and in future summaries, we will include descriptions of some of the options available for each command.

Summary: finger—provides information about users

name	options	arguments
finger	[-m, -l, -s]	[name . . .]

Description: When used with no argument, this command gives a list of who is on the system, giving the login name, the real name, the terminal, the idle time, the login time, and the office, if known, for each user. (This list of information constitutes the "short form.")

When used with one or more names, it provides the above information plus information about the home directory and the shell of the named users. (This augmented list of information constitutes the "long form.") The **finger** program will search for all users whose login name *or* real name matches the given name.

Options:

-m This option causes **finger** to search only for *login* names that match the argument name(s). Thus, **finger -m john** will give information only about a person whose login name is "john" and will ignore people named "john" but who have a different login name.

-l This forces **finger** to display out the long form.

-s This forces **finger** to display out the short form.

Example:

To find out the login names of every user named "John," and to print out just the one line summary, type

```
finger -s John
```

The result might look like this:

```
Login     Name              TTY  Idle        When      Office
jonny     John Grock        5                12:13     ACH000
buny0234  John Bunyon       17   <Jul  4 14:14>
daffy     John Duck         18   <Aug  2 06:02>         CB122
suzie     Susan John        19   <Aug 22 15:23>
john      Johannes Brahms   22   <Aug 17 09:42>         MU244
```

Notice that **finger** finds all "Johns," whether that be the first, last, or login name of the user. The "< >" indicate the user is not currently logged in. In searching for names, **finger** ignores whether or not a name is capitalized. The command

```
finger -s -m John
```

> would produce just the last line of this listing since the **-m** option restricts the **finger** command to searching only login names.

Although your system may not have **finger**, it will have stored somewhere the information that **finger** uses. Much of the information is kept in a file named **/etc/passwd**, and we will discuss this file in Chapter 12.

In the next chapter, we shall see how to communicate with our fellow computer people using electronic mail.

Review Questions

To help you fix in your mind the material from this chapter, we are providing you with some questions to test your knowledge. We also will provide the answers in order to keep you reassured.

A. Matching Commands

Match the command in the left column to the corresponding description in the right column.

1. who	**a.** Gives the date and time.
2. passwd	**b.** Tells who's logged in.
3. date	**c.** Produces a calendar.
4. cal	**d.** Gives information about users.
5. finger	**e.** Lets you choose a password.
6.	**f.** Deposits huge sums of money into a Swiss bank account.

B. Questions

1. Identify the arguments, if any, that appear in the following commands:

    a. finger zinger
    b. cal 1984
    c. cal 09 2025
    d. who

2. What's the difference (besides "or") between **passwd** and "password:"?

3. Which of the following is a basic purpose of the UNIX prompt, i.e., the "%" or "$"?

    a. To demonstrate UNIX's ability to produce unusual symbols.

b. To tell you UNIX is ready to accept a command.

c. To tell UNIX that you are finished.

4. What happens when you fail to hit [return]?

5. What does the phrase "hit [control–s]" mean?

6. How do you correct a typing error on the same line as the cursor?

Answers

A. 1–b, 2–e, 3–a, 4–c, 5–d, 6–f

B. **1.** a. **zinger** b. **1984** c. **09** and **2025** d. no argument. **2.** "password:" is a prompt from UNIX asking you to type in your password; **passwd** is a UNIX command that initiates the process of changing your password. **3.** b, of course. **4.** Nothing happens; UNIX just sits patiently, waiting to be told that you are done and that it is its turn to do something. **5.** It means you are to depress the [s] key and the [control] key simultaneously. **6.** It depends on the terminal you use. Generally, terminals use the [backspace] key, or the [rub] key, or [control–h], or the [#] key.

Exercises at the Terminal

The best way to learn UNIX is to use it. We hope you have been trying out the commands as you read about them. Here are some tasks you can try doing using the material in this chapter.

1. Login to your UNIX system.
2. Type **whp** and correct it to **who**.
3. If you don't have a password, give yourself one now. If you do have one, change it to a new one.
4. Find out how many people are logged in and who has been logged in the longest.
5. Find the time of day.
6. Find out on what day of the week you were born.
7. Find out on what day of the week is January 1, 1991.

3

Electronic Mail and On-Line Help: *mail, man,* and *learn*

In this chapter, you will find:

- Electronic Mail
  - The UNIX Mail System
  - Sending Mail to Yourself
  - Reading Your Mail
- Electronic Chit-Chat: *write*
- For Advanced Users
- The On-Line Manual
- Learning With *learn*
- Exercises at the Terminal

3   ELECTRONIC MAIL AND ON-LINE HELP: *mail, man,* and *learn*

Electronic Mail

Electronic mail is a fairly recent term for a mail delivery system that replaces conventional mail delivery with an electronic computer-based service. Electronic mail can also replace some types of telephone calls and inter-office memos. The form of electronic mail used with UNIX is sometimes called a "mailbox" system. Each user with a log-in account has a "mailbox" file that other users can send mail to.

An electronic mail system has several major benefits:

* You create the correspondence on your keyboard or terminal and you have word processing capabilities that make entry and corrections easy.
* You can mail identical copies to several users simultaneously.
* You can print paper copies and even have them typeset.

ELECTRONIC MAIL

U.S. MAIL

* The mailing process is much faster than postal letters—a message reaches its destination almost instantaneously.
* Electronic mail doesn't interrupt the recipient the way a phone call does; you can read your messages at your leisure.
* The letter can be electronically filed with all the inherent advantages of that process.
* The letters may be mailed locally, such as in a local UNIX time-share system, or letters may be routed through one of several world-wide distribution networks, such as USENET.
* No stamps, envelopes, or paper are required and no trips to the post office are needed.

The major disadvantage of this type of electronic mail is that the recipient must log into his or her account to notice whether mail has been sent or not. Other forms of electronic mail can overcome this disadvantage. For example, mail can be printed on paper at the receiving end and, then, be hand-delivered like an office memo or telegram.

The Unix Mail System

The UNIX mail system uses the command word **mail** (**Mail,** on some systems) to initiate both the sending and the receiving of mail. The mail system actually contains several dozen options for preparing, delivering, reading, and disposing of mail. These options are briefly described in the on-line manual (under **mail**). However, most new users can get along very nicely with the simple command sequence we will describe next.

Sending Mail to Yourself

If you want to remind yourself to do something the next time you log onto the UNIX system, the mail system provides an easy service. If your login name is Beth, and if you have the shell prompt appearing on the screen, you just type **mail beth** and push [return]. You can now begin drafting your letter. The UNIX mail system does not use a prompt here. Just keep typing, using [return] as you would a carriage return on a typewriter. When you complete the letter, push [control–d] or, on some systems, a lone period at the beginning of a new line. The sequence would look like this:

```
% mail beth
Take the dog to the vet.
```

```
Sign up for the exercise class at school.
Give a big party for Bob.
[control-d] <———————————————————————— (or a lone period)
%
```

The next time you log in, the greeting would include the happy announcement "you have mail."

Reading Your Mail

To read your mail is simplicity itself. First, you type **mail**. The system responds by telling you how many letters you have, who sent them, and when. To read the first letter, just type a 1, then push [return], and so forth. Here is a sample mail treat.

```
% you have mail <———————————————————————— (UNIX displays)
% mail <—————————————————————————————————— (You type)


Mail version 2.0 March 5,1982. Type ? for help. <—— (UNIX displays)
2 messages:
  1 Dick  Sat May 15 15:03 10/155
  2 Bob   Sat May 15 15:05 10/153



1 <———————————————————————————————————————— (You type)
Message 1: <———————————————————————————————— (UNIX displays)
From Dick Sat May 15 15:03:15 1983
To: Beth


Hi Beth,
Are you ready for the big beach party Saturday night?
I'll pick you up at 8:00 pm sharp!
Love,
Dick



2 <———————————————————————————————————————— (You type)
Message 2: <———————————————————————————————— (UNIX displays)
From Bob Sat May 15 15:05:24 1983
To: Beth
```

```
Hello beautiful blue eyes,
don't forget our big date
to go dancing Sat night
See you at 7:30,
Bobbybaby
```

```
[control-d] <——————————————————————————— (You type)
EOF <———————————————————————————————————— (UNIX displays)
%
```

The "EOF" stands for "end of file," which means that you have left the mail file as shown with the % prompt.

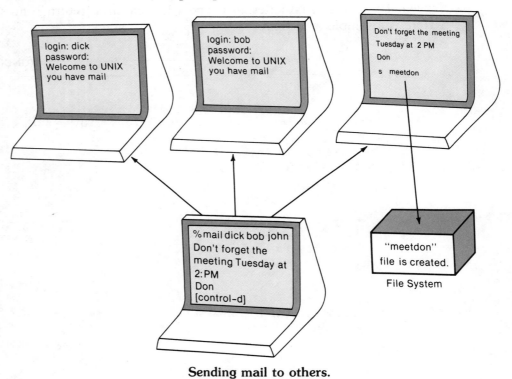

Sending mail to others.

What happens to the letters after you read them? They are automatically placed in a file in your home directory called **mbox**. But, you ask, supposing you want to store letter number 2 in a specific file (**bobstuff**, say)? Easy, just type

```
s bobstuff
```

immediately after reading letter number 2
or else

```
s2 bobstuff
```

at any time before you leave **mail**. These two commands differ in that the firs
command (**s**) saves the letter just displayed while the second command (**s2**)
specifically saves letter number 2. Either command appends the letter to the
contents of that file.

Another question?

Yes, supposing you don't want to save the letter. In that case, just type a

```
d
```

to delete the last message. The following two tables summarize the mail command for sending and receiving mail.

Summary: `mail`—sending mail		
name	**option**	**argument**
`mail`	none	[people . . .]

Description: Mail can be sent to one or more people, using login names
for the addresses. After you invoke the mail command and
push [return], there is no prompt or response from the system. You should begin the typing out of your letter and
when done, place a [control–d] or type a period on a separate line.

Options: None

Example: % **mail dick bob**
                 Hi Dick and Bob,
                 This is my first letter using the UNIX mail system.
                 Will you send me mail?

> **Thanks,**
> **Don**
> **[control–d]**
> %

Comments: Remember, when you finish writing the letter, you must type **[control–d]**. A file can be sent over mail by using the redirect commands as follows:

% **mail dick bob** < **filename**

This redirect command is discussed fully in Chapter 4.

Special
References: "Mail Reference Manual"—This manual lists many more options.

Summary: `mail`—receiving mail

name	options	argument
`mail`	`1,2,3 . . . .` `p,d,s` [filename]	

Description: The command word **mail** with no arguments is used to check mail out of the post office for reading. The options shown below can then be used to read and dispose of your mail. If no options are chosen for disposing of mail, the mail is automatically placed in a file in your directory called **mbox**.

Commands:
1,2,3. . . .	Reads message 1 each time you push 1, etc.
p	Prints the first message.
d2	Deletes message number 2.
s3 [file]	Appends message number 3 to contents of file or creates new file if none exists.
q	Quits mail. Mail that you have read and have not otherwise dispensed with will be appended to your **mbox** file. You can read unfinished letters later.

Example:

```
% mail
Mail version 2.0 January 13, 1981. Type ? for help.
1 message:
        1 bernd Fri Aug 27 15:51 6/127


1
Message 1:
From bernd Fri Aug 27 15:51:19 1982
To: beth

Hello Beth! Don't forget the champagne and marshmallows!
Burningly, Bernd


q
Saved 1 message in mbox
%
```

Electronic Chit-Chat: *write*

UNIX systems have a second form of electronic communication, one that lets you hold a conversation with another user. This method can work only if the person you want to talk to is logged in and wants to talk back. The first step is to see who is on the system; the **who** command will tell you this. Suppose you spot your old friend Hortense Grigelsby and that her login name is hortense. Then you would give the command

```
write hortense
```

She would then get this message on her screen:

```
Message from abner on tty 14 at 09:56 . . .
```

(We are assuming that your login name is abner.)

Meanwhile, on your screen, the cursor will advance to a line with no prompt. Now each line you type on your terminal will be transmitted to Hortense's terminal when you hit the [return] key. (The line also shows on your screen as you type it.) When you have finished your say, hit [control–d]. This

65

will restore your regular prompt to you and will send the message "EOT" (for "end of transmission") to Hortense's terminal, so that she will know you are done.

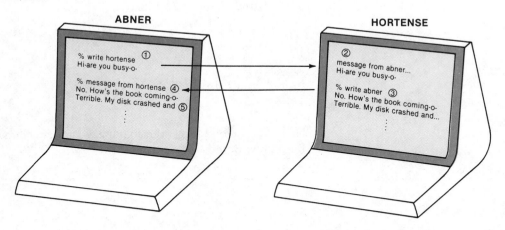

Abner writing Hortense and vice versa.

To get a two-way exchange, once she learns that you are writing her, she can enter

```
write abner
```

Then she can send you messages while you send her messages. On most systems, what she types can appear in the middle of your typing and vice versa. It is best to adopt a sensible code of behavior. A simple one to use, that is similar to CB radio, is to type

```
-o-
```

for "over" when you have completed a thought, and to type

```
-oo-
```

for "over-and-out" when you intend to quit. These are not commands, they are just ways to help you coordinate communication with your partner.

In Chapter 9, we will show you how to block **write** messages using the **msgs** command if you wish to work undisturbed.

Summary: `write`—write to another user		
name	**options**	**arguments**
`write`		user login name

Description: **write** transmits lines from your terminal to the other user's terminal. Transmission occurs when you hit the [return] key. Transmission is terminated by hitting [control–d]; this sends "EOF" to the other user.

Note: To block incoming messages from interrupting your work, use the **mesg** command described in Chapter 9.

For Advanced Users

Who is an advanced user? It might be someone with considerable experience with computers. It might be someone of unusual brilliance. Or, it might

be someone with a lot of time on her hands. It might be you. If so, we offer you some additional material to help take you beyond what this book offers. We can do this because the UNIX system itself contains information about UNIX. First, there is an extensive manual stored in the system memory. Secondly, there are some tutorial lessons on file. Each is useful, but each has its drawbacks. We will look at these two facilities in turn.

The On-Line Manual

There is a very large document called the UNIX Programmer's Manual. It is available in bound printed form; Volume 1 is also stored in a file on disk memory. This second version is called the "on-line" manual. All the UNIX commands and utilities are documented in this manual and you can easily summon this information to your terminal screen. Sound great? It is, except for one point. The manual is written for experienced UNIX programmers, not for beginners. (That's one reason we wrote this book!) This may not be a problem if the command you wish to study is a simple one like **date**. But, for other cases, you may have to put in a goodly amount of trial-and-error work to see how to apply the information to your needs. But, then, that's a great way to learn!

How do you tap into this fount of knowledge? By typing **man** followed by the name of the command you wish to study. For example, to learn all there is to know about **date**, type

```
man date
```

(Don't forget the space between **man** and **date**.)

To learn more about the **man** command itself, type

```
man man
```

(Don't forget the [return] key.) Be prepared to wait a bit; it sometimes takes the system quite awhile to find the desired entry. (Oddly enough, the entries are scattered throughout the system.) Here is an excerpt from the UNIX on-line manual as it might appear if we typed **man who**.

```
WHO(1)              UNIX Programmer's Manual              WHO(1)


NAME
     who - who is on the system
```

```
SYNOPSIS
  who [who-file] [am I]

DESCRIPTION
  who, without an argument, lists the login name, terminal
name, and login time for each current UNIX user.
  Without an argument, who examines the /etc/utmp file to
obtain its information. If a file is given, that file is
examined. Typically, the given file will be /usr/adm/wtmp,
which contains a record of all the logins since it was
created. Then, who lists logins, logouts, and crashes
since the creation of the wtmp file. Each login is listed
with user name, terminal name (with '/dev/' suppressed),
and date and time. When an argument is given, logouts
produce a similar line without a user name. Reboots
produce a line with 'x' in the place of the device name,
and a fossil time indicative of when the system went down.
  With two arguments, as in who am I (and also, who are
you, which does the same thing), who tells who you are
logged in as.


FILES
  /etc/utmp

SEE ALSO
  getuid(2), utmp(5), r(1C), cuid(1C)
```

This example follows the typical format of the UNIX Manual entries.

First, under the heading of "NAME," there is the name and a brief description of the command. Next, there is a SYNOPSIS which shows how the command is used:

```
who [who-file] [am I]
```

This form indicates that the **who** command has two optional arguments, indicated by the presence of brackets. The first is a who–file, whatever that is. It is not in boldface (on the screen, boldface may show up as reverse video, i.e., black letters on a white background), so one would not type "who–file" literally but would, instead, type the actual name of the appropriate file. In this case, the description gives a possible choice. The second possible option is in boldface, meaning that "am I" is to be typed literally.

Then comes a description. As you can see, the description presupposes knowledge about the system (such as what /etc/utmp is), but you can just filter out the parts that don't yet concern you.

Next comes a section called "FILES." It contains a list of files used by UNIX to run this particular command.

The "SEE ALSO" section lists some related commands and utilities. The numbers in parentheses tell which section of the manual contains the description. Thus, **who(1)** is in the first section and **utmp(5)** is in the fifth section.

The UNIX manual, Volume One, has 8 sections:

1. Commands
2. System Calls
3. Subroutines
4. Devices & Special Files
5. File Formats & Conventions
6. Games
7. Macro Packages & Language Conventions
8. Maintenance

Unless you are quite advanced, you probably will be most interested in Section 1 and, perhaps, Section 6.

Summary: man—find manual information by keywords

name	options	arguments
man	[-k]	[keyword . . .]

Description: When used with no argument, this command searches the entire on-line manual for the first section containing the keyword. It then prints a description of the command similar to the printed version of the manual.

Options: **-k** This option produces a one-line summary of each manual section containing the keyword in the Table of Contents.

> **man cat**
> Example: This command will display on the screen the on-line manual
> explanation of the command **cat**.
> Note: **man** is usually quite slow in carrying out its service,
> have patience.

Learning With *learn*

The best way to learn UNIX is to work with it. This is the motivating idea
behind **learn**, which gives CAI (Computer-Aided Instruction) courses for several UNIX-related subjects. When you invoke **learn**, the system gives you an
interactive lesson at your terminal. It presents information, asks questions,
and tells you whether or not your answers are correct. The "learn" tutorial,
like most programmed instruction, is of limited value and is sometimes frustrating to newcomers. It seems to work best for experienced programmers,
perhaps because they have learned to take computer output with a grain of
salt. To use this utility, just type

```
learn
```

The screen will then present something like

```
These are the available courses-
  C
  editor
  eqn
  files
  macros
  morefiles
If you want more information about the courses, or if you have
never used learn before, type 'return'; otherwise type the
name of the course you want, followed by 'return'.
```

If you hit [return], this is what you will read:

```
These are the available courses-
  C
  editor
  eqn
  files
```

```
macros
morefiles
If you want more information about the courses, or if you have
never used 'learn' before, type 'return'; otherwise type the
name of the course you want, followed by 'return'.


files-basic file handling commands.
editor-ed text editor; must know about files first.
morefiles-more on file manipulations and other useful
  stuff.
macros-''-ms'' macros for BTL memos & papers; must know
  editor.
eqn-typing mathematics; must know editor & macros, need
  DASI terminal.
C-writing programs in the C language; must know editor.
```

This is probably the proper order, but after you have the "files" course and know the basics of "editor," try anything you like.

You can always leave "learn" by typing **bye** (and a [return]). You can stop the **learn** program from typing by pushing [interrupt] (or [break] or [rubout] or [delete], depending on your terminal).

To quote the Manual,

> "The main strength of **learn**, that it asks the student to use the real UNIX, also makes possible baffling mistakes. It is helpful, especially for nonprogrammers, to have a UNIX initiate near at hand during the first sessions. . . . Occasionally, lessons are incorrect, sometimes because the local version of a command operates in a nonstandard way. Such lessons may be skipped, but it takes some sophistication to recognize the situation."

What can happen most often is that you will answer a question correctly but the system will not recognize the answer and will say you are wrong. It then asks you if you wish the question repeated. If you know you are right, just answer "no" and the program will go on to the next question. If you keep these cautions in mind, you should be able to **learn** much.

Exercises at the Terminal

1. Read your **mbox** file (if you have one) to see if it contains any old letters.
2. Send yourself mail, perhaps some reminders of things to do today. When the message arrives at your terminal that you have mail, read it, and save it in a file called **today**.
3. Try the command **who** to see if anyone you know is using a terminal right now. If so, use the **write** command to ask him or her if you can practice sending some mail.
4. Send mail to someone you know (or would perhaps like to know).
5. If you read the section concerning the "on-line" manual, try using the manual on a command you already know about. Then, experiment with it. You can't hurt it.

Files and Directories: *cat, ls,* and *more*

4

In this chapter, you will find:

- Introduction
- Files and the UNIX Directory System
- Listing Directories: *ls*
  - Choosing Directories
  - Some *ls* Options
- Reading Files: *cat*
- Reading Files: *more* {BSD}
- Creating Files With *cat*
- Input and Output
- More on Redirection
- Review Questions
- Exercises at the Terminal

4   FILES AND DIRECTORIES: *cat, ls,* and *more*

Introduction

The UNIX file and directory system is wonderfully simple yet versatile. The best way to learn its features is to use them, so we strongly urge you to experiment with the commands we will present, even if you don't really need to use them yet.

You need to know several things to use the file and directory system with ease and understanding. First, you need to know the structure of the system. That will be the first topic of the chapter, and we will drop in a few reminders and amplifications as we continue.

Secondly, you need a way of finding out what files you have; the **ls** command will help you there. The **cat** and **more** commands will handle the next necessity, that of seeing what is in the files. These last three commands form the core of your relationship with your files.

Of course, it would be nice to have a way to create files, and that will be the subject of Chapters 5 and 6. However, we will give you a head start in this chapter by showing you a quick and easy way to produce files. (Actually, you already have learned one way—sending mail to yourself!)

That's whats coming up, so let's begin by seeing how UNIX organizes files.

Files and the UNIX Directory System

Files are the heart of the UNIX system. The programs you create, the text you write and edit, the data you acquire, and all the UNIX programs are stored in files. Anything you want the computer to remember for you, you must save in a file. One very important skill to acquire, then, is the ability to create files; we will start you off on that in this chapter. But unless you can keep track of your files, it doesn't do much good to create them. The UNIX directory system is designed to help you with the extremely important task of keeping track of your files.

Just as a telephone directory contains a list of subscribers, a UNIX directory contains a list of files. It also can contain a list of subdirectories, each of which can contain lists of more files and subdirectories. Let's look at the most basic example of a directory—the "home directory."

When you are given an account on the system, you are assigned a "home directory." When you log in, you can think of yourself as being "in" your home directory. (Later you will learn to change directories but, for now, let's keep you confined to your home directory.) Now, suppose you create a file. You will have to give it a name. (See the box on file names.) Suppose you call it **ogre**. This name will then be added to the list of files in your home directory and, in future instructions, you can refer to the file as **ogre**. After you have created a few files, you can visualize your home directory as looking like the following sketch. (We will use thick lines for directories, thin lines for files.) Also, you can think of your directory as being your personal filing cabinet and of the files as being labeled file folders.

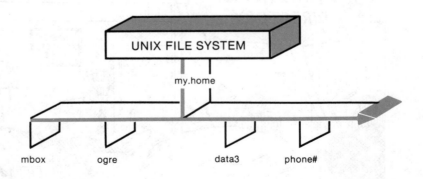

A home directory.

Of course, every other user has his home directory, too, so UNIX needs a way to tell home directories apart. UNIX accomplishes this by giving your home directory a name, usually your login name. Next, UNIX needs a way of keeping track of all these home directories. It does this with a new directory—a directory of directories. Typically, this directory would be called **usr**, and the home directories are termed "subdirectories" of **usr**. The following diagram will help you visualize this.

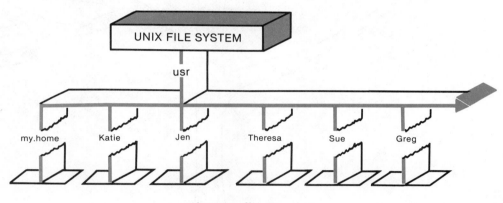

The *usr* directory.

Notice that the **usr** directory in this example contains some files as well as directories. In general, any directory can contain both files and subdirectories.

Is **usr** the ultimate directory? No, that distinction goes to a directory called / and known informally as **root**. (Computers are usually not that informal; they insist on /. However, **root** is easier to say, so we'll use that name.) All other directories stem directly or indirectly from **root** which, of course, is why it is called **root**. The following sketch (The directory system) represents a complete directory system.

The drawing looks a lot like a tree; the directories are the trunk and the branches, and the files are the leaves. For this reason, the UNIX directory system is often described as having a tree structure. (Here the metaphors get a bit confusing, for the **root** directory is the trunk of the tree.)

A different analogy portrays the system as a hierarchy like, say, the organization of an army. At the top is the **root** directory. Serving under **root** is the next rank of directories: **usr**, **bin**, and the like. Each of these, in turn, commands a group of lower-ranking directories, and so on. The next figure represents the hierarchal view.

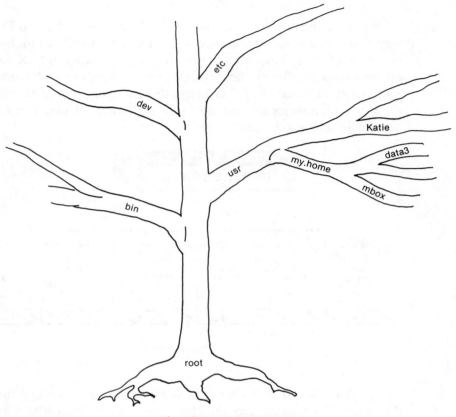

The directory system.

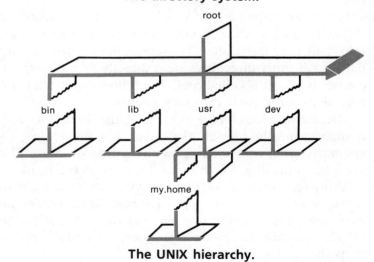

The UNIX hierarchy.

The directory system, then, provides structure for the organization of files. It also provides a clear way of specifying the location of a file, and we will explore that in Chapter 7.

What can you do in the UNIX directory system? You can expand it by adding subdirectories to your home directory, and subdirectories to those subdirectories. You can change directories, moving your field of action to, say, one of your subdirectories. And, you can place files in any directory or subdirectory that you control.

File And Directory Names

UNIX gives you much freedom in naming your files and directories. The name can be from one to fourteen characters long, and you can use about any character you want. However, you will be better off if you avoid using characters that have a special meaning to UNIX. In particular, avoid using the following characters: / \ " ' * ; - ? [ ] ( ) ~ ! $ { } < >. (It is not, necessarily, impossible to use these characters, just inconvenient.) You can use digits as part of a file name with no difficulty; in fact, you can give names like **22** if you like. However, it does make sense to make the names as descriptive as possible.

UNIX uses spaces to tell where one command or filename ends and another begins, so you should avoid spaces in names. The usual convention is to use a period or underline mark where you normally would use a space. For example, if you wanted to give the name **read me** to a file, you could call it **read.me** or **read_me** instead.

Uppercase letters are distinguished from lowercase letters, so **fort**, **Fort**, **forT**, and **FORT** would be considered to be four distinct names.

UNIX makes no distinction between names that can be assigned to files and those that can be assigned to directories. Thus, it is possible to have a file and a directory with the same name; the **snort** directory could have a file in it called **snort**. This doesn't confuse UNIX, but it might confuse you. Some users adopt the convention of beginning directory names with a capital letter and beginning filenames with a small letter.

Listing Directories: *ls*

The **ls** command is used to list the contents of a directory. Let's take a hypothetical example and see how this command is used. Samuel Spade is a new student enrolled in a burgeoning computer science course (called cs1) at a very large university. His UNIX login name is sammy and his instructor has identified his account in the UNIX hierarchy as shown in the following diagram. (In this case, a directory other than **/usr** is being used to house the student accounts.)

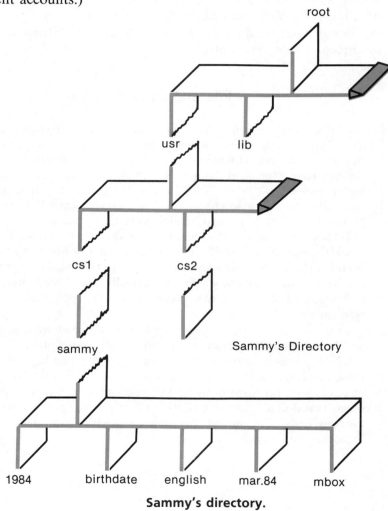

Sammy's directory.

We assume that Sammy is properly logged in and has established contact with the shell as indicated by the % prompt. At this point, the shell is ready to execute his every whim (command). In our hypothetical situation, if Sammy types

```
ls
```

the system would respond with

```
1984    birthdate    english    mar.84    mbox
```

These are the names of the four files and one subdirectory in Sammy's account. The directory is **english**, and it is listed along with the files. How can we tell it is a directory? We can't tell just by looking at this list. Either we have to remember that it is, or else we can use the **-F** {BSD} or the **-l** options that are described a little later.

Well, that is pretty simple, and you probably won't need to know more than this at first. But there is much more to **ls** than what we just have seen. For one thing, you can list the contents of just about any directory, not just your own. Secondly, in the words of one version of the on-line manual, "There are an unbelievable number of options."

We will look into some of these matters now. If you want to skip ahead, that's okay, but remember to come back to these pages when you need them.

Choosing Directories

If you just type **ls**, you get a listing of your "current working directory." Right now, that would be your login directory but, later, when you learn how to change directories, it will be whatever directory you are currently working in (just like the name says!). To get a listing of files and directories in some other directory, you just follow **ls** with the name of the directory you want to see. For instance, the command

```
ls english
```

would show what is in the directory **english**. Note that there has to be a space between **ls** and the directory name. The directory names may be a little more involved than this example; you will learn all about that when you get to the section on "pathnames" in Chapter 7.

Some *ls* Options

You tell UNIX which options you want by using option flags, just as we described for **finger** in Chapter 2. The flag should be separated by spaces from the command name and from any following arguments. Suppose, for example, that Sammy types

```
ls -s
```

The **-s** option is a "size" option; it gives the size of the file in blocks. (Files are built from blocks having a size of 512 bytes, in our example.) The UNIX response would look like this:

```
total 30    26 birthdate   1 mar.84
      1 1984     1 english     1 mbox
```

Thus, the file **birthdate** contains 26 blocks or 26 × 512 = 13,312 bytes.
This might give you a small surprise; try

```
ls -a
```

If Sammy does this, he will find some strange entries!

```
.      .cshrc   1984       english   mbox
..     .login   birthdate  mar.84
```

The **-a** option stands for "all," and it lists some things normally invisible to the reader. As we will discuss later, the single period is short for the directory itself, while the double period is short for the parent directory. These entries are part of the scheme that binds directories together, and they need not concern us here. The other two new entries, **.cshrc** and **.login**, are special files used by UNIX to set up operating conditions in Sammy's directory. We will discuss them in Chapter 9.

The bulkiest and most informative option is the **-l**, or long, option. For Sammy, this option would produce the following listing:

```
total 30
-rw-r--r-- 1 sammy    231 Aug 18 12:34 1984
-rw-r--r-- 1 sammy  13312 Jul 22 16:05 birthdate
drwxr-xr-x 2 sammy    112 Aug 29 10:15 english
-rw-r--r-- 1 sammy     52 Aug 01 17:45 mar.84
-rw-r--r-- 1 sammy    315 Aug 28 09:24 mbox
```

The "total" entry shows the number of blocks used. After that comes one line for each file. The first character in each line tells if the entry is a file (shown by a "-") or a directory (shown by a "d"). Next come several letters and hyphens. These describe "permissions" to read and use files; we'll take that matter up when we discuss **chmod** in Chapter 10. Then comes a numeral that gives the number of "links." (See the **ln** command in Chapter 7.) Next comes Sammy's login name; this column tells who "owns" the file. Next comes the actual length of the file in bytes. Then comes the date and time the file was last changed. Finally, there is the file name.

You can use more than one option by stringing together the option letters. For example, the command

```
ls -la
```

would produce a long listing for all the files revealed by the **-a** option.

The following summary will give a few more options for your pleasure.

Summary: ls—list contents of directory

name	option	argument
ls	[-a,c,l,m,r, s,F,R,+ others]	[directory . . .]

Description: **ls** will list the contents of each directory named in the argument. The output, which can be a list of both files and subdirectories, is given alphabetically. When no argument is given, the current directory is listed.

Options:
-**a** lists all entries.
-**c** lists by time of file creation.
-**l** lists in long format, giving links, owner, size in bytes, and time of last file change.more.
-**m** lists in a stream output using commas for separation.
-**r** reverses the order of the listing.
-**s** gives the size in blocks of 512 (may vary) bytes.
-**F** marks directories with a / and executable programs with an "*" {BSD}.

-R lists recursively any subdirectories found; that is, lists not only the contents of the current directory but, also, the contents of all its subdirectories, and so on. {BSD}

Example: **ls -cF**
                  This command will list the contents of the current directory in the order that they were created, marking a subdirectory with a / and the executable files with an *.

Comments: Remember that directories contain only the "names" of files and subdirectories. To read information contained in a file, use **cat** or **more**. As with many UNIX commands, different UNIX systems may use different letters for options.

Reading Files: *cat*

cat is short for the word "concatenate," which means to link together. However, some people prefer to think of it as catalog. It can be used to display the contents of one or more files on the terminal screen. To display one of the files in Sammy's account, e.g., **mar.84**, you would type

```
cat mar.84
```

The system would then print whatever was in the file named **mar.84**. Here we assume it looks like this:

```
    March 1984
  S  M Tu  W Th  F  S
              1  2  3
  4  5  6  7  8  9 10
 11 12 13 14 15 16 17
 18 19 20 21 22 23 24
 25 26 27 28 29 30 31
```

As you can see, this file contains a calendar for the month of March. Apparently, Sammy has mastered the **cal** command (Chapter 2) and has learned how to save the output. (See "redirection" later in this chapter and, again, in Chapter 9.)

To read another file, for example, the one called **mbox**, you would type

```
cat mbox
```

If you make a mistake and type

```
cat box
```

UNIX will appeal to your sympathies with

```
cat: can't open box
```

The **cat** command and some of its options are summarized in the following table.

Summary: cat—catenate and print		
name	**option**	**argument**
cat	-n,-s,-v {BSD}	[file . . .]

Description:	**cat** reads each file in sequence and writes it on the standard output (terminal). For long files, use the **more** command.
	If no file name is given, or if "-" is given as a file name, **cat** reads the standard input (the keyboard); a [control–d] will terminate keyboard input. (This latter process is described later in this chapter.)
	If the file is too large for a single screen, try using [control–s] and [control–q] to stop and start the file information appearing on the screen, or use the **more** command {BSD} described below.
Options:	**-n** numbers lines starting at 1 {BSD}
	-s eliminates multiple consecutive blank lines {BSD}
	-v prints a visible representation (such as ^B) for "invisible" characters (such as [control–b]) {BSD}
Example:	**cat -s file2**
	This will print **file2**, eliminating occurrences of two or more consecutive blank lines.

87

Comments:	If no input file is given, **cat** takes its input from the terminal keyboard. Later in this chapter, we show that **cat** and redirect together are very useful. Note: The redirection operator uses the symbol >. You can use **cat > file5** to create a new file called **file5** and can enter text into that file. You can use **cat file2 file3 >> file4** to append **file2** and **file3** to the end of **file4**.

Reading Files: *more* {BSD}

The major problem with **cat** is that it won't wait for you. For example, if we assume the file **1984** is a full calendar, then there isn't enough room to fit it on the screen. **cat** doesn't care. **cat** will fill the screen full, and then continue adding more information at the bottom of the screen, scrolling the screen upwards. The first few months go by too fast to read, let alone reminisce. To solve this problem, a new command, **more**, was invented. **more** stops when the screen is full; after you've read the screen, hit the space bar, and **more** advances one more screenful. **cat** works for short files; **more** should be used for long files. To use **more** on **1984**, type

```
more 1984
```

and see the file one full screen at a time.

Summary: more—used to view long files one screenful at a time {BSD}		
name	**option**	**argument**
more		[file---]
Description:	**more** displays the file one screenful at a time. At the end of each screen of information, **more** prints the fraction of the file that has been read so far. To advance the text one line,	

> push [return]. To advance the text one screenful, push
> [spacebar]. To exit **more**, push [rubout] or [break] or [q].
>
> Comment: **more** has several useful features, such as the ability to search
> ahead for a key word. If you are interested in learning more
> about **more**, the on-line manual is the place to look.

The three commands, **ls**, **cat**, and **more**, are probably the most often used commands in the UNIX system.

Creating Files With *cat*

Now that you can list files and display the contents of text files, you undoubtedly are eager to create files of your own. After all, that's where the action is! The best way to create files is to use one of the UNIX editors that we will discuss in Chapters 5 and 6. That will take a bit of practice on your part; luckily, however, we can use **cat** again (a versatile animal) to produce files much more simply.

Suppose, for example, you wish to create a file called **poem** to contain an original composition. You can use this procedure:

```
cat > poem
A bunch of officers
Sat in their tunics
Hoping to learn
more about UNIX
[control-d]
```

When [control–d] is typed, your words are funneled into the file **poem**. To check if the procedure worked, just type **cat poem** and see the glory of your work shine again on the screen.

You now can create files, so please go ahead and create some; then you can try out this chapter's commands as you read along. Right now, however, we are going to take a brief side excursion to explain why this last procedure works. If you are eager to move ahead, you can skim through the explanation, but do pay attention to the parts on redirection.

How does this command work? There are two tricks involved. The first trick is that if you *don't* tell **cat** what file to look at (i.e., if you type **cat** and [return] without providing a file name), it will look at whatever you type in next on the terminal. Indeed, it considers *your input* to be a file. A [control–d] tells UNIX that you are done pretending to be a file; until you type that, you can put in as many lines and [return]'s as you like. Secondly, we have used the magic of "redirection," a UNIX ability we will discuss fully in Chapter 10. The > is a redirection operator; it takes information that ordinarily would be sent to the screen and channels it to the following file instead. (You can remember this easily by seeing that the > character looks like a funnel!)

Let's look at each trick separately. First, suppose you type

```
cat
```

with no file name following it. (Remember to hit [return], however.) Then, the cursor (the white square of light) drops down to the next line, but you don't get a prompt. You, then, can type whatever text you like, hitting [return] to start new lines. When you are done, type [control–d]. Up to this point, it is almost like sending **mail**. Once you hit [control–d], **cat** takes what you wrote and sends it to your screen. Now you have a copy (on the screen) of what you just typed. In other words, **cat** does what it always does; it prints a copy of the file on the screen. The only difference is that, in this case, the file was your fresh input instead of a stored file. The exchange could look like this:

```
% cat
Help! I have lost my trained fleas!          <──────────── original
Help! Help me, please!                        <──────────── original
[control-d]
Help! I have lost my trained fleas!          <──────────── copy
Help! Help me, please!                        <──────────── copy
%
```

The final line (the % sign) tells you that UNIX is done. The preceding two lines constitute the output produced by **cat**.

What about the redirection part? Any command that normally sends output to the screen can be followed by the operator > and a file name. This will cause the output to be sent to file instead of to the screen. For instance,

```
who > turkeys
```

will place the list of users who are logged on into a file called **turkeys**. Where does the file come from? It is created on the spot! As soon as UNIX spots the redirection operator, it looks at the name following it and creates a file by that name.

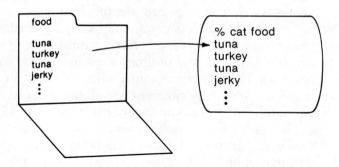

(A) *cat* **file to screen.**

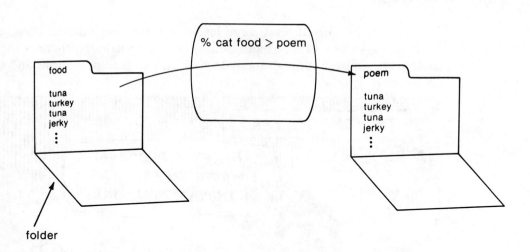

(B) *cat* **file to file using redirection.**

cat **being redirected.**

What if you already have a file by that name? It is *wiped out* and replaced by the new version. As you can see, this is an area in which you will want to be very careful. A careless command like the preceding example could wipe out your previous **turkeys** file of famous turkeys from history! Note, however, the box in Chapter 7 that outlines ways to protect your files.

Look back again at our example with the excellent poem. Notice how the command line (**cat** > **poem**) contains all the necessary instructions: where to get the material (" ", i.e., the keyboard), what to do with it (**cat** it), and where to put the results (into the file **poem**).

Of course, this method doesn't allow you to make corrections to the file. To gain that ability, you really do need to learn about the editors.

This method of creating files involves the concepts of "input" and "output," so we will take a quick peek at just what this means.

Input and Output

UNIX deals with at least three levels of input and output. First, a computer has a variety of input and output devices. Secondly, there is the information transmitted through these devices; it, too, is termed input and output,

depending on its destination. An interactive system such as UNIX normally accepts input from the keyboard (the characters you type) and "routes" its output (the characters it produces) to the screen. The keyboard and the screen are termed the standard input and standard output devices. (As a courtesy to you, the user, a copy of your input is "echoed" to the screen so that you can see what you have typed. The system doesn't have to echo, so be thankful for small kindnesses.)

A command also can have an input and output. For example, **cat** takes its input from the file name following it, and, normally, it sends its output to the output device, the screen. On the other hand, you don't have to supply **date** with an input, but it does give you an output. The redirection operators deal with the input to and output from commands.

More on Redirection

The > operator is a very useful tool. It can be used with any command or program that normally sends output to the screen. For example,

```
cal 03 1984 > mar.84
```

would first create the file **mar.84**, then execute the **cal** command. The output of **cal**, which would be the calendar for March 1984, is placed in the **mar.84** file.

Note that > redirects output from a command to a file, not to other commands or programs. For example,

```
poem > cat
```

does not work because **poem** is not a command.

Let's look at one more example of redirection. Assume you have files called **bigbucks** and **morebucks**. What will the following command do?

```
cat bigbucks morebucks > laundry
```

Let's answer the question step by step.

1. What's the input? The files **bigbucks** and **morebucks**.
2. What's the operation? **cat**, or concatenate.

3. What's the output of the operation? The input files printed in succession.
4. What's the output destination? The file **laundry**.
5. What's the final result? The file **laundry** contains combined copies of the files **bigbucks** and **morebucks**.

Now for one more word of CAUTION: Do not try a command of the form:

```
cat bigbucks morebucks > bigbucks
```

While you might think this would result in adding the contents of **morebucks** to what was in **bigbucks**, the right-hand side of the command starts things off by erasing **bigbucks** before any **cat**ing is done. When UNIX gets to the **cat** part, **bigbucks** is already empty!

All in all, **cat** is a pretty useful command. You can use it to see the contents of a file, to create new files, and to make copies of one or more files. And, unlike the domestic variety, the UNIX "cat" obeys instructions!

Review Questions

The basic commands of this chapter will become second nature as you begin to depend on the UNIX file system to help you handle information. Here are some review questions to give you confidence in using the system and matching commands to functions.

Match the functions shown on the left to the commands shown on the right. The answers are given after the questions.

1. `cat dearsue`
2. `more butter`
3. `cat story.1 story.2`
4. `ls`
5. `who > userlist`

a. Lists the contents of a file, one page at a time.
b. Lists contents of the present directory.
c. Prints the contents of **story.1** and **story.2** on the screen.
d. Prints out the contents of the file **dearsue**.
e. Places a copy of who is presently logged into the system in the file **userlist**.

Answers:

1–d, 2–a, 3–c, 4–b, 5–e

Exercises at the Terminal

Even if you have been following the chapter while sitting at a terminal, you might like to try these exercises to illustrate the major commands and to practice their use.

1. List the contents of your home directory.
2. Use both **cat** and **more** on each file (assuming you only have three or four files to look at).
3. After using a command that works as you expect, try the command again but with an error in it to see what happens. For example, try **lss** or **cat date** or **dates** or **more file33**.
4. Can you use **cat** and *redirect* to place a copy of all your files into a new file? Hint: Try **cat a b c d > e**. If this worked, try to add today's date to the top of the new file **e**. (Hint: It's all right to change file names.)
5. Try to read the file(s) you created in Problem 4, using both **cat** and **more**.
6. Send mail to yourself using the method you were shown in Chapter 3.
7. Read your mail and save any letters in a new file, perhaps calling it **letters1**.
8. Create a new file using **cat** and call it **Today**. Put in a list of some of the things you have to do today.
9. Try out some of the options with both the **cat** and **ls** commands; for example, you might try **cat -n Today**, or **ls -c**.

5

Using Editors: The *ed* Line Editor

In this chapter, you will find:

5   USING EDITORS: THE *ed* LINE EDITOR

Introduction

The UNIX editors are the key to creative use of the computer. These editors allow you to create and alter text files that might contain love letters, form letters, sales data, programs in FORTRAN, Pascal, or BASIC, word processing, interactive programs, and much more. This chapter and the next will introduce the major features of two useful UNIX editors: the **ed** (for editor) editor, and the **vi** (for visual) editor. The **ed** editor is a "line" editor that has been the standard workhorse for UNIX during the late 1970s and early 1980s. **vi** is a cursor-oriented "screen" editor for use on crt's and is increasing in popularity in the 1980s.

Introduction to Editing

In the UNIX operating system, everything is stored in files, even the UNIX operating system itself. Earlier, we learned to place text, data, or programs into files by using either **mail** or redirection (>). The chief problem

with those two methods is that the only way to make changes or corrections to a file is to erase the entire file and start over.

The UNIX editors overcome this problem. They let you alter files efficiently and easily, providing you with the basic support you need for most UNIX tasks. In these sections, we will give an overview of how editors and editor "buffers" work. Then, we will describe the major features of **ed**. We will take up **vi** in the following chapter.

The Memory Buffer

Our files are stored in the system's memory. When we set an editor to work on a file, it leaves the original file undisturbed. Instead, it creates a copy of the file for you to work with. This copy is *kept* in a temporary workspace called the "buffer." The changes you make are made in this copy, not in the original file. If you want to *keep* the changes you have made, you must then replace the original file with your worked-over copy. This is simple to do; you just give the **w**rite (or **w**) command, and the original file is replaced by the updated version. (Note: This write command is an editor command; it is not the same write that is used in sending messages to other users.)

This "buffered" approach has a big advantage. If you really botch your editing job (accidentally deleting a page, for example), you haven't damaged the original file. Just quit the editor (using the **q**uit or **q**) command without writing, and all evidence and effects of your error(s) disappear, leaving the original file unchanged.

There is, we confess, a disadvantage to this method of operation. Your changes are not saved automatically. *You must remember to* write *your changes!* If you quit without doing so, your changes are discarded. Some versions of UNIX editors try to jog your memory if you try to quit without writing your changes, but some don't. The failure to save editing changes has led to many an anguished cry and slapped forehead across this great nation. It may even happen to you, but you have been warned.

Next, we look at how the editing process works.

Two Modes of Editor Operation

The **ed** and **vi** editors have two basic modes of operation: the Text Input Mode and the editing or Command Mode. An overview of these two modes can be seen in the following diagram.

When we first "enter" an editor, we are placed in the Command Mode. This means that any keyboard entry is interpreted to be a command like

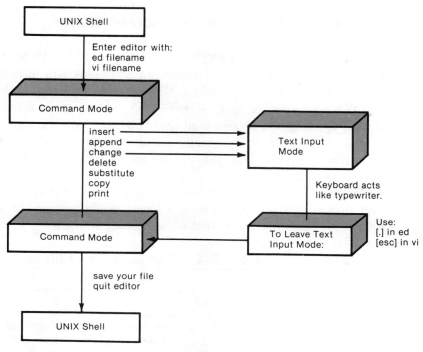

Two modes of operation.

those commands shown previously. In this mode, we could delete a word or a line or change a spelling error. We can enter the Text Input Mode by using the **append** command, that is, by typing the [a] key. Now any key entry will be interpreted as text to be stored in the buffer, not as a command as before. We now can enter text representing FORTRAN programs, sales data, or chapters in a book. Each editor has only *one* way to leave (exit) the Text Input Mode; use the [esc] key to leave **vi**, or use a period [.] as the first and only character on a line by itself to leave **ed**, as shown in the preceding diagram.

If you like what you have written in the Text Input Mode or modified in the Command Mode, then it can be permanently saved in memory by using the **write** command. The **write** command is quite versatile. You can save the entire buffer or a portion of the buffer using "line numbers." You can also save or write to the existing file (created when you first went into the editor) or you can write to a new file (creating the new file in the process). These "saving" techniques are almost identical in both UNIX editors. They will be discussed in detail later in the specific sections devoted to each editor.

You might be wondering which editor you should use. In the next section, we will present an overview of these two editors and how to use them.

Comparing the Line Editor and the Screen Editor

All UNIX systems running UNIX version 7, or UNIX System III, support the line editor, **ed**. Many of these same systems will also be supporting a screen editor, such as **vi**. Some UNIX systems support another editor called EMACS and other editors will surely be created in the future. Which editor should you use? We recommend that you start with the screen editor, **vi**, if it is available and if you generally use a crt terminal. Our experience at one college was that the great majority of those students exposed to both editors wound up using **vi**.

The following table gives a brief comparison of these two editors. However, many of the comments and terms might be new and will not seem important until you have tried some editing yourself.

Table 5–1. Comparing *vi* With *ed*

Function	ed	vi
Terminal	Tty, crt	Crt
Text Display	Fair. In **ed**, you display "lines" of the file but you must tell **ed** what lines you want to see.	Good. In **vi**, you always have a full page of text before you. Text can be "scrolled" or "paged."
Text Input Mode	Good. Has three commands to enter this mode.	Better. Has eleven commands to enter this mode.
Command Mode 1. Making changes within lines.	Cumbersome, since you must type the words you replace.	Easy, since you can type over the words you replace.
2. Handling large text files.	Somewhat cumbersome.	Easy, since you can "scroll" and "page."
3. Deleting lines.	Easy.	Easy.
4. Moving lines around.	Easy.	Easy.
5. Global searching and replacing.	Easy.	Easy.
6. Saving text.	Easy.	Easy.

The last three text editing features use almost identical commands. In fact, **vi** has access to all commands in **ed** by just prefacing those commands with a colon [:].

In the next section, we will take a detailed look at the line editor, **ed**. If you plan to use **vi**, you may easily skip to the next chapter.

The *ed* Line Editor

The **ed** line editor is the most widely available text editor on UNIX systems today. Its editing features include appending, inserting, deleting, moving and copying one or more lines of text, global searching and replacing of words, and block writing of text to memory. **ed** is a very powerful editor, yet easy to use since editing commands are generally structured with a simple format.

We will begin this section by describing how you get into and out of the editor. Then, the format for issuing commands in **ed** will be discussed. After that, we present examples of how to input and edit text. This section concludes with an **ed** command summary.

Calling the *ed* Editor

There are different expressions used for starting up an editor. We say you can "call" the editor or "invoke" the editor or "get into" the editor. No matter how you say it, the command issued from the UNIX shell is just

```
ed filename
```

The filename can be a file already in your directory. In which case, the file contents are placed in the **ed** temporary buffer for you to edit. If you have no file by that name, then a new file is created. When you call **ed** up with an existing file, the editor responds on the screen with the number of characters stored in the file. If the file is new, then **ed** responds with a question mark and the file name. If you wanted to edit an existing file, but mistyped its name, this convention would alert you that **ed** was starting up a new file. (The exact responses may vary slightly from version to version.) Let's look at two examples. If you invoke **ed** with the command

```
ed poem
```

then, the editor will respond with

```
? poem
```
(a new file is created and named "poem")

or

462   (existing file has 462 characters)

ed gives you the number of characters in the file, but it does not print the file on the screen unless you give it the appropriate print command.

The editor is now in the Command Mode ready to accept such commands as append, move, delete, write, quit, print, and so on. The commands that you give must follow a set format, which is described next.

The *ed* Command Format

A complete **ed** command, in general, has three parts: an address, a command, and a parameter. The address tells the editor which line or lines are affected. The command tells the editor what must be done. Examples of commands are **p** (for print a line onto the screen), **d** (for delete a line), and **s** (for make a substitution). The parameter provides additional information, such as what substitution will take place. Often, however, a complete command will have just one or two of these parts.

Here are a few examples of the command format.

Table 5–2. The *ed* Command Format

Sample command	Address range	Command	Parameter
1,2p	1,2	p	
3d	3	d	
3s/The/the/	3	s	/The/the/
p	None given, thus, print current line.	p	
.,$d	Current line to end of file.	d	

In time, we will explain all these commands and more, but in case you are impatient, here is a brief rundown of what they do. The first command prints lines 1 and 2. The second command deletes line 3. The third command substitutes the word "The" for "the" in line 3. The fourth command prints the current line. The fifth command deletes everything from the current line to the end of the file.

Locating Lines

Half of the difficulty in using editors is telling the editor *where* in the text file you wish to insert text or make changes. The **ed** line editor approaches this task by using "line numbers"; text in the **ed** temporary buffer is organized into numbered lines. A line is considered to be everything typed up to a carriage return, [return]. Each line in the buffer is numbered consecutively and renumbered whenever a new line is inserted, deleted, or moved. In addition to maintaining this list of text lines, the editor always maintains a notion of what is the "current line." You might imagine the current line to be a line pointed to by an "invisible" cursor as shown in the following sketch.

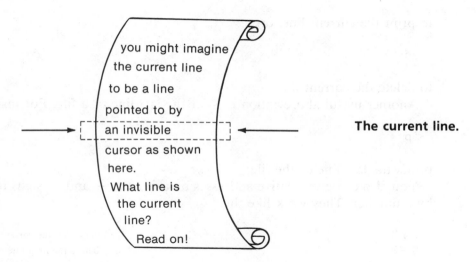

you might imagine
the current line
to be a line
pointed to by
an invisible   **The current line.**
cursor as shown
here.
What line is
the current
line?
Read on!

What line in the buffer is the current line? When you first invoke the editor with an existing file, the current line becomes the *last* line in the editor buffer. If you were now to type a command like print or append or insert, this command is carried out with respect to the current line. For example, if you use the print command, by typing

p

the current line is printed on the screen. On the other hand, if you type

3p

then, line 3 is printed. In this latter case, we gave the editor a specific line to work on. Now line 3 becomes the current line. In general, when you issue a command, the last line affected by that command is considered to be the new current line.

An abbreviation for the current line is the dot character (.). The current line is also called "line dot." Thus, we can speak of the line 3, or line 4, or line dot. Do not let the multiple use of the dot in **ed** confuse you. Recall that you can leave the Text Input Mode with a single dot placed alone on a line. Now, in the Command Mode, a dot is an address abbreviation for the current line in the line-editing editor. Thus, you can type

.p

to print the current line, or

.d

to delete the current line.

Another useful abbreviation is $ for the last line of a file. For instance,

$p

prints the last line of the file.

You also can give relative addresses by using the + and − signs followed by a number. They work like this:

.+3   (3 lines after the current line, and)
$−2   (2 lines before the final line of the file.)

You can specify a range of lines by giving two line numbers separated by a comma. For example,

3,8d

deletes lines 3 through 8, while

1,$p

prints all the lines in your file onto the screen, and

.−9,.+9p

prints 19 lines altogether, with the current line in the middle.

So now we have several ways of giving line addresses. We can give a line number or a range of line numbers, we can use the special symbols "." and "$" for the current line and for the final line, respectively, and we can use plus signs and minus signs to locate lines relative to the current line or the last line. But how do we find out what the line numbers are?

If the file is short, you can use **1,$p** to show the whole file on the screen. Then you can count the lines yourself. The second thing you can do is find the line number of the current line (line dot); you do this by typing an equal sign after the dot as follows:

```
. =
```

ed will respond by telling you the line number of the current line. (Remember that **ed** commands, like UNIX commands, should be followed by [return].) This command is particularly handy after you have moved around a bit using the **+** and **−** commands described above or when using the pattern searching described next.

Line Lengths

There is an interesting point about line lengths that may not be obvious to you. It is this: the length of a line on the screen may not correspond to how long the editor thinks the line is. The reason is that when you type text in, on most systems, the screen will start a new line when you exceed 80 characters or hit the [return] key (whichever comes first), but the editor will only start a new line in your file when you hit the [return] key. Thus, you could type in a line of, say, 150 characters before hitting a [return] key. This line would be "wrapped around" on the screen and would look like two lines. However, the editor would count it as just one line. Not only would this throw you off if you were counting lines, but it could produce surprising results when you send the file to a line printer. And it could really get you into trouble if you are writing programs; FORTRAN, for example, expects commands to be in columns 7 through 72.

The most straightforward approach to this problem is to use the [return] key as it is used on an electric typewriter. As you near the end of a line, hit the [return] key to start a new line. You should try to make this use of the [return] key an automatic habit when using an editor.

The **vi** editor has a "wrapmargin" command that produces automatic [return]'s at whatever point you specify. This useful feature is discussed in the next chapter.

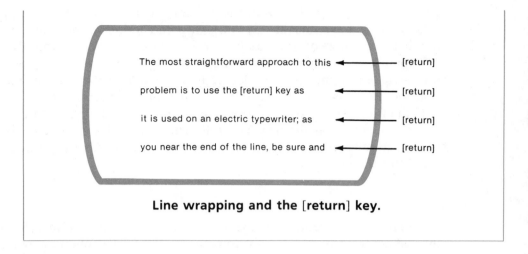

The most straightforward approach to this ◄———— [return]

problem is to use the [return] key as ◄———— [return]

it is used on an electric typewriter; as ◄———— [return]

you near the end of the line, be sure and ◄———— [return]

Line wrapping and the [return] key.

Pattern Searching

ed offers an interesting and useful alternative for finding lines. Instead of specifying the line number, you can give **ed** a pattern to look for. You do this by enclosing the pattern in slashes. For example, if you give the command

```
/bratwurst/
```

ed will search through your file for "bratwurst" and, then, print the line that contains the first example it finds; after that, it stops searching. The search starts after the current line and proceeds forward through the file. If **ed** doesn't find the pattern by the time it reaches the file end, it goes to the file beginning and proceeds to the original line. If it hasn't found the pattern yet, it will let you know by printing out a question mark.

ed interprets the pattern as a "character string" rather than as a word. A character string, or "string" for short, is just a series or string of characters. If you were to set **ed** looking for the string

```
/man/
```

it doesn't care whether that string is a separate word (man, in this case) or part of a longer word (the "man" in manual or command, for example). It will just find the first occurrence (either on the current line or after it) of the consecutive letters m-a-n.

A space in text is a character—the space character—and can be used as part of the search string. So the command

```
/man /
```

will find "man " and "woman ", but not "command," since there is no space after the "n" in "command."

Stepping Through Text

Here is another technique that is useful for finding lines of text. If you type

```
[return]
```

alone without any other command, **ed** will interpret that to mean

```
.+1p
```

That is, **ed** will advance one line and print it on the screen. So if you want to go slowly through your buffer looking for changes to make, the following sequence is easy to use.

```
1p
[return]
[return]
[return]
```

and so forth. When you find a line you want to change, you have two choices. You can address the current line by line number or you can use the default address, which is a line dot. That is, if you type

```
p
```

by itself, the address is the current line by default.

Here is an example of how you might read through a file called "energy" one line at a time.

```
ed energy
? 320
1p
    Energy consumption during the last six months
```

```
[return]
has been brought down 17%, thus saving our
[return]
company over $6,000,000. Everyone is to be
[return]
congratulated.
[return]
?
```

The ? at the end means there are no more lines of text in the buffer.

You also can step backwards a line at a time by typing a minus sign

```
-
```

followed by a [return]. This is short for

```
.-1p
```

Thus, there are four approaches to locating text in the buffer. The first approach is to use specific line numbers, such as 1, 4, $, etc. The second method is to use the "current" line as a reference point and move relative to this line "dot" by using the [+] and [−] keys. Thirdly, you can let **ed** search for particular words or patterns. Finally, you can use the [return] key to step through the file line-by-line.

Now that we can locate lines, we can turn our attention to creating and altering files.

The *ed* Text Input Mode

There are three commands in **ed** that will turn your keyboard into a type-writer for entering text (or data, or programs) into the editor's buffer. These commands are **a** for append, **i** for insert, and **c** for change. If no address is given, these commands affect the current line. Otherwise, append and insert must be given a single line address, and change can be given an address of one or more lines. **append** will place text after the addressed line and **insert** will place text before the addressed line. The lines addressed using **change** are all deleted making way for any new text you type in. The **append** command entering the Text Input Mode is illustrated in the following two examples.

The Append, Write, and Quit Commands: *a*, *w*, and *q*

Jack Armstrong has just received a terrific job offer and wants to draft a letter accepting the position. His first step is to invoke the editor using

```
ed jobletter
```

This creates a new empty file called **jobletter** and places Jack in the Command Mode, printing

```
?jobletter
```

(or something similar, depending on which UNIX system is being used). Since Jack wants to use the keyboard as a typewriter, he now enters the Text Input Mode by pushing

```
a
```

which stands for append.

Generally, there is no prompt to indicate the Text Input Mode. He now begins typing his letter:

```
Dear Sir:

      I am delighted to accept your offer as chief
      trouble shooter for the Eon Corp. for $250,000
      a year.

            Sincerely,

      Jack Armstrong
```

Recall that once **ed** is in the Text Input Mode, the keyboard acts like a typewriter. The [return] key is used as a carriage return to end each line. To indent lines, Jack can use either the [spacebar] key or the [tab] key.

Satisfied with his work, Jack now leaves the Text Input Mode by typing a lone period [.] at the beginning of a new line like this,

```
.
```

This may seem strange at first, but remember, when we use the keyboard as a typewriter, every key we push will place characters on the screen. The good people who built the **ed** editor had to find some rare keystroke that would never be needed in the typewriter mode so that Jack and you can use it to leave that mode. While a period is not a rare keystroke, it is rare to begin a line with a period.

After leaving the Text Input Mode and reentering the Command Mode, Jack can save his text using the **write** or **w** command as follows:

```
w
```

(Don't forget to follow commands with the [return] key!) If the command is successful, the editor will respond with the number of characters saved. (Note: This is an important clue that serves as a check to see if you have indeed left the Text Input Mode with a [.] on the last line. If you type w and the letter "w" appears on the screen, you are still in the text entry mode. Beginning users often forget this step.) Jack now leaves the editor with the quit command by typing

```
q
```

which stands for **q**uit.

This places him back in the UNIX shell and gives him back the shell prompt (%). He can now read and verify that his letter was properly saved with **write** by typing

```
cat jobletter
```

While rereading his letter, Jack has a new thought. He wants to add a post-script to the letter. So he "invokes" the editor with his new file by typing

```
ed jobletter
```

The editor responds with the number of characters in the file as shown.

```
176
```

Jack types in

```
a
```

which stands for **a**ppend and adds his new message by typing

```
PS. Could you advance me $25,000? Thanks
.
w
q
```

The **a** command at the beginning of an editing session appends the text at
the end of the file. Every time you first invoke **ed**, the imaginary cursor is at
the very end of the file. (Later, we show how the **append** command can add
text elsewhere within the buffer file, rather than just at the end of the file.)

Summary of Examples

Here's a complete summary of these first two examples:

```
% ed jobletter                              <———————— (Jack invokes 'ed)
? jobletter                                 <———————— (ed prints this)
a                                           <———————— (append command)
Dear Sir:                                   <———————— (Jack starts typing)


  I am delighted to accept your offer as chief
trouble shooter for the Eon Corp. for $250,000
a year.


          Sincerely,

          Jack Armstrong
.                                           <———————— (Jack ends text entry)
w                                           <———————— (writes to memory)
176                                         <———— (UNIX says 176 characters)
q                                           <———————— (Jack quits ed)
%                                           <———————— (shell prompts
                                            <———————— returns)


% ed jobletter                              <———————— (Jack invokes editor)
? jobletter 148                             <———————— (editor responds)
a                                           <—— (append after last line in file)


  PS.Could you advance me $25,000.          <———————— (Jack types this)
Thanks

.                                           <———————— (Jack ends text entry)
```

```
w                                      <——— (writes contents to memory)
192                                    <——————— (editor responds)
q                                      <——————— (Jack quits editor)
%                                      <——————— (shell prompt)
```

These examples illustrate the major features of the Text Input Mode using the **a** command. Later in this chapter, we will give examples of creating text using the insert command **i** and the change command **c**.

Meanwhile, a day has passed, and Jack wants to make some changes to his text. To do this, he needs the often-used "substitute" command **s**.

The Substitute Command: *s*

If you want to change the spelling of a word, or add new words to a line, you must use the substitute command **s**. Since **ed** is a line-oriented editor, our imaginary cursor can only distinguish lines. It *cannot* move within a line; this lack is the major drawback to a line editor. Thus, to tell the editor what word we want to change, we have to literally spell out the word as shown in the following entry:

```
3s/old word(s)/new word(s)
```

Recall that the number is an address. If you leave the number off, then the substitution is made to the current line.

You can also add a print **p** parameter (a parameter is like a command) to the end of the substitute command which will cause the editor to print the line *after* making the substitution. It would look like this

```
3s/old word(s)/new word(s)/p
```

The substitution patterns are strings, just like the search patterns, so you must exercise some care when using them. For example, suppose line 3 reads

```
He commanded the next man to paint the cows blue.
```

What would the effect of the command

```
3s/man/woman/p
```

114

be? Since the first occurrence of the string "man" is in "command," the result would be:

```
He comwomanded the next man to paint the cows blue.
```

For this example, a better command would have been

```
3s/man /woman /p
```

It would have skipped to the first occurrence of "man" followed by a space.

Now, let's go back to our previous example and see what changes Jack wants to make and how he does it. Jack begins by typing

```
ed jobletter
```

and gets the editor's response of

```
192
```

The first change that Jack wants to make is to replace the word "delighted" with "happy." "It's best not to sound overeager," he thought. He can make the change by typing **p** and stepping through the letter using the [return] key until he reaches the line he wants. It's easier, though, to use the search mode; in which case, the process could look like this:

```
/delighted/
    I am delighted to accept your offer as chief
s/delighted/happy/p
    I am happy to accept your offer as chief
```

He could have combined his two commands into one:

```
/delighted/s/delighted/happy/p
```

The first "/delighted/" identifies the line; the second "/delighted/" identifies the word to be changed. Too much typing for you? This command can be shortened to

```
/delighted/s//happy/p
```

If you have a search pattern followed by a substitution command, as we just did, and the search word is the one you want to replace (again, as we just did), you can use this form. The **ed**, upon seeing the two slashes in a row (no spaces) after the **s**, will understand that it should use the preceding pattern ("delighted," in this case) for the word to be replaced.

In any case, after Jack makes the change, the affected line is the current line. He makes one more substitution as follows:

```
s/chief/Chief/p
    I am happy to accept your offer as Chief
```

Since no new address was given, this change took place on the same line.

Finally, he wants to make a change on the next line. In order to read the next line, Jack again pushes the [return] key to get

```
    trouble shooter for the Eon Corp. for $250,000
```

Jack wants to delete the word "the" in this line so he uses the command

```
s/the //p
```

This command reads: Take the current line and substitute for the string "the " the blank space that is between the slashes (that is, nothing) and print the results. This gives

```
    trouble shooter for Eon Corp. for $250,000
```

Notice the space after the "the" in the substitution command. In the sentence, there is a space on each side of "the." If Jack just typed:

```
s/the//p
```

two spaces would remain between "for" and "Eon." The command he used eliminated one of the spaces, thus keeping the word spacing regular.

Jack can now record these changes using the **write** command and, then, leave the editor with the **quit** command.

Although the commands we've used so far (**append**, **print**, **substitute**, **write**, and **quit**) are enough to get you started, there are a few more commands that can augment your editing prowess considerably.

Additional Editing Commands in *ed*

We hope you have tried out the previous editing commands on a terminal and are ready to add additional editing power to your repertoire. Here is a brief summary of the new editing commands that we will cover next.

1. Commands that operate on lines.
   A. The move command, **m**
   B. The delete command, **d**
   C. The copy command, **t**
2. Commands that enter the Text Input Mode.
   A. The insert command, **i**
   B. The change command, **c**
3. Special commands.
   A. The global parameter, **g**

We will now illustrate these commands by considering the efforts of Paul the Poet, who is trying mightily to create a short poem. So far, Paul has produced a file called **April.Rain**. He cannot use the filename **April Rain** with a space between the names because UNIX interprets this as *two* files. Paul now wants to edit what he has, so he types

```
ed April.Rain
```

and, then,

```
1,$p
```

to print out the entire file as follows:

```
It's not raining rain on me,
   It's raining whippoorwills
In every dimpled drop I see
   Streaming flowing hills
```

Paul wants to make some changes. Specifically, he wants to delete the last line and put in a new line. He can do this in any one of three ways. First, he could delete line 4 with

```
4d
```

Then, he could add the new line with the **append** command, i.e., enter the new line after typing

```
3a
```

or, he could use the **insert** command after the delete command by entering the line after typing

```
4i
```

Note that the **insert** command inserts lines before the "addressed" line, whereas the **append** command inserts lines after the addressed line. Thus, the command **3a** will add text after line 3 and the command **4i** will add text before line 4. Command **3a** is thus equivalent to command **4i**.

The third way to make this change is to not use the delete command at all, but use the **change** or **c** command which deletes and replaces in one step. Paul does this by typing

```
4c
    Wildflowers on the hill
.
```

Now, Paul wants to start a second stanza with the same lines that started the first. That is, he wants to copy the first two lines and place them at the end of the buffer file. He does this by using the **t** command.

```
1,2t$
```

He can check his results by printing the current line (line dot) as follows:

```
p
```

which gives the last line copied

```
It's raining whippoorwills
```

To see if the preceding line was copied, Paul types the minus character, or — command as follows:

```
−
```

and, the editor responds with:

```
It's not raining rain on me,
```

Now Paul thinks of some new lines to add at the end of the poem so he types:

```
$a
  Where clever busy bumblebees
    Will find their board and room.
  .
```

Remember that the **$** symbol stands for the last line so **$a** means append after the last line.

"Aha," thinks Paul, "let's change whippoorwill to daffodil!" He can do this with the substitute command, as follows:

```
1,$s/whippoorwills/daffodils/p
```

Here the command **s** is the substitute command applied from line 1 to the end of the file ($). The last **p** prints any lines containing the substitution. Paul now wants to step through the poem from beginning to end using the [return] key. Here is how it looks on the screen:

```
1p
  It's not raining rain on me
[return]
    It's raining daffodils
[return]
  In every dimpled drop I see
[return]
    Wildflowers on the hills
[return]
[return]
  It's not raining rain on me
[return]
    It's raining daffodils
```

In a flush of growing excitement, Paul decides to change the last line before continuing. To double-check that he has the right line, he types

```
.p
```

and gets

```
    It's raining daffodils
```

He replaces that line by typing

```
.c
        But fields of clover bloom
.
```

"Aha," says Paul, "this is it!" He prints the entire poem using

```
1,$p
```

The editor responds with:

```
It's not raining rain on me
    It's raining daffodils
In every dimpled drop I see
    Wildflowers on the hill

It's not raining rain on me
    But fields of clover bloom
Where clever busy bumblebees
    Will find their board and room
```

(This poem is an adaptation of ''April Rain'' by Robert Loveman.)

120

Gleefully, Paul saves his work and quits the editor using

```
w
q
```

Making Searches and Substitutions Global: *g*

The search command and the substitution command share the property that each looks for the *first* occurrence of the pattern. A search ends as soon as it finds a line containing the search pattern, and a substitution acts only on the first occurrence in the line of the pattern. Suppose, for instance that we are editing a file whose text is as follows:

```
It was a hot, blustery day. Most folks stayed indoors. Not me.
A dog came ambling down the street. He wasn't a big dog,
and he wasn't a small dog; he was just an in-between dog.
```

Suppose for this and for the following examples that the first line is the current line. Then, the command

```
/dog/s//tiger/p
```

would produce the following result:

```
A tiger came ambling down the street. He wasn't a big dog,
```

That is, **ed** found the first line containing "dog" and replaced the first occurrence of "dog" with "tiger." We can make the command more universal or "global" by using the **g** parameter and command. There are two ways to use it in this example. First, we can put a **g** command in front of the search pattern. This will cause **ed** to find *all* lines containing "dog." The interchange would look like this:

```
g/dog/s//tiger/p
```

```
A tiger came ambling down the street. He wasn't a big dog,
and he wasn't a small tiger; he was just an in-between dog.
```

Still, however, only the first "dog" on each line is changed to "tiger." The second way to use the **g** remedies this. By putting a **g** parameter after the

121

substitution command, we make **ed** replace *every* occurrence of "dog" on a given line. By using a **g** in both places, we get a truly global substitution that affects all "dog" entries on all lines:

```
g/dog/s//tiger/gp
```

```
A tiger came ambling down the street. He wasn't a big tiger,
and he wasn't a small tiger; he was just an in-between tiger.
```

Moving Lines and Writing to Another File: *m* and *w*

So far, we have used the most common **ed** commands. However, it's worthwhile to show another use of the **w**rite command and, also, illustrate the **m**ove command.

The **w**rite command can be used to copy excerpts from a text file for use in another file. This can be done from the editor using a command like

```
3,7w AprilRain2
```

This command would place lines 3 through 7 in the file called **AprilRain2**, creating the file in the process.

However, let's assume **AprilRain2** was an existing file and you had just used the **w**rite command as described above. Now the existing file is *replaced* by lines 3 through 7. As you can see, the **w**rite command can be dangerous, since it can wipe out existing files. You need to be careful in choosing your file names.

Our last text-rearranging command is the **m**ove command **m**. For example, suppose that we have a file containing the lines

```
Apolexy
Bongo
Doobidoo
Cackle
```

Now, we want to make this list alphabetical. Suppose "Cackle" is on line 4. We can have it moved to just after line 2 by commanding

```
4m2
```

which will move line 4 to a position after line 2, and all is well.

We have just introduced the major features of the **ed** editor. There are some aspects of **ed** that we have left out, mainly in the use of "metacharacters" and "regular expressions." You can use the on-line manual **man ed** for more information about these features. We will conclude this section on **ed** with a comprehensive summary.

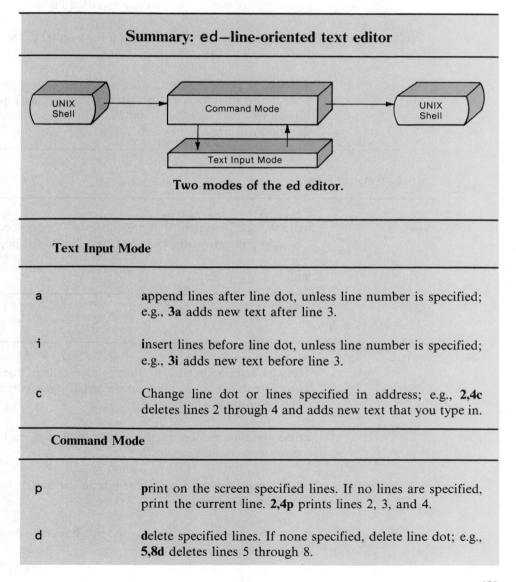

Summary: ed—line-oriented text editor

Two modes of the ed editor.

Text Input Mode

a   append lines after line dot, unless line number is specified; e.g., **3a** adds new text after line 3.

i   insert lines before line dot, unless line number is specified; e.g., **3i** adds new text before line 3.

c   Change line dot or lines specified in address; e.g., **2,4c** deletes lines 2 through 4 and adds new text that you type in.

Command Mode

p   print on the screen specified lines. If no lines are specified, print the current line. **2,4p** prints lines 2, 3, and 4.

d   delete specified lines. If none specified, delete line dot; e.g., **5,8d** deletes lines 5 through 8.

m	move specified lines to line named after **m**; e.g., **1,2m5** moves lines 1 and 2, placing them after line 5.
t	Copy specified lines to line named after **t**; e.g., **2,4t$** copies lines 2 through 4, placing them at end of buffer.
s/one/two/	substitutes the word "two" for the word "one" for the first occurrence of word "one" in the specified lines.
/nice/	Searches for the next line to contain the word(s) between the slashes; in this case, the string "nice."
g	global search or substitute generally used with **s** or /.../. **g/.../** finds all lines with the given pattern. **s/pat1/pat2/g** substitutes "pat2" for "pat1" for all occurrences of "pat1" in the specified lines.

Leaving the editor

w	write the specified lines that are addressed to a named file; e.g., **2,5w popcorn** writes lines 2 through 5 into file **popcorn**.
q	quit.

Addressing lines

.	This character addresses the current line, called "line dot." The current line is the last line affected by a command. Thus, **.p** prints the current line.
.=	Prints the line number of the current line; e.g., editor responds with a number like "5."
$	This character addresses the last line in the buffer; e.g., **$d** deletes the last line.
n	A decimal number **n** addresses the **n**th line; e.g., **3p** prints line number 3.

+	The + and − are used in conjunction with a reference line which may be specified with **n** or **$** or line dot, if unspecified; e.g., **$-5,$p** prints the last six lines of buffer.
−	
[return]	When used with no command, it is equivalent to **. + 1**, i.e., the next line. Very useful for stepping through the buffer.

Review Questions

Here are some questions to give you practice in applying the commands of this chapter.

A. Matching Commands to Functions

Match the commands shown on the left to the functions shown on the right. Assume all the commands are given in the Command Mode only; none are given from the Text Input Mode. The functions can be used more than once.

ed *Editor Commands*

1. $p
2. 2,4d
3. 3s/fun/funny/
4. 5,6m$
5. 5,6t$
6. 2,4/s/no/yes/g
7. /fun/
8. .=
9. 6a
    Chuckles is slow

Functions

a. Deletes lines 2 to 4.
b. Prints the number of the current line.
c. Copies lines 5 and 6 by placing them at the end of the file.
d. Moves lines 5 and 6 to end of file.
e. Substitutes funny for fun.
f. Substitutes yes for no in all occurrences in lines 2 to 4.
g. Prints the next line containing the string "fun".
h. Appends the line "Chuckles is slow" after line 6.
i. Prints current line.
j. Prints final line.

B. Questions

Here are some general questions.

1. When you invoke the editor with a file, e.g., using **ed file3**, how can you tell if it is a new file?
2. Why is the **q** command considered dangerous?
3. When you first enter the editor with an existing file and type **a**, the append command to add text, where is that text placed?

4. What command is used to save the editor buffer contents?
5. Where does the insert command **i** place new text?
6. Write out the command that will save the first three lines only of an editor buffer containing seven lines of text.
7. How do you exit the Text Input Mode?
8. Write out the command(s) to correct the following misspelled word, "sometome."
9. Write out the command(s) to delete the last five lines in ten lines of text.

Answers.

A. **1**–j, **2**–a, **3**–e, **4**–d, **5**–c, **6**–f, **7**–g, **8**–i, **9**–h

B. **1. ed** responds with the number of characters. **2.** It doesn't save your work. Give a **w** before **q**. **3.** At the end of the file. **4. w. 5.** Before the cursor. **6. 1,3w newfile. 7.** Use a lone dot "." at the beginning of a new line. **8. s/sometome/sometime/p** will also print the line. **9. 6,10d.**

Exercises at the Terminal

Here are some exercises to practice your editing techniques.

1. Enter the following text into a new file called **letterrec1**.

    Dear Sir:
        This is a letter of recommendation for john doe.
        john doe is a good worker.
        john doe has a fine character.
        john doe is a-ok.

            sincerely
            jane doe

2. Now, do the following:
    A. Save the letter.
    B. Correct all spelling errors.
    C. Capitalize jane, john, and doe.
    D. Delete the last sentence containing a-ok.
    E. Save the corrected letter as **letterrec2**.
    F. Leave the editor.
    G. Use **cat** to print both copies on the screen at the same time.
3. Go into the shell, list your files with **ls**, and do the following:
    A. Make a copy of one of your files, e.g., **mbox**, calling it **mbox2** or something similar.

B. Now, invoke the editor with this copy of a file and:
   (1) Insert the line, "This is a test", somewhere in the text.
   (2) Move 3 lines.
   (3) Replace all occurrences of the word "the" with "thee."
   (4) Copy 2 lines and place them in the beginning of the file.
   (5) Delete the last 4 lines.

6

The *vi* Screen Editor

In this chapter, you will find:

6 THE *vi* SCREEN EDITOR

Introduction

The **vi** editor is a much more sophisticated editor than **ed**. Its chief advantage is that it lets you move a cursor to any portion of the text you desire and to work on just that part. Thus, you can change a single letter or a single word in a line or you can insert new text in the middle of a line much more easily than you can with a line editor, such as **ed**.

The **vi** is an interactive text editor designed to be used with a crt terminal. It provides a "window" into the file you are editing. This window lets you see about 20 lines of the file at a time, and you can move the window up and down through the file. You can move to any part of any line on the screen and can make changes there. The additions and changes you make to the file are reflected in what you see on the screen. The **vi** stands for "visual," and enlightened users refer to it as "vee-eye." A complete description of the 100 or so commands in **vi** would overwhelm the beginning **vi** user; for that reason, we have chosen to divide our presentation of **vi** commands into three parts. These three parts represent three levels of expertise.

To begin, here is a brief overview of **vi**, showing the three levels of commands we have chosen to describe. A beginning user should read Part 1 which lists the "Basic commands to start using **vi**" and, if possible, should practice them before seriously studying the next levels.

1. Basic commands to start using **vi**.
   - A. Commands to position the cursor—**h, j, k, l** and [return]
   - B. Commands to enter the Text Input Mode—**a, i, o, O**
   - C. Commands to leave the Text Input Mode—[esc]
   - D. Commands that delete or replace—**x, dd, r**
   - E. Commands that undo changes—**u, U**
   - F. Commands to save and quit the editor—**ZZ, :w, :q!, :wq**
   - G. Commands from the "shell" for erasing—[del], or [control-h], or [#]
2. Advanced **vi** commands to enhance your skill.
   - A. Commands to position the cursor including "scrolling," "paging," and "searching"—[control-d], [control-u], **e, b, G, nG**, [control-g], **/pattern, $, 0**
   - B. Commands that will operate on words, sentences, lines, or paragraphs—**c, d, y**
   - C. Abbreviations for words, sentences, lines, or paragraphs—**w, b, e,** >, <, **0, $, {, }**

     D.   Commands to print storage buffers—**p**, **P**
     E.   Joining lines—**J**
  3. Additional **vi** Commands.
     A.   There are 60 or so additional commands to do more of the same kinds of editing as described above. In addition to these commands, there are "special" features of **vi**, such as "mapping" and adjusting **vi** to fit your terminal type.

The article "An Introduction to Display Editing With Vi" by William Joy and Mark Horton, available from the University of California, Berkeley (see Appendix B) gives the full story on **vi**.

Starting *vi*

Although **vi** is a very sophisticated editor with an enormous number of commands, the basic structure of **vi** is very simple. There are two modes of operation, the Command Mode and the Text Input Mode, as shown in the following diagram.

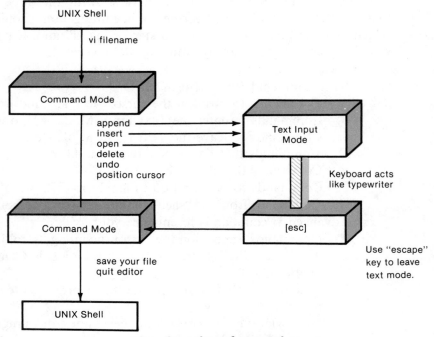

The *vi* modes of operation.

In this section, we will limit ourselves to the minimum number of commands that you will need to start using **vi**. Even though these commands are just a few of the total commands in **vi**, they cover the four major features of editing:

cursor positioning

text insertion

deletions and changes

permanently storing information

The method of starting **vi** is identical to the way we started the **ed** editor. You must be in the UNIX shell as indicated by a shell prompt (%). The command given is

```
vi filename
```

Just as in **ed**, the "filename" may be a file already in your directory; in which case, the file contents are copied into a temporary buffer for editing. If you do *not* have a file by that name, then a new file is created. When you call the **vi** editor, it responds on the screen with the contents of the file, followed by a series of tilde (∼) marks and, at the bottom of the screen, the name of the file.

Suppose you already have an existing file called **ohio**. If you type

```
vi ohio
```

the editor displays the contents of the file which, in this case, is assumed to be

```
What is the capital of Ohio?
Columbus
~
~
~
~
~
~
~
"ohio" 2/38
```

We assume you put the text shown on the screen into the file earlier. The first number (the "2" in 2/38) at the bottom tells how many lines there are. The second number (38) gives the number of characters. The editor is now in the Command Mode and the cursor is positioned in the upper left-hand corner of the screen; in this case, on the letter "W."

Any changes, deletions, or additions that we wish to make are made with reference to the cursor position. So the next question is, "How do we move the cursor?"

Moving the Cursor

More than 40 commands in **vi** help you position the cursor in the buffer file. In the first part of "Moving the Cursor," we will show you how to get anywhere on the screen (and, therefore, in a text file) using the five basic keys shown in the following sketch. Part 2 of "Moving the Cursor" will be given later in the section "Cursor Positioning Commands." In the second part, we will demonstrate many more cursor moving commands.

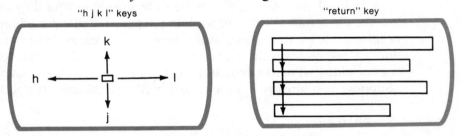

Basic cursor positioning keys.

Some terminals have "arrow" keys to move the cursor. However, most experienced typists prefer the [h, j, k, l] keys since they are close at hand, under the fingers. (At least they should be.) The [return] key is similar to the [j] key in that it moves the cursor down one line. However, the [return] key always positions the cursor at the *beginning* of the next line down, whereas, the [j] key moves the cursor straight down from its present position, which could be in the middle of a line.

If you have never tried moving the cursor, you should try it out at your earliest convenience. It's fun and easy to do. Make sure to practice cursor positioning on an existing file, since the cursor cannot be moved in a new file that doesn't contain any text. That is, these keys will only move the cursor over lines or characters of text that already exist in a file. This situation is shown in the following drawing titled "Positioning the cursor."

If you have an empty file, the editor "knows" that and thinks "why waste time trying to move the cursor if you have nothing to edit." This might lead to the question of "How do you enter text into a new file if you can't move the cursor?" The answer naturally leads to our next subject.

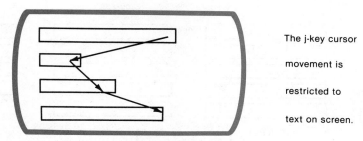

The j-key cursor movement is restricted to text on screen.

Positioning the cursor.

The Text Input Mode

We will show you four commands that let you use your keyboard to type text into a file. These commands are

> **a** for **a**ppend
> **i** for **i**nsert
> **o** and **O** for **o**pen

Each of these commands is referenced to the cursor location.

If you start **vi** on a new file, the cursor is restricted to the upper-leftmost position on the screen. The cursor cannot be moved by any of the cursor moving keys. However, if you use the **append a**, **insert i**, or **open O** commands, then text can be entered starting in the upper left-hand corner of the screen, just as you normally start writing on a piece of paper. You might wonder, "How can you place text in the middle of the line; for example, a title?" The answer is that you use the [space bar] key *after* entering the Text Input Mode.

If you start **vi** on a new file and use the **open** command **o** or **O**, then the cursor is moved one line up (**O**) or one line down (**o**), and is ready to receive text from the keyboard.

Illustrations of these text insertions while in the Text Input Mode are shown in the sketches on the next page.

The usual way to start a new file is to type **vi** and follow it with a space and the filename that you want to use. When the editor is ready, type **a** and [return]. Then, start typing away as if you were using an electric typewriter. Hit the [return] key to start a new line. If you make a typing error, you can use [control–h] or your regular erase key to back up and correct yourself. On many terminals, the erased letters don't disappear from the screen until you type over them, but they are erased from the buffer regardless.

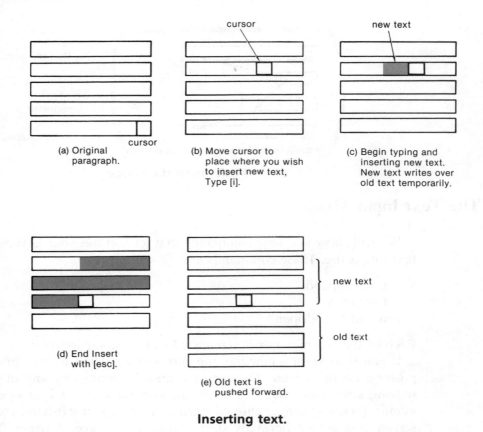

cursor

new text

(a) Original
   paragraph.

(b) Move cursor to
   place where you wish
   to insert new text,
   Type [i].

(c) Begin typing and
   inserting new text.
   New text writes over
   old text temporarily.

(d) End Insert
   with [esc].

(e) Old text is
   pushed forward.

new text

old text

Inserting text.

An example of beginning a new file and using the **append** command to insert text in it would look like this:

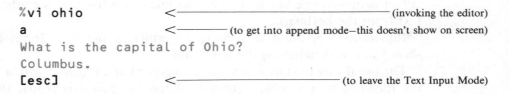

```
%vi ohio                    ←————————————————————— (invoking the editor)
a                           ←——————— (to get into append mode–this doesn't show on screen)
What is the capital of Ohio?
Columbus.
[esc]                       ←————————————————————— (to leave the Text Input Mode)
```

You can leave the Text Input Mode by pushing the [esc] key; the cursor remains where you left it.

Now assume that we have an existing file with two lines of text and the cursor was moved to the position shown below using the [l] key (ell) key.

```
              |
              |
              |
              |
              ↓
What is the capital of Ohio?
Columbus
```

The cursor is assumed to be on the letter "o" in the word "of". What happens when you use these four text input commands?

Each command puts you in the Text Input Mode for entering text. You can enter one letter or dozens of lines of text. The major difference between the commands is *where* the new text is entered. For example,

a   enters whatever you type *after* the cursor, "pushing" the rest of the line to the right. (On many terminals, you don't see the words pushed over until after you hit the [esc] key to leave the text mode. The new text will appear to obliterate the old text while you type, but the old text reappears when you hit [esc].)

i   enters whatever you type *before* the cursor, again pushing the rest of the line to the right.

o   opens up a line *below* the cursor, places the cursor at the beginning of the new line, and enters whatever you type.

O   is like **o** except that it opens a line *above* the present cursor position.

Suppose we try out each of the commands just described and enter 33333 from the keyboard (typewriter). Here is what each command would do to the text:

```
What is the capital of Ohio?                    (cursor on "o" in of)
Columbus


What is the capital o33333f Ohio?                       (append a)
Columbus


What is the capital 33333of Ohio?                       (insert i)
Columbus


What is the capital of Ohio?                            (open o)
33333
Columbus
```

137

```
33333
What is the capital of Ohio?                                    (open O)
Columbus
```

To end each of these Text Input Modes, you push the [esc] key. This places you back in the Command Mode.

You might be wondering what happens to the original text if you type in more than just five 3's. Suppose you insert several sentences before the letter "o". Where does "Ohio" go to? It just moves to the right of the screen as far as possible, and if more text is introduced, "Ohio" drops down to the next line. This is called "wraparound" and is shown by the following sketches:

THE CAT AND THE DOG FIGHT

EVERY CHANCE THAT THEY GET

1. Everything you type is kept on the screen, "wrapping" around as necessary.

THE CAT AND THE DOG FIGHT

EVERY CHANCE THAT THEY GET

2. Text "inserted" or "appended" in vi appears to write over existing text (until you push the [esc] key).

THE CAT AND THE DOG TEASE

EACH OTHER AND FIGHT EVERY

CHANCE THAT THEY GET

3. After pushing [esc] key, the old text reappears, wrapped around as necessary.

Wordwrap and inserting text.

Line Lengths and Automatic Right Margins

In the preceding chapter, we told you about the distinction between the length of a line on the screen and the length of a line in the file, and we stressed the importance of using the [return] key to start new lines. In **vi**, you can have the right margin set and can have new lines started automatically. Suppose, for example, you want the right margin set 15 spaces from the end of the screen. Then, while in the Command Mode, give this command:

```
:set wrapmargin=15
```

There should be no spaces in **wrapmargin=15**. Now, enter the Text Mode and try typing some text. When you reach the sixty-fifth column (that's 80 − 15), the editor will start a new line, just as if you had hit the [return] key. Actually, the editor is even cleverer than that; if you are in the middle of a word that would take you past the sixty-fifth column, **vi** will move the whole word to the next line. This means your right margin may not be even, but your lines won't end with broken-off words.

The **wrapmargin** command will stay in effect until you quit the editor. It is just one of several such commands available. Others do such things as adjust the tab widths, cause a new line to start with the same left margin as the preceding line, and tell the editor to check for matching parentheses. Each of these commands can be set semipermanently as shown in Chapter 10 and as described in the article by William Joy and Mark Horton that was mentioned earlier.

Now that we have these four versions of "Ohio," how can we "clean" them up? To "clean up" text or a program is a commonly used expression in a computer environment. It means to make it right, and to remove all unnecessary garbage. Unfortunately, there always seems to be a lot of "cleaning up" of files to do. This leads to our next set of commands for deleting and changing words and lines.

Deleting and Changing Text

There are three oft used commands for making small changes to the contents of a file. These are the **x** command for erasing one character, the **r** command for replacing one character, and the **dd** command for deleting one line. All three commands are made while in the Command Mode and all three leave you in the Command Mode after using them. Of course, all three commands use the cursor on the screen as the reference point for making changes.

Let's use the following example to illustrate the use of these commands. Suppose you have an existing file called **ohio** and you begin by typing:

```
vi ohio
```

The editor responds by displaying:

```
What is the capital o33333f Ohio?
33333
Columbus
~
~                                          (the left column is filled with tildes ~~~)
~
~
~
~
''ohio'' 3/49
```

The cursor starts out in the upper left-hand corner on the letter W.

To eliminate the 3's in the word "o33333f", you first use the [l] key (ell key) to move the cursor to the first number 3. Then, type:

```
x
```

This deletes the first 3 and very conveniently moves the rest of the line to the left. You can repeat the process four times more. That is, type:

```
xxxx
```

to delete the remaining 3's. The screen should look like this:

```
What is the capital of Ohio?
33333
Columbus
```

The cursor is left on the letter "f" in the word "of". Now, to get rid of the remaining 3's, we must move the cursor down one line. There are two ways to do this. You can use the [j] or the [return] key. The [j] key moves the cursor straight down. However, since there is no text below the "f", the closest point is the last number 3 in the next line.

The [return] key would position the cursor at the beginning of the line, on the first number 3. Actually, when you want to delete a line, it doesn't matter where in the line the cursor is located. You just type

```
dd
```

and the line is deleted. On some terminals, the editor places an @ symbol on the deleted line and moves the cursor down to the next line. It looks like this

```
What is the capital of Ohio?
@
Columbus
```

The @ symbol means that the line does not exist in the buffer even though you still see the space it left behind on the screen. Some terminals are "smart" enough to actually remove the line on the screen right after you delete it; the screen is redrawn with the remaining text moved up line by line to replace the deleted line.

Suppose that you wanted to make one last change. You wanted to capitalize each letter in the word "Ohio". First, you move the cursor up to the letter "h" by pushing the [k] key to move up one line, and then the [l] key to move to the right. Once you are on the letter "h", you type the following sequence:

```
rH
```

The first letter you type is **r**, the **r**eplace command. You replace whatever is under the cursor with the next keystroke, which in this case is a capital H [shift–h]. The cursor remains on the letter H.

In order to replace "i" with "I", you move the cursor one letter to the right using the [l] key and now type

```
rI
```

You can repeat the process and type

```
rO
```

to complete the change.

You may think that there ought to be a better way to make these changes. There is. In fact, there are two slightly easier ways, but in order to keep this introduction to **vi** simple, we have postponed discussion of these until later in the chapter.

Now that we have "cleaned up" our file, let's take one last look at it before we save the changes that were made. On the screen, it looks like this:

```
What is the capital of OHIO?
Columbus
```

Undoing Changes: *u* and *U*

Sometimes you may make a change and suddenly wish you hadn't done so. When that time comes, you will bless the "undo" commands. As the name implies, these commands undo what you have just done. The **u** command, which can only be given in the Command Mode, of course, negates the preceding command. If you delete a line with a **dd**, then typing **u** will restore it.

If you use the **i** command to insert the word "mush" in a line, then **u** will remove it. (You must go back to the Command Mode to undo.)

The **U** command is more general. It will undo *all* the changes you've made on the current line. For instance, consider the example where we used the **r** command to change "Ohio" to "OHIO". Hitting the **u** key would undo the last command (which was replacing "o" with "O") so that command would restore "OHIO" to "OHIo". But the **U** key would undo all the changes, restoring "OHIO" to "Ohio".

Many people, when starting out, find the **undo** commands to be extremely valuable.

The next section discusses saving text and quitting the **vi** editor.

How To Leave the *vi* Editor

Probably the single most frustrating experience you can have with a computer is to *lose* several hours worth of work. It is possible to do this in an editor with one or two careless commands. When considering leaving the editor, you might ask yourself this basic question: "Do I want to save the changes made during this editing session?" There are three possible answers; Yes, No, and Maybe.

The different ways you can save information and leave the **vi** editor are summarized as follows:

Command	What it Does
`ZZ [return]`	Writes contents of temporary buffer onto disk for permanent storage. Uses the filename that you used to enter **vi**. Puts you in the shell.
`:wq [return]`	The same as ZZ. **w** stands for **write**, **q** stands for **quit**.
`:w [return]` `:q [return]`	Writes the buffer contents to the memory, then quits the editor. A two-step version of **:wq**.
`:q! [return]`	Quits the editor and abandons the temporary buffer contents. No changes are made.

All of these commands must be made from the Command Mode and they will all place you back into the shell as indicated by the prompt (% or $). We have shown you use of the [return] key once more to clarify these important commands.

To leave the **vi** editor and save any changes made, it is best to use **ZZ** while in the command mode. You could also leave the editor with either **:wq** or **:w** [return] **:q**. However, you run the risk of absent-mindedly typing **:q!** instead. (This may not sound very likely to you. Of course, it didn't sound very likely either to the many people who have made this error.)

To leave the editor *without* saving changes, the normal way is to use **:q!**. You might use this command if you started to edit a file and did not like the way the changes were shaping up. The **:q!** leaves the original file unchanged and lets you abandon the editor's temporary buffer.

If you're not sure about saving changes, the best step is to save both versions of the file, the original and the changed version. This is done by using the **write** command with a new filename. For example, it might look like this:

```
:w ohio.new
```

or

```
:w ohio2
```

Thus, if you are editing **ohio** and make some changes, this command creates a new file under the new name. Here we show two common ways to create similar names; by adding a ".new" or a "2" to the existing name. After creating this new file, the **vi** editor will provide you with a confirmation as follows

```
''ohio.new'' [New file] 2/39
```

You can now safely leave the editor with **:q** or with **:q!**.

The difference between the commands **:q!** and **:q** is that **:q** will only leave the editor if there have been no changes since the last **w** command. Thus, it provides some protection against accidentally quitting the editor. The command **:q!** leaves the editor in one step.

Actually, when you are involved in long editing sessions, it is advisable to use the **write** command every 15 to 20 minutes, or so, to update your permanent file copy. Some users use **cp** to make a copy of a file before editing. Thus, they can update their copy every 15 to 20 minutes and can still retain the original version. All of these comments pertaining to saving text will apply equally to all types of files, no matter whether they are programs, data, or text files.

If you have been trying out these commands, you now have the basic skills needed to edit a file. You can create a file with the **vi** command, insert text with the **a**, **i**, **o**, and **O** commands. You can delete letters and lines with **x** and **dd**. You can replace letters with **r**. You can undo rash changes with **u** and **U**. You can save your results and exit the editor.

These **vi** commands should be enough to allow you to easily edit or create short files. You should practice them, if at all possible, before going on to the next section. Some of you will find that these commands are good enough for all your needs. If you seek greater variety and control, read on.

Additional *vi* Commands

If you need to edit or create short text files once or twice a week, you will usually find that the basic **vi** command list, discussed in the previous section, will be satisfactory for most work. However, if you must edit long texts, you may begin to long for greater editing power; **vi** has plenty of editing horse-power. In this section, we will shift into high gear to further explore the magic of the **vi** editor.

Since cursor positioning in the text buffer file is so important, especially in medium-size and long files, we will show you how to place the cursor anywhere in the file with just a few keystrokes. Then we will explore three commands known as "operators" that can make changes to words, lines, sentences, or paragraphs. Two of these operators actually provide you with temporary storage buffers that make relocating lines and paragraphs within a text file very easy to do.

Cursor Positioning Commands

We have already used five basic keys to position the cursor—the h, j, k, l, and [return] keys. Now we will add seven more keys and a searching function that will position the cursor easily over any size text file. We will start by considering four keys [b, e, $, Ø] that are useful in short text files. Then we add two keystrokes, [control–d] and [control–u], that are handy for medium (1–5 screen pages) text files. At this point, we will also explain "scrolling" and "paging." Then, we will complete our cursor positioning repertoire by looking at two commands used to position the cursor in large (5–100 or more screen pages) text files. These are the nG and /pattern commands.

The four keys [b, e, $, ∅] have a certain symmetry in their operation. Here is what they do:

b   Moves the cursor to the beginning of a word. Each time you push the [b] key, the cursor moves to the *left* to the beginning letter of the preceding word.

e   Moves the cursor to the *end* of a word. Each time you push the [e] key, the cursor moves to the *right* to the end letter of the next word.

Both the [b] and [e] keys will move to the next line, unlike the [h] and [l] keys which can only move the cursor back and forth to the end of the line. The [b] and [e] key operations are shown in the following drawing.

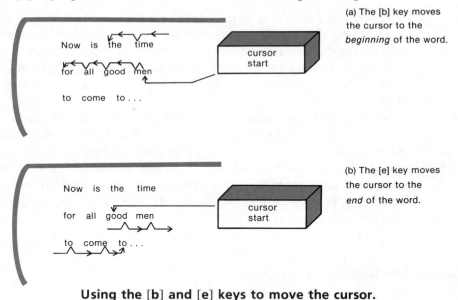

(a) The [b] key moves the cursor to the *beginning* of the word.

(b) The [e] key moves the cursor to the *end* of the word.

Using the [b] and [e] keys to move the cursor.

In a similar way, the [∅] and [$] keys move the cursor to the beginning and end of a *line* (rather than a word) as follows:

∅   This is the number zero key. It moves the cursor to the *beginning* of the line.

$ Moves the cursor to the *end* of the line.

These two keys can only be used on the line containing the cursor. The cursor does not jump to the next line as it does with the [b] and [e] key commands. Recall that the [return] key will jump lines and is similar to the sequence [j] [0]. The [0] and [$] operations are shown in the following drawing.

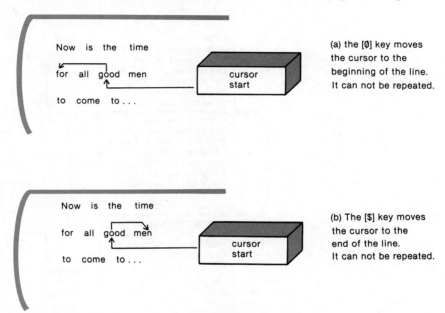

Using the [0̸] and [$] keys to move the cursor.

Now, let's take a closer look at how text moves on the screen.

Screen Scrolling and Paging

Sometimes, there is more text in the buffer than can fit on the screen at one time. You may have noticed that if this happens, you can bring more text into view by trying to move the cursor past the bottom (or top) of the screen. The cursor stays put, but a new line moves up (or down) into view. This is called "scrolling." So far, the [j], [k], and [return] keys, discussed in the previous section, as well as the [b] and [e] keys, will cause the screen to scroll. To visualize scrolling, imagine that the text is arranged on one long continuous page (like a scroll) and that only a portion of it appears on the screen at any particular time. Your crt screen, then, is like a window into the text, usually showing 24 text lines with 80 characters per line. See the following sketch. Imagine that the window moves while the text remains fixed.

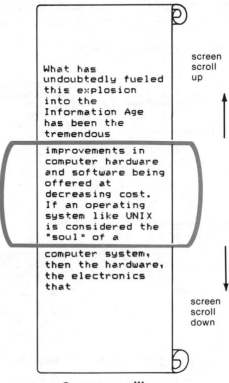

Screen scrolling.

The direction of scrolling usually refers to the direction the window moves past the text. For example, when we give the command to scroll down, the window moves downward and the text below the original window comes into view. When we scroll up, we "push" the window up and reveal portions of the text that precede the text in the original window location.

Different terminals will behave differently, even though the same **vi** commands are used. Some terminals can scroll down but will not scroll up. If a terminal cannot "scroll" up, then it must "page" up.

"Paging" means that the screen is completely erased and redrawn in a new position. Paging has the same end effect as scrolling 24 lines, but the process is different.

The cursor positioning keys [b], [e], [j], [k], and [return] will generally "page" or "scroll" the screen one line at a time. However, since a screen usually contains 24 lines, moving the text one line at a time in a large text file is unnecessary and time consuming. **vi** has two handy "scrolling" (or "paging") commands that solve this problem. They are the commands [control–u] and [control–d]. Recall that to get a [control–d], you push the [control] key and the [d] key simultaneously.

Here is a summary of these two cursor positioning keys.

[control-d]   Scrolls or pages the cursor *down*, usually 12 lines at a time.
[control-u]   Scrolls or pages the cursor *up*, usually 12 lines at a time.

Generally, most users prefer scrolling to paging since it is easier to follow the positioning of the cursor in the text file as the file moves up or down. Recall that paging erases the screen and redraws it, so you cannot follow the cursor to its final position.

If you have really *long* text files, even several [control–d] keyings can take too long. For example, this chapter contains about 1400 lines of text. This would require over 100 [control–d] keyings to reach the end of the file. Fortunately, there is an easier way. The command

nG

where "n" is an integer number will place the cursor on the line number "n". Thus, we could type

1400G

to move to line 1400. A similar command is the lonesome **G** command (capital G), which moves the cursor to the end of the file. Thus, if you type

G

while in the Command Mode, the cursor is positioned at the end of the file. To get to the beginning of the file, tell the editor that you want the first line; that is, type

1G

One very useful command related to the **nG** command is the [control–g] command, which tells you the line number the cursor is currently on. This is valuable in two ways. First, if you remember the number or write it down, you can come back to the spot later. Secondly, if you want to copy a portion of a file, [control–g] can be used to get the beginning and ending line numbers of the section. You can then save the section by using the **write** command with line numbers. The **write** command would look like this:

```
:120,230w chapter4.2b
```

This command would copy lines 120 to 230 and place them in a newly created file called **chapter4.2b**. If a file already existed with that name, the **w** command either destroys the file or does not work, depending on your particular version of **vi**.

Pattern Searches

Another way to position yourself in the file is by giving the editor a word or string of characters to search for. If you are in the **vi** command mode, you can type the character, /, followed by a string of characters that are terminated by a [return]. The editor will position the cursor at the first occurrence, in the text, of this string that comes after the cursor. For example, if you want to find the words, "happy day", just give the command

```
/happy day
```

If the first occurrence of "happy day" was not the one you wanted, you can move to the next occurrence by typing **n** for **n**ext. These searches will "wrap around" the end of the file and go back to the beginning to continue the process for as long as you type **n**.

If you prefer to search backward through the file instead of forward, the **?** will do that for you. Thus, the command

```
?malodorous
```

will start from the current cursor location and search backwards through your file for the word "malodorous." Again, the **n** will continue the search for the next preceding example. The search will wrap around to the end of the file when you reach the top.

Once you have the cursor where you want it, you are again in a position to make changes, move text around, or add new text to the file. We will look at these activities next.

Operators that Delete, Duplicate, Change, and Rearrange Text

We learned, in the section on basic **vi**, how to delete a line using the command **dd**. This delete command is actually made up of two parts; the delete "operator" **d** and the operator's "scope," the *line* symbolized by "d" again. The command **dw** uses the delete operator **d** but has as its scope a "word" as defined by the cursor and symbolized by "w." We can represent these types of commands as follows:

Operator + Scope = Command

In this section, we will discuss three operators and nine scopes. The operators are the "**d**elete," "**c**hange," and "**y**ank" operators. They can operate with the following scopes: words, lines, sentences, and paragraphs. We will then use the commands formed by these operators to delete, duplicate, change, and rearrange text. Sometimes, these kinds of changes are referred to as "cut and paste," describing the old-fashioned changes made with scissors and glue. This electronic version of "cut and paste" is more powerful, however, since we can "cut" more precisely and can make multiple copies for pasting.

The three operators and their scopes are summarized in the following lists. (We also include a description of the "put" command, for it teams up with the "yank" and the "delete" commands.)

Command	*Operator*
d	*Delete* operator. Deletes text, but stores a copy in a temporary memory buffer. The copy can be recovered using the "put" command, **p**.
y	*Yank* operator. Places a copy of text (word, sentence, line, etc.) into a temporary memory storage buffer for positioning elsewhere. The original text is left unchanged. The copy is "pasted" relative to the cursor position using the "put" command, **p**.
p	*Put* command. Works with the *yank* and the *delete* commands. Puts whatever was last deleted or yanked in place after or below the cursor.
c	*Change* operator. This is equivalent to a **d**elete operation and an **i**nsert command. It deletes a word, sentence, etc., and enters the Text Input Mode to allow the typing in of changes. Must be ended with an [esc].

These operators act with the following scopes, which are symbolized as shown.

Scope	Operation
e	The scope is from the cursor to the *end* of the current word; e.g., if the cursor is on the "u" in "current" and you type **de**, then "urrent" is deleted.
w	The scope is from the cursor to the beginning of the next *word* including the space.
b	The scope is from the letter before the cursor backwards to the *beginning* of the word.
$	The scope is from the cursor to the end of the line.
0	The scope is from just before the cursor to the beginning of the line.
)	The scope is from the cursor to the beginning of the next sentence. A sentence is ended by ".", "!", or "?" followed by either an "end of line" (provided by the [return] key) or 2 spaces.
(	The scope is from just before the cursor back to the beginning of the sentence containing the cursor.
}	The scope is from the cursor to the end of a paragraph. A paragraph begins after an empty line.
{	The scope is from just before the cursor back to the beginning of a paragraph.

You might notice that there is no symbol for a *whole line*. The creators of **vi** decided that since an operation on a whole line is done so often, the easiest way to do it would be to hit the operator key twice. Thus, **dd** and **cc** and **yy** are commands affecting the whole line.

Of course, the commands formed by these operations and their scopes need to be practiced to be appreciated. The following paragraphs give a few examples to illustrate their format and action.

The Delete Operator

The delete operator is easiest to visualize since it is a one-step process. Consider the short line.

123 456 789. ABC.

Assume the cursor is on the 5, then

de deletes to the *end* of the word, thus
deleting 56 and leaving   123 4 789. ABC.

dw deletes to next *word*, thus deleting 56
and leaving   123 4789. ABC.

db deletes to *beginning* of word, thus
deleting 4 and leaving   123 56 789. ABC.

d0 deletes to *beginning* of line, thus
deleting 123 4 and leaving   56 789. ABC.

d) deletes to end of *sentence*, thus deleting
56 789. and leaving   123 4ABC.
   (Since there were two spaces after the
decimal point in 4789., **vi** interpreted
the decimal point to be a period at the
end of a sentence.)

dd deletes the whole line.

A really neat way to practice these deletions is to use the "undo" command **u**. Since the **u** command *undoes* the last command, you can easily try out one of the deletions just described and, then, use the **u** command to get back to the starting point. Here is an example. Assume you have the text

123 456 789. ABC.

with the cursor on the "5".

Just type **dw** to see the 56 and two spaces deleted, and then type **u** to get back to the original text. It would look like this:

```
123   456   789.   ABC.                      type dw to get
123   4789.   ABC.                            type u to get
123   456   789.   ABC.
```

For fun, you can hit **u** again, and undo your undo!

All of the **d**elete operations and the **u**ndo commands are used in the Command Mode and they keep you in that mode. Now, let's consider the "change" operator.

The Change Operator *c*

The **c**hange operator **c** can use the same scopes as the delete operator **d**. In fact, the **c**hange operator deletes the exact same characters as the delete operator. The difference between the two operators is that the **c**hange operator places you in the Text Input Mode. You then can use the keyboard as a typewriter and can enter as much text as you like. Existing text moves to the right and "wraps around" as necessary to make room for your text insertion. You leave the Text Input Mode just as always by using the [esc] key. Some versions of **vi** include a marker with the **c**hange operation in order to mark the last character to be deleted using the $ symbol. Here is an example of a small change being made. Suppose you are in the **vi** command mode and have the following text on the screen with the cursor on the "6".

```
1234.   5678.   90.
```

You now type

```
ce
```

and the editor deletes to the *end* of the word leaving

```
1234.  567$.  90.
```

on display. Notice that the final character scheduled for replacement, the number 8, is replaced by the "$" symbol. The cursor is still on the 6, the first character scheduled for replacement. Now, if you type

```
Helloooo![esc]
```

you get

```
1234.  5Helloooo!.  90.
```

The **ce** command lets you change everything from the cursor to the *end* of the word. The other change commands, **c)** and **c}**, etc., operate in a similar way, but with different scopes. If you don't want to change or delete text but just want to make a copy elsewhere, then the yank operator and the put command are just what you need.

Using the "yank" and "delete" Operators With the "put" Command

You can use **d**elete and **p**ut commands to move text around in a file. **Y**ank and **p**ut commands, on the other hand, are ideal for *copying* and moving text around. The nine "scopes" allow you to mark precisely various parts of words, lines, sentences, and paragraphs. The yank and delete commands store these pieces of text in a temporary buffer that can be copied onto the screen with a **p**ut command. As usual, the commands are made with respect to the position of the cursor. As far as the **p**ut command is concerned, yank and **d**elete work identically. The difference to you is that yank leaves the original text unchanged, while **d**elete removes it.

Here is an example using **y**. Assume you are in the **vi** Command Mode with the following text on the screen and the cursor on the 6.

```
1234.  56789.
```

If you now type

```
y$
```

you will have stored a copy of 6789. in the temporary buffer. You can now move the cursor to another position (for example, at the end of the line) and type

155

p

This *puts* a copy of the buffer contents immediately after the cursor as in an append command. It would look like:

```
1234. 56789. 6789.
```

You might be wondering if the **p** command empties the buffer or if the buffer contents can be used again. You can, in fact, use it repeatedly to *put* down as many copies as you like. The only way to change the buffer's contents is to yank or to delete something else. The new text then replaces the old yank contents.

It seems too bad that the **d**elete command and the yank command have to share the same buffer. Also, what if you wanted to save some text for longer periods of time in an editing session. You might think that there should be more buffers for temporary storage! In fact, there are, and this is the subject of our next section.

Deleting, Duplicating, and Rearranging Text Using Temporary Buffers

As we explained earlier in the chapter, when you wish to edit an existing file, a copy of that file is brought from memory to the editor buffer. The use of memory buffers is so convenient that the **vi** editor actually has over 30 such temporary memory areas that are used for duplicating, rearranging, and temporarily storing text. In addition, if you accidentally delete lines of text, you cannot only recover the last deletion made but the eight previous ones as well. These deletions are stored in a set of temporary buffers numbered 1 to 9. You can get the **n**th previous block of deleted text back into your file by using the command **"np**. (The double quote mark alerts the editor that you are about to give the name of a buffer.) This command will place text after the cursor. A similar **p**ut command is **P**, which places the buffer contents before the cursor. Thus, the command

```
"1p
```

will recover the last deletion made and put it *after* the cursor, and the command

"1P

would place the last deletion *before* the cursor.

The **u**ndo command **u** is especially helpful if you want to search through deletion buffers 1 through 9. For example, you can display the contents of buffer number 4 by commanding

"4p

and if you don't want to keep it, type

u

You could repeat this to take a quick look at several buffers.

There is a better way to save, duplicate, and rearrange text than to use buffers 1 through 9 as described above. The problem with buffers 1 through 9 is that buffer No. 1 always has the last deletion made. Thus, if you move some text, and then make a deletion, the contents of the buffers change. If you plan to move or copy text, it is better to use a set of buffers that are unchanged by the ordinary delete operations. There is such a set, and the members are named with alphabetic letters from "a" to "z." To use these buffers, you precede the **d**elete operation with the name of the buffer in which the text is to be stored. Again, you need to use the quote symbol (") to inform the editor that you are using a buffer name. For example, the command

"c5dd

will delete 5 lines and store them in buffer c. These lines can be put back in their same place or in several places in the file by using the **put** commands, **p** and **P**, as follows:

"cp

This will put the contents of buffer c after the cursor. You can move the cursor and repeat the command to place additional copies of buffer c anywhere in the file.

These alphabetically labeled buffers will also store your **y**ank contents if you wish to just *copy* and store information. The commands are used identically. Consider the following example. Assume you have the following text on the screen for editing purposes.

```
Ancient Adages
Bountiful Beauties
Credulous Cretins
Diabolic Dingos
```

and the cursor is on the "Bountiful Beauties" line. Now you type

"fdd

The editor deletes the line containing the cursor and stores the contents in a buffer labeled "f," leaving on the screen

```
Ancient Adages
Credulous Cretins
Diabolic Dingos
```

If you now move the cursor to the bottom line and type

"fp

you will get

```
Ancient Adages
Credulous Cretins
Diabolic Dingos
Bountiful Beauties
```

The deleted contents that are stored in buffer "f are now printed.
Now, if you were to start with the same original text, but substitute **yy** for **dd**, then the screen would display

```
Ancient Adages
Bountiful Beauties
Credulous Cretins
Diabolic Dingos
Bountiful Beauties
```

Here we see that the yank command leaves the original text (the second line) in its place, while letting us place a copy elsewhere.

Just as before, the **d**elete and **y**ank commands "share" storage buffers for saving deleted or copied text. The text stored in buffer f ("f) will remain in the buffer until new text is placed there or until you leave the **vi** editor. Thus, these buffers are extremely helpful for rearranging text.

These **d**elete and **y**ank commands may be repeated using commands like

```
"g7yy
```

which copies seven lines of text and stores them in a buffer named g.

Moving Larger Blocks

You can extend the range of these operator-scope combinations by prefixing the command with a number. The number indicates the *number* of lines, words, sentences, etc., that you wish affected. For example,

```
20dd
```

would delete twenty lines, and the command

```
5cw
```

would let you change 5 words. If you use this last command, a $ will appear in place of the last character of the fifth word, so that you can see which words would be replaced. You are free, of course, to replace the 5 words with 1, 2, or 7 words, if you want.

If you want to move rather large blocks of material, you probably will find it more convenient to use the **t** and the **m** commands of the **ed** editor. You don't have to change editors to do this, for these commands are available from **vi**, too. We will show you how to get to **ed** commands shortly.

Joining and Breaking Up Lines

All of these "cutting and pasting" operations can leave the text on the screen somewhat messy looking. A paragraph might look something like that shown in the following illustration.

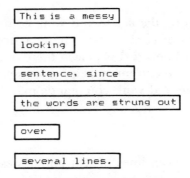

A messy looking paragraph.

How can we "clean" it up? (That is, how can we get the line lengths to be more equal?) There are three major ways to join sentences together. The *slowest* way is to retype the lines leaving out the blanks. A much easier way is to use the **J** command in **vi** which joins the next line down to the current line. For example, if you are in **vi** and have four short sentences, each on a line by itself, then you can place the cursor on the top line and type

J

three times. This would join the sentences on the same line and wrap them around, if necessary, as shown in the next sketch.

```
1.  The tall man strolls away.        The tall man strolls away.  An alarm

2.  An alarm sounds.                  sounds.  RUN!   A dead end.

3.  RUN!                              Sentences joined and wrapped around.

4.  A dead end.
```

Four short sentences.

Joining sentences.

If you wind up with lines that are too long, just insert a [return] where you wish to break the line. You can do this most easily by placing the cursor on the space where you wish to make the break, and then use the **r** command to replace the space with a [return]. You can reshape your line lengths as you see fit by using this and the **J** command.

Another way to clean up text is to use one of the text-formatting utilities discussed in Chapter 12. We will conclude this long chapter by mentioning some additional commands that are available in **vi** and by giving the **vi** summary.

Additional Commands and Features of vi

We hope that the commands you have learned so far will meet most of your editing needs. In order to keep this chapter fairly simple, we have omitted about 60 additional commands that are available in most versions of **vi**.

The **vi** editor has several features in addition to its commands, and you may wish to learn about them. These additional features let you do many things, including

* specifying your terminal type
* adjusting the screen size
* adjusting indentation, tabs, and wrap margin settings
* using macros and abbreviations to simplify a complex operation or a long keystroke entry
* editing two or more files at the same time
* using **ed**-like commands

The last feature deserves further mention, especially since we have already used it several times without telling you. To use an **ed**-like command, enter the Command Mode, then hit the [:] key. This will give you a :-prompt at the bottom of the screen. Now you can give most of the commands listed in the **ed** chapter. As soon as the command is executed, you are returned to the standard **vi** command mode. We use the term "ed-like" because the editor invoked by this command is not **ed**; it is a line editor called **ex** that is similar.

If you prefer a longer stay in line editor **ex**, you can give the **Q** command while in the **vi** command mode. This, too, will give you a :-prompt at the screen bottom, but you will stay in the **ex** mode until you type **vi** to return.

The examples that we have used so far have involved the **write** commands (such as **:w** and **120,230 w chapter4.2b**) and the **quit** commands (**:q**, **:wq**, and **:q!**).

Of the other **ed** commands available, the most useful are those that let you deal with large blocks of material. Two important examples are the **copy** command **t** and the **move** command **m**. These perform the same tasks as delete-and-put and yank-and-put, respectively, but they work only on entire lines. Briefly, the command:

   `:20,300m500`

will move lines 20 through 300 to just after line 500. The command:

   `:20,300t500`

places a copy of the lines 20 through 300 just after line 500, but leaves the original lines 20 through 300 in place.

Another **ed** command that is very useful is the global search-and-replace command. For example, the command:

   `:g/e/s//#/g`

will find every "e" in the file and replace it by a "#". Try it, it is visually stimulating. Just remember that you can undo this change with the **u** command. For more detail on the preceding commands, see the chapter on **ed**.

The **vi** editor also has a read-only option that is called up by typing **view** instead of **vi**. This is useful if you want to use the cursor-positioning keys to *read* text without worrying about accidentally adding or changing the file. Of course, you can do the same thing by leaving **vi** with a **:q!**. This command quits **vi** without writing any changes made.

More information about using the **vi** features and commands is presented succinctly in the article by William Joy and Mark Horton titled "An Introduction to Display Editing with Vi" (see Appendix B).

A Summary of the Screen Editor vi

The screen editor **vi** has an abundant set of commands that rivals the best word processing systems in terms of flexibility and power. It can also be used by the beginning user who limits his or her commands to a few basic commands, such as those discussed in the section on basic **vi** commands. It is very important to remember that **vi** has two modes of operation—the Command Mode and the Text Input Mode. One important point to consider about the Command Mode is that most of the commands are used to position the cursor or to find text. The rest of the commands either delete something or place you into the Text Input Mode.

Summary: vi—screen-oriented text editor

The *vi* modes of operation.

Entering Text Input Mode—End this mode with an [esc]

---

a | Appends text after the cursor. You can type as many lines and [return]'s as you wish.

i | Inserts text before the cursor. You can insert as many lines of text and [return]'s as you wish.

o | Opens a new line below cursor. Ready for your text input.

O | Opens a new line above cursor. Ready for your text input.

R | Replaces characters on the screen, starting at the cursor, with any characters you type.

Command Mode—These commands, after execution, return you to the Command Mode

---

r | Replaces a single character under the cursor with a single character that you type.

/happy | Search sequence; looks for next occurrence of pattern following /; in this case, the word "happy."

?lark | Search sequence; like /, but searches backwards from the cursor.

n	Used after / or ? to advance to the next occurrence in the buffer of the pattern.
u	Undoes the last command.
U	Undoes all the changes on the current line.
x	Deletes character under the cursor.
[del] or #, or [control–h]	This backspace feature of the shell also works in the editor. These commands move the cursor character by character leftward within a line, erasing each character from the buffer.
[control–d], [control-u]	Scrolls or pages the screen down or up, one-half page at a time.
nG	Positions the cursor at line **n** in the files.
[control-g]	Identifies the line where the cursor is located by line number.

Operators in the Command Mode (see following scopes)

d	Deletes indicated text starting at the cursor. For example, use **dw** to delete a word and **dd** to delete a line; **3dd** deletes 3 lines. Deleted text is stored temporarily in a buffer whose contents can be printed out with the **p** command. Also, **d** can be used with named buffers in the manner described for **y** below.
c	Deletes indicated text starting at the cursor and enters the Text Input Mode. Thus, **ce** deletes from the cursor to the *end* of the word, allowing you to add text between those positions.
y	Copies indicated text, starting at the cursor, and stores it in a buffer. There are nine unnamed buffers (1-9) that store the last nine delete or yank operations and 26 named buffers (a–z) that can be used for storage. The double quote mark (") is used to tell the editor the name of the buffer. Thus, **"cy$** will

store text from the cursor to the end of the line in a buffer named c.

p The **p**ut command, used to put down "delete" and "yank" buffer contents after the cursor or on the next line. Command **p** puts the last item yanked or deleted back into the file just after the cursor, and **"cp** will put the contents of buffer c after the cursor.

P The "put" command. Identical to **p**, except it places the buffer contents before the cursor.

Scopes for Use With Operators

e The scope is from the cursor to the *end* of the current word; eg., if the cursor is on the "u" in "current," and you type **de**, then "urrent" is deleted.

w The scope is from the cursor to the beginning of the next *word*, including the space.

b The scope is from the letter before the cursor, backwards, to the *beginning* of the word.

$ The scope is from the cursor to the end of the line.

∅ The scope is from just before the cursor to the beginning of the line.

) The scope is from the cursor to the beginning of the next sentence. A sentence is ended by ".", "!", or "?" and followed by an "end of line" (provided by the [return] key) or by 2 spaces.

(The scope is from just before the cursor back to the beginning of the sentence containing the cursor.

} The scope is from the cursor to the end of a paragraph. A paragraph begins after an empty line.

{ The scope is from just before the cursor back to the beginning of a paragraph.

	Leaving the Editor
:w	Writes the contents of the buffer into the current file of the same name. Can be given a new filename to write to. Also, can send partial buffer contents using line numbers, such as **:3,10w popcorn.**
:q	Quits buffer after a :w command.
:wq	Write and quit, placing buffer contents in file.
:q!	Quits buffer without making changes in file. Dangerous.
ZZ	Write and quit, placing buffer contents in file. Used to avoid accidentally hitting a :q or :qw.
	Using the ed Editor While in vi
:	Gives a colon (:) prompt at the bottom of the screen and lets you make one **ed** command. You are returned to the **vi** mode when the command finishes execution.
Q	Quits **vi** and places you in the **ed** editor, giving you a Command Mode prompt, the colon [:], at the bottom of the screen. You can get back to **vi** just by typing the command **vi** while in the Command Mode.

Review Questions

A. **Match the commands shown on the left to the functions shown on the right. Assume all the commands are given in the Command Mode only, none are given from the Text Input Mode.**

vi Editor Commands   *Functions*

1. 35G   **a.** Scrolls screen down 1/2 page
2. 3yw   **b.** Moves cursor down 1 line
3. r2   **c.** Stores 4 lines in buffer c
4. /fun   **d.** Prints line number of the current line

5. [control–g] **e.** Moves cursor to left one character
6. 2dd   **f.** Replaces character under cursor with number 2
7. j   **g.** Yanks out 3 words
8. "c4dd   **h.** Substitutes funny for fun
9. [control–d] **i.** Deletes 2 lines
10. h   **j.** Puts cursor on line 35
       k. Finds the word "fun"

B. General Questions

1. When you invoke the editor with a file, that is, type **vi file3**, how can you tell if it is a new file?
2. Why is the or **:q** command considered dangerous?
3. When you first enter the editor with an existing file and type **a**, the append command to add text, where is that text placed?
4. What command is used to save the editor buffer contents?
5. Where does the insert command **i** place new text?
6. Write out the command that will save the first three lines only of an editor buffer containing seven lines of text.
7. How do you exit the Text Input Mode?
8. Write out the command(s) to correct the following misspelled word, "some-tome."
9. Write out the command(s) to delete the last five lines in ten lines of text.

Answers

A. 1–j, 2–g, 3–f, 4–k, 5–d, 6–i, 7–b, 8–c, 9–a, 10–e

B. **1.** The left column of the screen fills with tildes (~) **2.** None of the changes you've made are saved **3.** After the cursor **4. :w, ZZ 5.** Before the cursor **6. :1,3w** filename **7.** Use [esc] **8.** Position cursor over "o", type **ri 9.** Position cursor on first line to be deleted and type **5dd**

Exercises at the Terminal

Here are some exercises to practice your editing techniques. You can use either editor.

1. Enter the following text into a new file called **letterrec1**.

    Dear Sir:
      This is a letter of recommendation for john doe.
      john doe is a good worker.
      john doe has a fine character.

john doe is a-ok.

sincerely
jane doe

2. Now, do the following:
   A. Save the letter.
   B. Correct all spelling errors.
   C. Capitalize jane, john, and doe.
   D. Delete the last sentence containing a-ok.
   E. Save the corrected letter as **letterrec2**.
   F. Leave the editor.
   G. Use **cat** to print both copies on the screen at the same time.
3. Go into the shell, list your files with **ls**, and do the following:
   A. Make a copy of one of your files, e.g., **mbox**, calling it **mbox2** or something similar.
   B. Now, invoke the editor with this copy of a file and:
      (1) Insert somewhere the line, "This is a test."
      (2) Move 3 lines.
      (3) Replace all occurrences of the word "the" with "thee."
      (4) Copy 2 lines and place them in the beginning of the file.
      (5) Delete the last 4 lines.

7

Manipulating Files and Directories: *mv, cp,* and *mkdir*

In this chapter, you will find:

- Introduction
- File Names, Pathnames, Heads, and Tails
- Basic File and Directory Manipulation Commands
- Directory Commands: *mkdir, rmdir, cd,* and *pwd*
  - The Make Directory Command: *mkdir*
  - The Change Directory Command: *cd* or *chdir*
  - The Print Working Directory Command: *pwd*
  - The Remove Directory Command: *rmdir*
- File Commands: *rm, cp, mv,* and *ln*
  - The Remove Command: *rm*
  - The Copy Command: *cp*
  - The Move Command: *mv*
  - The Link Command: *ln*
- Searching Through Files: *grep*
- Marvelous Metacharacters!! Wildcards—Character Substitutions
- Dictionary Abbreviations: ''.'', ''..'', and ''~''
- Review Questions
- Exercises at the Terminal

7   MANIPULATING FILES AND DIRECTORIES: *mv, cp,* and *mkdir*

Introduction

Now that you have the basic file *reading* commands from Chapter 4, you can get into the real fun of directory and file manipulation. However, before we do that, we will take a brief look at how UNIX names files so that they don't get mixed up. We will then conclude this chapter by showing you some typing shortcuts that you can use with metacharacters (abbreviations).

File Names, Pathnames, Heads, And Tails

What happens if Bob, Lola, and Nerkie (each of whom has his or her own UNIX account on the same system) each decide to create a file called **whiz**? Does UNIX become confused? Does Lola find Bob's work in her file? Of course not! UNIX is much too clever for that. To understand what happens, you first should review the tree structure of the UNIX directory system. The full name of Lola's **whiz** file includes the name of the directory it is in. The full names of all three **whiz** files would be

```
/usr/bob/whiz
/usr/lola/whiz
/usr/nerkie/whiz
```

These are called the "pathnames" of the files because they give the path through the directory system to the file. The very last part of the pathname (the part after the last /) is called the **tail**, and the rest of the pathname is called the **head**.

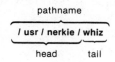

A pathname, a head, and a tail.

The head of the first file tells us that the **bob** directory branches off the **usr** directory and that the **usr** directory branches off the / directory (our old friend, **root**). For this example, all three pathnames have the same tail; i.e., **whiz**. On the other hand, they all have different heads (**/usr/bob/**, **/usr/lola/**, and **/usr/nerkie/**), so UNIX has no problem distinguishing between them.

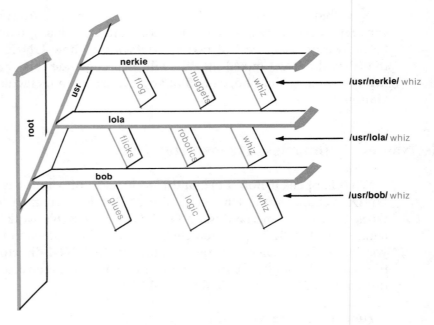

Pathnames and the directory tree.

The slash (/) takes on two roles in a pathname. The slash at the very beginning stands for the **root** directory. The other slashes serve to separate the name of a directory from the name of the following directory or file.

When a file is in your working directory, you can be casual and call it by its tail name. When the file is in a different directory, however, you need to tell UNIX which directory the file is in. One foolproof method is to use the pathname. For example, if Nerkie wishes to read Bob's **whiz** file, he can enter the command

```
cat /usr/bob/whiz
```

There are other ways, using abbreviations and conventions, to identify files but, if you are in doubt, use the pathname!

Let's look at one more example. Lola has created a directory called **bigstuff** and, in it, she has placed the file **walrus**. The pathname of this file is

`/usr/lola/bigstuff/walrus`

The tail name is

`walrus`

The head is

`/usr/lola/bigstuff/`

If Lola is in the directory **/usr/lola/bigstuff** and wants to read the files, she can simply call the file **walrus**.

However, if she is in her home directory (**/usr/lola**), she can refer to the file as **/usr/lola/bigstuff/walrus**, or, more simply, as **bigstuff/walrus**.

This illustrates an important special case. If a file is in a subdirectory of the one you are in, the only part of the pathname you need use is the subdirectory name and the tail.

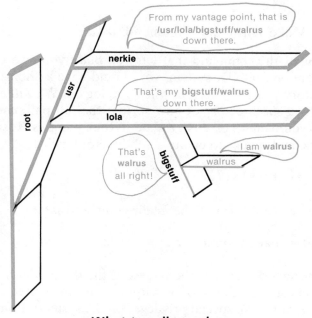

What to call a *walrus*.

Basic File and Directory Manipulation Commands

As a walrus once said, "The time has come to talk of many things." We will now look at the standard usage for the following commands:

```
rm, cp, mv, ln, mkdir, rmdir, cd, and pwd
```

They will let you manipulate your files and directories with ease and versatility. There is more information here than you may need immediately but, eventually, you will use it all. Again, we urge you to try out these commands as you read along. Use the redirected **cat** command or one of the editors to create some files to work with. (They need not be as inspired as our poem in Chapter 4!)

Directory Commands: *mkdir, rmdir, cd*, and *pwd*

Directories give you a place to keep your files. The first three commands let you create, remove, and move through directories. The last command tells you where you are.

The Make Directory Command: *mkdir*

This is the command that lets you build you own directory subsystem. If you are on a UNIX system, you should have a "home" directory; this is the directory you are placed in when you log on. We will assume that your directory is a subdirectory of **/usr** so that the full pathname of your directory is **/usr/yourname** (i.e., **/usr/roscoe** if your name is Roscoe). The procedure is simple and quick; to create a subdirectory called, say, **formletters**, you enter

```
mkdir formletters
```

The general form of the **mkdir** command is

```
mkdir name1 name2 . . .
```

where **name1**, etc., are the names of the directories you wish to create. You can make directories only within your own directory system (unless, of course, you have special privileges on the system). If **name1** is a tail and not a pathname, then the new directory is attached to the directory you are in when

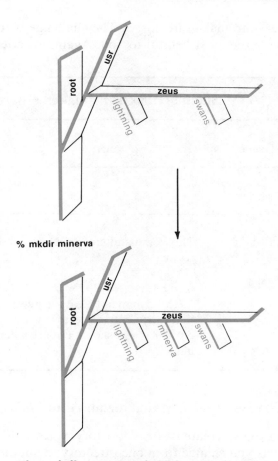

% mkdir minerva

The *mkdir* command: before and after.

making the command. For example, if Bob is in his home directory and issues the command

```
mkdir foibles
```

the result is a new directory whose pathname is **/usr/bob/foibles**. After doing this, Bob could switch from his home directory to the **foible** directory (see **cd**) and make the command

```
mkdir gambling
```

to create the directory **/usr/bob/foibles/gambling**

It's easy to make directories. The challenge is to design the directory system that's the most helpful to you. Again, experience is a great teacher.

Summary: `mkdir`—makes a new directory

name	options	arguments
mkdir		[directoryname . . .]

Description: This command creates a new subdirectory in the present directory.

Example: **mkdir Chapter4**
This command creates a new subdirectory called **Chapter4** that exists in the directory where you entered the command. Note that you should not use a blank space in your directory names.

The Change Directory Command: *cd* or *chdir*

Once you've created a new directory, you would like to use it. The **cd** command lets you change from one directory to another. The general form of the command is:

```
cd directoryname
```

The change directory command was once called **chdir**, but it is used so often that newer versions of UNIX have shortened the name to **cd**. Once it is executed, the named directory becomes your "working directory." For example, if you enter the commands

```
cd /usr/lola/quarkdata
ls
```

the result will be a list of files in the directory **/usr/lola/quarkdata**. Of course, there is a question of "permissions." If Lola gave this command, she would have the power to alter the files in this directory. If Bob gave the command, normally he could look but not touch. (The standard setup allows you to look at someone else's files but not alter them. However, you can copy the file and alter the copy.) The **chmod** command, discussed in Chapter 10, lets you change the permissions governing your files.

The command

```
cd
```

with nothing following it, will place you in your home directory.

Summary: `cd`, `chdir`—change directory		
name	**options**	**arguments**
`cd`		[directoryname]

Description:	This command makes the named directory your current working directory. If no directory is given, the command takes you to your home directory.
Example:	**cd /usr/reggie/foods/carbo**
	This command would place you in the **/usr/reggie/foods/ carbo** directory.

The Print Working Directory Command: *pwd*

Once you have the power to change working directories, you have the possibility of forgetting which directory you are in. The command **pwd** causes UNIX to print the full pathname of your current working directory. If, when you try to copy or move a file, UNIX claims that the file doesn't exist and you know it does, try **pwd**. You may find that you are in a different directory than you thought and that you need to use a full pathname for a file. The use is simple. If you type

```
pwd
```

and if UNIX replies

```
/usr/src/cmd
```

then you are currently in the **/usr/src/cmd** directory.

Summary: pwd—print working directory		
name	**options**	**arguments**
pwd		
Description:	This command prints out the pathname of the current working directory.	

The Remove Directory Command: *rmdir*

Sometimes you find you have no more use for a directory; the **rmdir** command lets you get rid of it. The standard form of the command is:

```
rmdir dir1 . . .
```

The command removes the one or more directories listed after the command. The command will not remove non-empty directories or, normally, directories belonging to others.

UNIX gives you the tools to organize your files efficiently and easily. We have given you the rules governing several useful commands, but it is up to you to make good use of them. The first step is to practice with them, creating new directories, populating them with files, and then copying and moving files. Get comfortable with the procedures.

Next, give thought to your own needs. Don't hesitate to create new directories. It's a good idea to use different directories to house different projects or different types of material. Give your directories and files names that tell you what the contents are; use names like **chapter3** and **unixbook** rather than **file1** and **directory2**. UNIX gives you the opportunity to make your directory system a model of clarity and convenience—take advantage of it!

Summary: `rmdir`—remove directories

name	options	arguments
`rmdir`		directoryname(s) . . .

Description: **rmdir** removes the named directories, providing that they are empty.

Example: **rmdir budget65 budget66**
This command removes the directories **budget65** and **budget66** if they do not contain any files.

File Commands: *rm, cp, mv,* and *ln*

Handling old-fashioned files involved much paper shuffling. These four UNIX commands let you do the modern equivalent—electron shuffling—with much greater ease.

The Remove Command: *rm*

This command removes files. If you don't use it, your directories can become a jungle choked with unused and superceded files. The command is simple to use; you just follow **rm** with a list of the files you wish gone. Each file name should be separated by a space from the others. Thus,

```
rm dearjohn dearjoe dearfred dearigor
```

removes four files.

As you can see, it is very easy to remove files; in fact, it is so easy and so irreversible, that you should stop and ask the following questions:

1. Am I sure I no longer want this file?
2. Is this the file I think it is?
3. Am I really sure about my answers to Questions 1 and 2?

Summary: rm—remove files		
name	**option**	**argument**
rm	−i, −r	filename(s) . . .

Description: **rm** removes each file in the argument list.

Options: −**i** asks, for each file on the list, whether or not to delete it; the user responds with **y** or **n** for yes or no.
−**r** deletes a directory and every file or directory in it.

Example: **rm** −**i Rodgers**
This will cause UNIX to query **rm**: remove Rodgers? And you reply with a **y** or **n**.

Special caution is needed when using **rm** with the "wildcard" substitutions discussed later in this chapter. We'll remind you again when you reach that section. You may want to use the **−i** option described in the following summary.

Ordinarily, you can't remove directories with **rm**; use **rmdir** if that's what you want to do. The **−r** option given in the following summary *does* let you remove directories, but you had better be certain that you really do want to remove *everything*. **rmdir** is safer because it only removes empty directories.

Normally, you are not allowed to remove files from someone else's directory. To make things fair, someone else can't remove yours.

The Copy Command: *cp*

The **cp** command is used to create a copy of a file. There are several reasons you should have a copy command. One is to create backup copies of files. A file you are working on can be wiped out by a systems problem or (believe it or not!) by slips on your part, so "backups" are a good idea. (A backup is a second copy of a file.)

A second reason is that you may wish to develop a second, slightly different version of a file, and you can use a copy as a convenient starting point. Another need may develop from the fact that UNIX is a shared system. A colleague may write a program or collect some data you can use, and a copy function gives you an easy way to place it in your own directory. The simplest form of the copy command is:

```
cp file1 file2
```

The command works from left to right; **file1** is the original and **file2** is the copy. This is the way the command functions. First, it creates a file called **file2**. If you already have a file by that name, it is *eliminated* and replaced by the new empty file. Then, the contents of **file1** are copied into **file2**. You, of course, would use whatever names you want for the files; you aren't limited to **file1** and **file2**. For example, Sam Softsell might use the command:

```
cp buypasta buytacos
```

to copy the contents of his **buypasta** file into a **buytacos** file.

Sam should be careful that he doesn't already have a valuable file called **buytacos**, for it would have been wiped out by the last instruction. This is one of the less friendly aspects of UNIX but, for some versions, it can be avoided. See the box on file protection.

To copy a file from another directory into your own, you need to know the full directory name of the file. If you enter

```
cp bigthought idea
```

UNIX will search only your directory for a file called **bigthought**. If the **bigthought** file is in, say, Bob's directory (assumed to be **/usr/bob**), then the proper command is:

```
cp /usr/bob/bigthought idea
```

Here **/usr/bob/bigthought** is the pathname of the original file. (At the end of this chapter, we will show some abbreviations that will let you reduce the amount of typing you need do when dealing with long pathnames.) Incidentally, Bob can use **chmod** (Chapter 10) to keep others from copying his files.

A second form of the copy command is:

```
cp file1 file2 ... directory2
```

This copies the list of files given into the named directory, which must already exist. This instruction will become more useful to you once you begin establishing additional directories. The new files retain the tail name of the originals. For example, suppose Sam Softsell has a subdirectory called **backup** in his home directory of **/usr/sam**. The command:

```
cp pasta backup
```

creates a file named **pasta** in the **backup** directory. There are two points to note here.

First, although both files are named **pasta**, they exist in different directories and, thus, have different pathnames. For the preceding example, the pathname of the original file is **/usr/sam/pasta** and the pathname of the copy is **/usr/sam/backup/pasta**.

Secondly, if the directory named **backup** didn't exist, UNIX would assume that this command was in the first form we described. In other words, it would just copy the file **pasta** into a file called **backup**, all in the original directory.

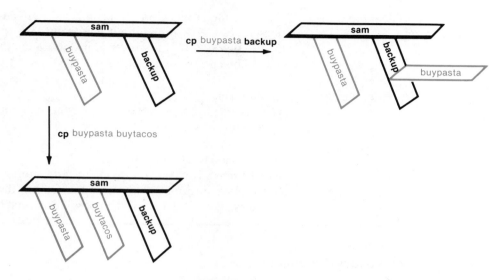

Copying files.

Sometimes, UNIX may give you messages like "cp: cannot create file2" or "cp: cannot open file1." This is UNIX's way of confessing bafflement at your instructions. Check to make sure that you typed the names correctly, that you're not trying to place files in someone else's directory, or that, perhaps, you need to use a full pathname.

Summary: cp—makes copies of files		
name	**options**	**arguments**
cp	[−i] {BSD}	file1 file2 file(s) . . . directory

Description:	The command **cp file1 file2** creates a copy of the first file (**file1**) and gives it the name **file2**. If a file named **file2** already exists, it will be replaced by the new one. The second form of the command (**cp file(s) . . . directory**) makes copies of all the files listed and places them in the named directory.

Option:	**−i** If the target name for the copy is used already, this option causes UNIX to inquire if you really wish to overwrite the existing file. If you answer **y**, it does; any other answer causes the **cp** process to terminate. {BSD}
Examples:	**cp flim flam** This command makes a copy of the file **flim** and calls the copy **flam.**
	cp /usr/snoopy/stormy /usr/ruff This command makes a copy of the file **stormy** (from the **/usr/snoopy** directory) and places the copy in the **/usr/ruff** directory; the pathname of the copy is **/usr/ruff/stormy.**

The Move Command: *mv*

This command lets you change the name of a file and lets you move a file from one directory to another. The simplest form of this command is:

```
mv file1 file2
```

The effect of this command is to change the name of **file1** to **file2**. The file is left unchanged, but a new name is moved in. Suppose Lola LaLulu wants to change the name of a file from **a.out** to **findanswer**. She could solve her problem with the command:

```
mv a.out findanswer
```

Suppose, however, she already had a file called **findanswer**? **Mv** is as ruthless as **cp**; it would wipe out the old file in order to make the name available for the contents of **a.out**. However, see the box on file protection.

You can use the **mv** command to change the name of a directory, too. The form is

```
mv oldname newname
```

and is the same as that for changing a file name. In other words, **mv** doesn't care whether **oldname** is a file or a directory, it will just proceed and give it the new name.

The final use of **mv** is to move files to an existing directory. The form is:

```
mv file1 file2 ... directory
```

We can think of this command as moving one or more files to the specified directory. This is a very handy housekeeping command. For example, if Lola, an exotic physicist studying those exotic subatomic particles called quarks, has accumulated four files of quark data, she can create a directory called **quarkdata** (using **mkdir**) and, then, could type:

```
mv quark1 quark2 quark3 quark4 quarkdata
```

to gather the four files together in the new directory. This form of the command leaves the tail of the pathname unchanged. For example, the preceding command would change the pathname of **/usr/lola/quark1** to **/usr/lola/quarkdata/quark1**. (At the end of the chapter, we will see a much quicker way to make the same move!)

Of course, this use of **mv** won't work if the destination directory doesn't exist or if you don't have permission to "write" in that directory.

If you give a command like

```
mv chair kitchen
```

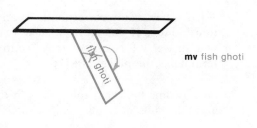

mv fish ghoti

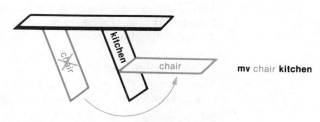

mv chair **kitchen**

Two smooth moves.

how does UNIX know whether you want **kitchen** to be a file or to be a directory? Well, UNIX may be clever, but it isn't psychic; it doesn't know which

Summary: mv—move or rename files		
name	**options**	**arguments**
mv	[−i] {BSD}	filename1 filename2 or filename(s) directoryname

Description: **mv** allows the user to change the name of a file. The first form of the command shown above changes the name of "filename1" to "filename2".

However, since filenames can include the full pathname, it is possible to use the command to move a file to a new directory as shown in the second form of the command.

Option: **−i** If a new name corresponds to an existing one, this option inquires if you really wish to overwrite the old file. If you answer y for yes, the move continues. Any other reply terminates the move. {BSD}

Examples: (We assume here that the user is in the **/usr/flisk** directory and that **hobo** is a subdirectory of that directory.)

mv mrak mark
This changes the name of the file **mrak** to **mark**.

mv mark hobo
This changes the name of the file **mrak** (pathname **/usr/flisk/mrak**) to **/usr/flisk/hobo/mark**, thus moving the file to the **hobo** directory.

mv mray hobo/mary
This changes the name of the file **mray** (pathname **/usr/flisk/mray** to **/usr/flisk/hobo/mary**, thus changing the directory and the tail of the pathname.

you want. It *does* know, however, whether or not you already have a directory called **kitchen**. If you do have such a directory, UNIX puts the **chair** file there. If you don't have a directory called **kitchen**, UNIX assumes you want **kitchen** to be a filename.

Protecting Files

Many UNIX systems provide means to protect files from being accidentally "overwritten" by **cat, cp, mv,** and the like. The C shell, for example, allows the following command {BSD}:

```
set noclobber
```

Noclobber means that using **cat** (or any other command) with the > redirection operator will not erase (or "clobber") existing files. If you type this when you log on, it will remain in force until you log out. If, for example, you have files called **dog** and **pony** and have this option in effect, when you try

```
cat dog > pony
```

you will get a message like

```
pony: File exists
```

and the command will not be executed. If you insist on having your way, the command:

```
cat dog >! pony
```

will override the noclobber protection. The "!" tells UNIX that resistance is useless; it must obey your command.

Setting the noclobber option does nothing to halt possible mischief from **cp** and **mv**. In many UNIX implementations, however, **cp** and **mv** have a polite option that can be invoked by attaching a "flag" option to the command. The forms are as follows:

```
cp —i file1 file2
mv —i file1 file2
```

The "flag" in this case is the −i; note that it is separated by a space from the command and by a space from the file names. If files **dog** and **pony** both exist and you command

```
cp − i dog pony
```

UNIX will respond with

```
overwrite pony?
```

If you discover you made a mistake, respond with **n** for no. If you really *do* want to write over the **pony** file, respond with **y** for yes, and UNIX will proceed.

Are you lazy (not likely!), forgetful (well, maybe), or efficient (of course!)? It's possible to let UNIX set the **noclobber** and −i options automatically when you log in. You need to know how to place instructions in your **.login** file to do this. We will discuss that in Chapter 10.

The Link Command: *ln*

This command allows you to assign multiple names to a single file. This allows you to refer to the same file by different pathnames. This can be handy when you have many subdirectories, for it lets you "link" one file to several different directories. (The names you assign are the links between the file and the directories.)

A general form of this command is:

```
ln file1 name2
```

name2 can be either a new name you wish to give to the file or it can be an existing directory name. If it is a proposed filename, the result of executing this command is that **file1** will now have two names: **file1** and **name2**. If **name2** is the name of a directory, then **file1** will also be known by the tail of its old name (**file1**) in the directory **name2**. Let's clarify these two cases with two examples.

Suppose Tana the Wonder Dog is in her home directory (**/usr/tana**) and gives the command:

```
ln soupbone chews
```

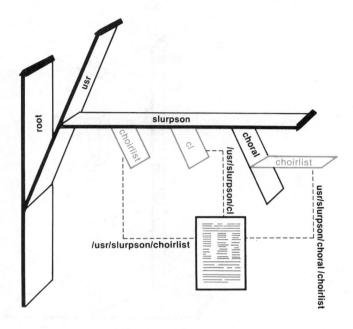

Different links to the same file.

UNIX checks to see if the name **chews** has been used yet. If it hasn't, then UNIX gives the new name to the file while still keeping the old one. (A **ls** command, for example, would show both; and a **ls −l** command would show that each had two links.) Tana then could call up the file by either name. What if there had already been a file called **chews** in the home directory? Then, **ln**, being more polite than **cp** or **mv**, would tell you so and would not make the new link. What if **chews** already was a subdirectory? Then, the situation would be like the next example.

Now suppose Tana has a subdirectory called **tidbit**. The command:

```
ln soupbone tidbit
```

adds the **soupbone** name to the **tidbit** directory, but leaves the original name undisturbed. Thus, the same file is now in two directories and has two pathnames: **/usr/tana/soupbone** and **/usr/tana/tidbit/soupbone**. These are the same file, not copies. When Tana is in her home directory and wants to see the file, she can type (after all, she is a wonder dog):

```
cat soupbone
```

189

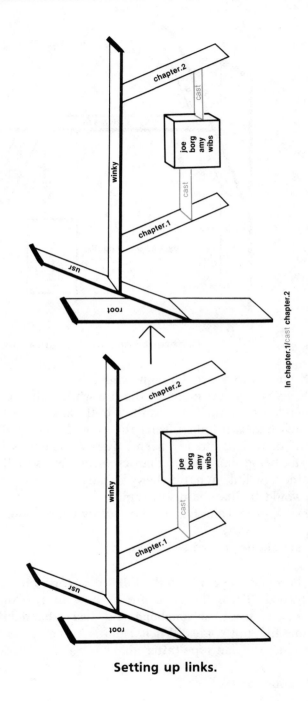

Setting up links.

(short for **cat /usr/tana/soupbone**).

If she switches to the **tidbit** directory (see **cd**), she can see the contents of the file by typing:

```
cat soupbone
```

(short for **cat /usr/tana/tidbit/soupbone**).

Without the **ln** command, she would have had to type:

```
cat /usr/tana/soupbone
```

to see the **soupbone** file when in the **tidbit** directory. When you have paws and have to type, you appreciate all the shortcuts you can get.

Suppose Tana, while in her home directory, now issues the command:

```
rm soupbone
```

Soupbone, of course, disappears from her home directory. Does this mean that the contents of the file disappear? No. The file still exists in the **tidbit** directory! Only when all of the names or links to the file have been removed will the file itself be erased.

Summary: ln—make file links		
name	**options**	**arguments**
ln		filename1 [filename 2] or filename(s) directoryname

Description: This command lets you add one or more names to an existing file providing a cross-reference system. Each name located in your directory has equal priority for reading or writing to the file. However, if a file is linked to another user, generally only the originator of the file can write in it (see the `chmod` command in Chapter 10).

The form "**ln** filename1" creates a link between the current working directory and filename1. Filename1 can include a full pathname, therefore, it is linked to a file in another directory.

The form "**ln** filename1 filename2" is like the preceding action, except the name of the new file is filename2.

The form "**ln** filename(s) directoryname" lets you put new file names or links into other directories.

Examples: (We will suppose the current working directory is **/usr/francie/spring** and there is a file called **math** in the **/usr/francie** directory.

ln /usr/francie/math
   This command creates the filename **math** in the current directory (**/usr/francie/spring**) and links that name to the file called **math** in the **francie directory**. The full pathname of the new link is **/usr/francie/spring/math**.

ln /usr/francie/math trig
   This command does the same as above except that the newly created filename is **trig** instead of **math**. The full pathname of the new filename is **/usr/francie/spring/trig**.

ln hist eng /usr/francie
   This command puts the two filenames **hist** and **eng** from the current directory into the **/usr/francie** directory.

Suppose you have established several subdirectories and you want them to have access to the same mailing list. You could, of course, place a copy of the mailing list in each directory, but that would use up too much disk space. By using the **ln** command, you can link the file containing the list to a name in each of the directories. In effect, the same file will exist in each directory. An additional advantage is that if you update the file from one directory, you've updated it for all the directories.

There are limitations to **ln**. One is that you can't use **ln** to assign two names to the same directory.

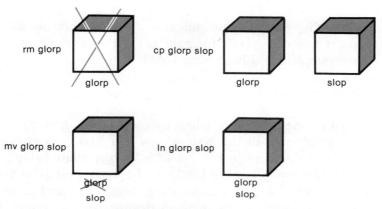

A comparison of *rm, mv, cp,* and *ln*.

Searching Through Files: *grep*

grep is a command whose beauty of function far exceeds its beauty of name. **grep** performs the invaluable service of searching your files for a key word or phrase and telling you what it finds. Suppose, for example, you have several inventory files (**infile1**, **infile2**, **infile3**, and **infile4**) and want to find out which one contains the description of your widget. The following command will serve that high purpose:

```
grep widget infile1 infile2 infile3 infile4
```

grep will search each file in turn and will print out those lines that contain the string of characters "widget."

The form of this command is:

```
grep pattern file(s)
```

In Chapter 11, we explore **grep**'s abilities much more fully. For the moment, we will point out just two more aspects.

First, if the pattern has a space in it, enclose the pattern in single quotes so that **grep** will know that the second word is part of the pattern and not a file to be searched. For example, if you were interested only in a glaxon widget, you could type:

```
grep 'glaxon widget' infile1 infile2 infile3 infile4
```

Secondly, the wildcard substitutions described in the next section can make it easier to specify file names. For instance, as you will soon learn, the first example could have been typed:

```
grep widget infile?
```

grep is one of the most heavily used UNIX commands. As you become more involved with the system, you will find **grep** growing on you. Don't worry if it does; it's just a sign of a healthy relationship.

One of the pleasures of UNIX is the freedom it gives you in creating files and directories and in manipulating them. Whether you are a collector keeping an inventory, a businessman dealing with accounts, mailing lists, and sales records, a researcher working with experimental data and computer programs, or a homeowner monitoring your budget and your energy usage, easy file handling is a key to happy computing.

Marvelous Metacharacters!! Wildcards—Character Substitutions

You can get tired and bored punching in file names and directory names, especially when you have to use the full pathnames. UNIX provides some tricky ways to save time. We'll look here at some alternative ways to identify file names.

One of the cleverer abilities of UNIX is pattern searching. That is, it can find filenames that match a "pattern" which you supply. You can have it list all your files that start with **chubby,** or have it remove all your files that end with **old,** or have it **cat** all your files having names with exactly four characters. The secret is in the use of special characters that can be used to stand for one or more characters in a file name. The special characters are "**?**" and "*****". The rules are these:

1. A **?** matches any one character.
2. An ***** matches any grouping of zero or more characters, except that it will not match a period that is the first character of a name. (This protects special files used to set up your home directory; those files have names like **.login** or **.profile**.)

Some examples should make the workings of these rules clear.

First, suppose that your directory contains the following files:

```
co.5     coward    hog    huge      part2.2    thug
cow      coy       hug    part2.1   start2.3
```

The command **ls** alone will list all these files, while the command **ls cow** will list only the **cow** file. The command:

```
ls co?
```

however, will list **cow** and **coy**, but not **co.5** or **coward**. We can describe the process this way. You provide the pattern of "**co?**"; this means a **co** followed by exactly one character (which can be any character). UNIX searches for filenames that match this pattern, and it finds **cow** and **coy**. It doesn't list **co.5** or **coward** because they both have *more* than one character after the **co**. Here are other examples of using **ls** and **?** with the sample directory above.

1. command: **ls hu?**
   response: hug
2. command: **ls hu??**
   response: huge
3. command: **ls ???**
   response: cow coy hog hug
4. command: **ls ?o?**
   response: cow coy hog

The process of finding out which of your files match the pattern you give is called "filename expansion." For instance, in the last example, we could say that the pattern **?o?** was expanded to match **cow**, **coy**, and **hog**. Note that you use two **?**'s to represent two characters, etc.

The ***** character is more general yet. As promised, it will represent any number of characters. Here are some sample commands and the responses using it.

1. command: **ls h***
   response: hog hug huge
2. command: **ls *g**
   response: hog hug thug
3. command: **ls hug***
   response: hug huge

4. command: `ls *hug`
   response: `hug thug`
5. command: `ls *.*`
   response: `co.5 part2.1 part2.2 start2.3`

Let's take a closer look at how these examples work. The first example lists all files beginning with **h**. The second command lists all files ending in **g**. The third command lists all files starting with **hug**. Note that in this case, the * even matches the "null character" (i.e., no character at all). (The pattern **hug?** matches **huge** but not **hug** because **hug?** has exactly four characters. However, **hug*** matches both **hug** and **huge**.) The fourth command matches all names ending with **hug**; again, the null character is matched. The final example matches all names containing a period in them, except for files whose name begins with a period. (Recall that **ls** doesn't show such files unless you use the −**a** option.)

The "*" and "?" characters, as well as the ">" character, belong to a group of characters having special meanings and uses in UNIX. They are called "metacharacters," an imposing term that hints at their latent power. Besides metacharacters, UNIX also possesses metasequences. An example is the pattern-matching sequence [ ]. Like **?**, this sequence matches one character, but more restrictively. The trick is to place between the brackets a list of characters to be matched. Here are some examples:

1. command: `ls co[xyz]`
   response: `coy`
2. command: `ls [cdeghr]o[gtw]`
   response: `cow hog`

The first example matches all 3-character names beginning with **co** and ending in **x**, **y**, or **z**. The second example would also have matched **cog** and **how**, among others, if you had had them in your directory. Note that the [ ] sequence matches one character and *only* one character. For example, [**nice**] matches an **n**, or an **i**, or a **c**, or an **e**; it does not match **ice** or **nice**.

You can specify a range of characters using the [ ] notation. For instance, [**2–8**] represents the digits 2, 3, 4, 5, 6, 7, and 8, while [**A–Z**] represents all the capital letters. Thus,

`ls [A-Z]`

would match all file names consisting of a single capital letter, and

```
ls [A-Z]*
```

would match all file names starting with a capital letter and ending in anything. The last example points out that you can combine the different pattern-matching operations into one command.

Very interesting, you say, but of what use is this? In part, the usefulness depends on what sort of names you give your files. Consider the earlier example that we gave of the **mv** command:

```
mv quark1 quark2 quark3 quark4 quarkdata
```

Lola could have accomplished the same result with

```
mv quark? quarkdata
```

or

```
mv quark[1-4] quarkdata
```

Of course, the first instruction would also move any other files matching that pattern, such as **quarky** or **quarkQ**.

Here's another example. Suppose you created a directory called **backup** and you wanted to place copies in there of *all* the files in your home directory. The following entry would do the job.

```
cp * backup
```

In general, one should be cautious using a solo *. Consider, for example, what the command

```
rm *
```

does. Since * matches anything, the command removes all of the files in your current working directory. Well, you're hardly likely to give that command unless you mean it, but it can crop up accidentally. Suppose that Lothario wishes to get rid of 20 files called **Hortense1**, **Hortense2**, etc. He could type:

```
rm Hortense*
```

and all would be well. But, if he accidentally hit the space bar and typed:

```
rm Hortense *
```

UNIX would first look for a file called **Hortense**, remove it if found, and then proceed to * and remove all files. Here is another example. You wish to *cat* the file **Fourtney.Bell**. If you have no other files starting with **F**, you can type

```
cat F*
```

If you have other files starting with **F**, perhaps

```
cat Fo*
```

or

```
cat F*l
```

will work, depending on the names of the other files.

The wild cards are great time-savers. The more you work and play with UNIX, the more often and the more naturally you will use their help.

Directory Abbreviations: ".", "..", and "~"

UNIX also offers you some useful abbreviations for directory names. We now will unveil them.

If Nerkie wants to copy two files called **tillie** and **max** from Bob's subdirectory **gossip** into his own subdirectory **lowdown**, he could type, as we have seen,

```
cp /usr/bob/gossip/tillie /usr/bob/gossip/max
/usr/nerkie/lowdown
```

UNIX offers some shortcuts to those of you who desire less typing. They are abbreviations for particular directories. Here they are:

Your current working directory:	.	(a simple period)
The directory from which yours branches:	..	(two periods)
A home directory: {BSD}	~	(a tilde)

The first two representations are general, while the last one is used just by the C shell. A tilde by itself represents the user's home directory, and a tilde followed by a login name represents the home directory of the person with that login name.

Here are some abbreviations and what they stand for, assuming Nerkie uses them while in the **/usr/nerkie** directory.

```
~                    /usr/nerkie
~bob                 /usr/bob
~lowdown             /usr/lowdown
~/lowdown            /usr/nerkie/lowdown
~bob/gossip          /usr/bob/gossip
.                    /usr/nerkie
..                   /usr
./lowdown            /usr/nerkie/lowdown
```

Note the difference between ~**lowdown** and ~/**lowdown**. The first one would cause UNIX to look for the home directory of a user named "lowdown," while the second would lead UNIX to look through Nerkie's home directory for a subdirectory called **lowdown**.

If Nerkie uses **cd** to switch to the **/usr/nerkie/lowdown** directory, the meanings of the first five examples are unchanged, but the next two become:

```
.     /usr/nerkie/lowdown
..    /usr/nerkie
```

Here is one way Nerkie could shorten his typing. He could stay in his home directory and type:

```
cp ~bob/gossip/tillie ~bob/gossip/max lowdown
```

(Because Nerkie is in his home directory, UNIX will recognize **lowdown** as a subdirectory of Nerkie's home directory.)

Another possibility is that he could change directories and move into Bob's directory before giving the copy command:

```
cd ~bob/gossip
cp tillie max ~/lowdown
```

Yet another possibility is that he would first switch to his own subdirectory:

```
cd lowdown
cp ~bob/gossip/tillie ~bob/gossip/max .
```

These directory abbreviations can be combined with the wild-card substitutions. For instance, Nerkie can copy the entire file contents of Bob's **gossip** subdirectory into his own **lowdown** subdirectory with:

```
cp ~bob/gossip/* lowdown
```

If Nerkie already is in the **lowdown** directory, he could have done the copying with:

```
cp ~bob/gossip/* .
```

The directory abbreviations often come in handy when you decide to make wholesale revisions in your directory system. They give you a convenient way to shift large blocks of file about.

Review Questions

The hierarchical structure of the file system is one of the major features of the UNIX operating system. Here are some review questions to give you confidence in using the system.

A. Matching Commands

Match the functions shown on the left to the commands shown on the right. The answers are given at the end of the chapter.

1. cd ..
2. pwd
3. mv dearsue dearann
4. mail sue
5. cat part.? > final
6. ls
7. mkdir D2
8. grep sue dearann
9. rm fig*
10. cp ~hoppy/stats

a. Makes a new subdirectory named D2.
b. Lists contents of working directory.
c. Changes the name of **dearsue** to **dearann**.
d. Initiates sending mail to sue.
e. Prints all lines containing the word "sue" in the file **dearann**.
f. Copies the file **stats** in hoppy's home directory into a file called **stats** in the current working directory.
g. Gives your current working directory.
h. Concatenates all files whose names consist of **part.** followed by one character, and places the result in the file **final**.
i. Moves your working directory up one level.
j. Removes all files whose names start in **fig**.

B. Creating Commands

Use the hypothetical file structure shown in the following figure to create the commands that will accomplish the following actions (in some cases, there is more than one way).

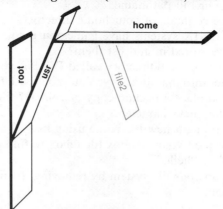

Your hypothetical working directory.

Assume that you are in the directory called *home*.

1. List all files and directories in your account.
2. Read the file named **file2**.
3. Make a copy of **file2** and call it **file5**.
4. Make a subdirectory called **D2**.
5. Put yourself in subdirectory **D2**.
6. Move **file2** into **D2**.
7. While in directory **D2**, list all files in directory **home**.
8. Create a subdirectory **D3** at the same level as **D2**; i.e., not a subdirectory of **D2**. (Hint: This is a 2-step sequence.)
9. Place today's date in a file in **D3**, calling it **f8**.
10. Remove subdirectory **D3**.

Answers:

A. 1–i, 2–g, 3–c, 4–d, 5–h, 6–b, 7–a, 8–e, 9–j, 10–f

B. 1. ls 2. cat file2 3. cp file2 file5 4. mkdir D2 5. cd D2 6. mv ~home/file2 . or mv ../file2 . or cd home and mv file2 /D2/file2 7. ls ../ or ls ~home 8. cd to go to your home directory, then mkdir D3 9. date > /D3/f8 or cd D3 and date > f8 10. First, cd D3, second pwd to make sure you're there, then rm * (a powerful command!), then cd to get back home and, finally, rmdir D3.

Exercises at the Terminal

Even if you have been following the chapter while sitting at a terminal, you might like to try these exercises to illustrate the major commands and to practice their use.

1. Find your full pathname.
2. List the contents of your home directory.
3. Some UNIX systems have games on them. Can you find the directory that they are stored in and list them?
4. Create a new subdirectory called **D7**. Put yourself in **D7** and try to copy any two files into that directory. You should use full pathnames for the experience.
5. Can you place a backup copy of your **D7** files into a new subdirectory called **D8** using metacharacters?
6. Try creating a new file name using **ln**.
7. Use **grep** on your mailbox file **mbox** to find the occurrence of a word such as "dear" or "hello."
8. Clean up your file system by removing the files from **D8** and, then, removing **D8** itself.

8

Using Programming Languages: FORTRAN, Pascal, and C

In this chapter, you will find:

8   USING PROGRAMMING LANGUAGES: FORTRAN, Pascal, and C

New UNIX user Wendell Turnbull Krumpnose rushed to the computer room clutching the magnetic tape that he had just received in the mail (ordinary mail, this time, not electronic mail). The tape contained a FORTRAN program that made home solar energy calculations.

"Here, guys, please load this on the system for me."

Since Wendell was such a nice guy, the technicians gladly dropped what they were doing, loaded the tape on a tape drive, and read the contents of the tape into a file called **solcalc** in Wendell's directory. Wendell sat down at his terminal, eager to use the new program.

But how? Wendell thought for a moment (that being the usual unit of time he devoted to thought). "Commands like **cat** and **ls** really are programs, and I run them just by typing their names. So maybe all I have to do is type **solcalc**." He did so, and UNIX replied with

```
solcalc: Permission denied.
```

Hmm. Maybe he should try typing the FORTRAN commands himself. He picked a line at random (**real rval**) from the program listing and typed it to see what would happen. UNIX responded with

```
real: Command not found.
```

Hmm. Perhaps a different approach was needed. "Help!" he cried, and the technicians hurried in with concerned looks upon their faces. "What can we do to assist you?" they chorused.

Wendell explained his problem, and they quickly set him straight. The computer has its own private language, and it isn't FORTRAN. UNIX systems, however, have a special program called **f77** that translates FORTRAN into the simple instructions that the host computer can understand; this process is called "compiling." Soon, under the benevolent tutelage of the staff, Wendell was able to master the needed skills. He changed the name of his file to **solcalc.f** so that **f77** would recognize that it was a FORTRAN file. Next, he typed

```
f77 solcalc.f
```

and waited while **f77** labored mightily for him. Finally, **f77** produced a ready-to-go program and placed it in a file called **a.out** (a favorite UNIX name for such files). Now to use it! All Wendell had to do now was type the word **a.out**, and the program ran. His original idea had not been that bad, he had just applied it to the wrong file.

Eventually, Wendell thought of modifications he wanted to make in the program. The program had many subsections called subroutines, and it seemed a shame to have to recompile the whole program when his changes were made to just one subroutine; compilation uses a lot of computer time. Again, his friends helped him out and showed him how to use the UNIX editors to place each subroutine in a file of its own. Now, when he submitted the collection of files to **f77**, the compiler not only gave him a ready-to-run program (**a.out**), it also gave him a compiled version of each subroutine. From now on, if Wendell needed to change a subroutine, he needed just to recompile that one subroutine and let **f77** combine it with his compiled versions of the rest of the program. With support like this, Wendell could not avoid fame and riches.

* * * *

Running a Program

How do you run a program on a computer? This is a pretty important question for many people. Perhaps you know a computer language or two yourself; perhaps you have purchased, borrowed, or otherwise acquired a program from elsewhere; perhaps you are just learning to program. Once you get a program, it is a simple matter to run it using UNIX. In this chapter, we will outline some of the basic concepts that concern programs, discuss some of the languages with which you can work, and explain how to run programs in C, FORTRAN, and Pascal. We won't tell you how to write programs, but this chapter will get you started in the process of using programs.

Languages, Compilers, and Interpreters

Once upon a time, not so long ago and not so far away, you needed to have mastered much technical lore and have great skill to run a computer. Now, it is getting easier and easier every day to use them. People haven't gotten any smarter, and neither have the computers. (But computers have gotten faster, cheaper, more compact, more powerful, and are capable of storing more information, so they are not doing too badly!) What has changed is that clever people have written clever programs to make it easier for the non-specialist to deal with computers. In particular, the development of programming languages, of compilers and interpreters, and of operating systems makes programming much simpler. What do all these terms mean? To clarify these points, we will survey how a computer is used.

Computers are machines that follow instructions. If you devise a set of instructions to accomplish some particular task, that is a program. Thus, the trick to use to get a computer to work for you is to give it the right instructions. This is not that easy to do, for the computer, itself, understands only a limited set of rather basic instructions called the "instruction set." Furthermore, it knows these instructions not by name but by a code (binary code) that uses only ones and zeros. The most basic way to program a computer, then, is to feed a string of these binary-coded instructions to the computer. This is called working in "machine language." Programming in machine language is tedious and exacting; it certainly is not going to capture the imagination of the general public. Also, each type of computer would, in general, have its own machine language, so every time a new machine was acquired, the users would have to learn the new language and rework their old programs. Thus, users were driven by their own laziness to develop a universal language that could be used on many different machines.

Now, that is an interesting problem. How do you create programs to run on any machine when each machine has its own primitive machine language? One way is to do it in two steps. The first step is to create a more universal language that humans can understand easily, and, perhaps, even love. Such a language, of course, is incomprehensible to a computer. The second step is to write a translation program that translates the new language into the machine's own language. This translation program is called a "compiler." Each kind of computer, then, would have its compiler written in its own machine language; the compiler, then, lets the computer understand the universal language.

What universal language resulted from this plan of attack? By now, hundreds of languages have been created along these lines, but none is regarded as universal (except, perhaps, by its creator). Several, however, do have a widespread popularity, including such stalwarts as FORTRAN, COBOL, BASIC, Pascal, APL, PL/M, LISP, Logo, and C. UNIX systems usually are supplied with most of these languages and can have the others installed. This means that UNIX-compatible compilers or interpreters exist for these languages. (An "interpreter" is a particular kind of compiler used for interactive languages such as Logo and BASIC. See the following box.)

207

Compiled Languages and Interpreted Languages

Compiled languages and interpreted languages represent two approaches to using languages on a computer. The compiling approach was developed in the days when the usual way of using a computer was to feed it punched cards, punched tape, or magnetic tape. This meant that the user had to prepare the entire program in advance and then submit the whole thing to the computer. A compiler would then take this entire block of programming and work it into a language acceptable to the computer. Thus, the end result of the compiler's toil was a complete program arranged in machine language. You could save this program and, next time, use it instead of the original. Hence, once your program was successfully compiled, you didn't have to compile it again unless you needed to change it. Since compilation is a slow process, you will save much time when you avoid compiling programs.

The development and rapid spread of the video keyboard terminal opened up a much more exciting way of communicating with a computer—direct interaction. Now we have an electronic "Simon says" machine. You tell the computer to do this, and it does; you tell it to do that, and it does. But, compiled languages don't fit into this scheme very easily; nothing gets done until after you type in the entire program and, then, have it compiled and run. Interactive languages, such as BASIC and Logo, get around this by translating each line *as you type it in*. For example, suppose you type the following three lines in BASIC:

```
LET X = 6
LET Y = 2 + X
PRINT Y
```

Immediately after you enter the first line, the computer creates a storage area, names it "X," and stores the value 6 in it. Immediately after you enter the second line, the computer creates a storage area, names it "Y," adds 2 to 6, and stores the value of 8 in Y. Immediately after you enter the third line, the computer prints the value 8 on your terminal screen, letting you see how clever it is. The program that does the work of translating your instructions into machine actions is called an "interpreter."

Suppose, though, you want to collect a few instructions together into a program before having them acted upon. BASIC and Logo allow you to do this. However, when you do finally run the program, it is still interpreted line by line rather than as a block. That is, the interpreter looks at one line of instructions, converts it to the proper code, executes the translated instruction, and only then looks at the next line.

The chief difference, then, between a compiler and an interpreter is that the compiler translates entire program chunks at a time while an interpreter translates single lines at a time. Each method has its advantages and disadvantages. The main advantage of the interactive approach is the direct and rapid feedback you get. Do it right, and you see your success immediately. Do it wrong, and you find out right away. Also, you get to correct it right away. The main disadvantage is that interactive systems are relatively slow. For example, if a program cycles through the same instruction several times, that instruction has to go through the translation process each time. Compilers more or less reverse the situation. You don't get any feedback until you complete the program and try to compile and run it. On the other hand, once the program works properly, you have an efficient machine-language version. Compilers are fairly intelligent programs and, by looking at program segments larger than a line, they can put together a more efficient translation than an interpreter does.

We've indicated the role of languages and of compilers and of interpreters. What about operating systems? Operating systems, such as UNIX, handle such tasks as feeding a program to a compiler, loading the resulting machine-language program into the computer, and running the program. Thus, modern computers are set up so that you can have them attend to all the grungy details while you act as the master planner.

Let's take a brief look at some of the more common languages.

FORTRAN

FORTRAN is an acronym for "FORmula TRANslation." This language was developed in the 1950s to deal with scientific and engineering programming. As the name suggests, FORTRAN is particularly suited to working with equations and formulas. Since then, of course, computers have been used for a wider and wider range of problems, and FORTRAN has been modified to meet these new needs. The latest version, FORTRAN 77 (so named because its standards were defined in 1977), is a general-purpose language, capable of dealing with numeric and nonnumeric problems. Many people in computer science feel that FORTRAN is dated and is not state-of-the-art, but there is a tremendous body of programs and software available in FORTRAN. FORTRAN still is used widely in engineering, science, and education. Thus, the language will continue to be an important one for a long time.

COBOL

COBOL (for COmmon Business-Oriented Language) was developed a little after FORTRAN and was intended to meet the needs of business programming. At that time, computers were huge and expensive so it was mainly only the giant companies that had them. Thus, much of the business programming for the major corporations has been done using COBOL. Small businesses, on the other hand, acquired computers when computers became smaller and cheaper. Business programming, on this smaller scale, more typically has been done in BASIC, for this language is better suited for small computers.

BASIC

BASIC (for Beginners All-purpose Symbolic Instruction Code) was developed in the 1960s at Dartmouth College to help students, with no computer background, learn to use a computer. It is an easy language to learn and to use, and its simplicity and small memory requirements have made it a natural choice for microcomputers. It's probably the most widely used language in the world. It is used for business applications, educational purposes, research, and computer games. It is an interactive language with all the advantages and disadvantages that that implies. The original version had severe limitations in such things as highly restricted variable names, so now several enhanced versions are available. These versions are more powerful, but the existence of more than one version can cause problems when you try to shift a program from one machine to another.

Pascal

Pascal (named after the 18th Century mathematician Blaise Pascal) was developed in the 1970s by Niklaus Wirth, a Swiss mathematician. By that time, people had been programming long enough to evolve a feeling for good programming principles. Wirth developed Pascal to embody these ideas. His main intent was to provide a language that would help, even compel, computer science students to develop a good programming style. However, the use of Pascal has grown beyond education and, today, Pascal is a very popular general-purpose language. Its use is being promoted in industry, where experience has shown it to produce programs that are more reliable and understandable than the older FORTRAN, BASIC, and COBOL programs.

C

C was developed by D. M. Ritchie at the Bell labs in the 1970s. In many ways, it is based on the same ideas as Pascal, but it was developed with an eye to systems programming, that is, the writing of programs to be used in running a computer system. For example, most of UNIX is written in the C language, including the FORTRAN and Pascal compilers. Although that is the orientation of the language, it can be used as a general language. On UNIX systems, programs written in C generally use less computer space than similar programs written in other languages.

Logo

Logo was developed in 1966 with the design goals of being simple to use, yet extremely powerful. It grew from work in Artificial Intelligence and is used in educational research. It is an interactive language that integrates in a uniform manner the facilities for graphics, calculation, and list processing. It is not yet widely available on UNIX, but its use is expected to grow rapidly in the next few years.

Compiling and Using Programs

Writing a program involves several major steps. The first is deciding what you want the program to accomplish. The second is working out a logical approach to accomplish the goal. The third step, called "coding," is used to express that approach in a programming language. We aren't going to tell you how to do any of these things (we'd like to, but that would take another book or two), but we will show you what to do once you get that far.

C, FORTRAN, and Pascal each have their own compiler. They are all used in much the same fashion, so we will go through two examples in C and, then, summarize the use of the other two compilers.

Compiling a C Program

To get the feel of using UNIX compilers, you may want to run through this example at a terminal. We begin with a very simple example of a program in C. It's simple enough that you don't really have to know C to work through this example.

```
#include <stdio.h>


main( )
{


  char name [72];


  printf("Hi! What's your first name?\n");
  scanf(" %s", name);
  printf("Hello, %s!\n", name);
  printf("You have a very nice, intelligent-sounding name.\n");


}
```

To use this program, your first step is to use an editor to create a file. If you've been good and have read the preceding chapters, you know how to do that. The name of the file should end in **.c**; this will identify the file as a C program to the C compiler. For example, you could call the file **lets.c**. If you copy this program into a file, be sure to type it exactly as it appears here. Don't substitute ('s for {'s or ['s and don't omit the semicolons. The indentations and blank lines are used to clarify the organization of the program to a human reader; they are ignored by the compiler. The "# include" statement tells the compiler where to look for some standard routines (such as the "scanf" routine), and it is not needed on some systems.

Suppose, now, that you have this program in the file **lets.c**. Your next step is to feed the program to the C compiler. The UNIX C compiler is called **cc** (clever name, eh?), and the feeding consists of typing **cc** and following it with the name of the file you wish to compile. In this case, you would type

```
cc lets.c
```

There will be a brief wait while **cc** does its work. If you made a detectable error in typing the program, **cc** will tell you so. It even will tell you exactly what it thinks is wrong; whether you can make sense out of the message depends on what you know about C. Of course, you may never make errors and, so, will need not worry about error messages.

Once **cc** is finished, the standard UNIX prompt will return. If you list your files, you will find a new one called **a.out**. This is the name **cc** gives to the file in which it places the machine-language version of your program. The program is ready to work; just type

```
a.out
```

to run it. If you want to save the program, it is a good idea to rename **a.out** so that you don't clobber your old program the next time you compile another program!

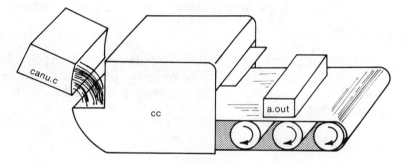

Feeding a program to *cc*.

Now let's extend the example a little. First, use an editor to add a new line to **lets.c** so that it now looks like this:

```
#include <stdio.h>


main( )
{


   char name [72];


   printf("Hi! What's your first name? \n");
   scanf(" %s", name);
   printf("Hello, %s!\n", name);
```

```
printf("You have a very nice, intelligent-sounding name.\n");
addsome();
```

```
{
```

We've added the line with **addsome( )** in it. Now, create a new file called **addsome.c** and enter the following text in it:

```
addsome()
{
   printf("I am happy to have felt your fingers on me.\n");
}
```

Now we have two files. One (**lets.c**) contains the main program, and one (**addsome.c**) contains a subordinate program (called a "function" in C) that is used by the main program. To get this combination to work, we compile both files simultaneously:

```
cc lets.c addsome.c
```

Once this is done, you can **ls** your files and see that you have three new files: **lets.o**, **addsome.o**, and **a.out**. When you type **a.out**, your new program will run. What about **lets.o** and **addsome.o**? They contain the object code (see next box) for **lets.c** and **addsome.c**, respectively. They, too, can be fed to the **cc** compiler. Because they already are in machine code, they will be processed faster than the original files. Thus, if you lose your **a.out** file, you can reconstruct it with any one of the following instructions:

```
cc lets.c addsome.c
cc lets.c addsome.o
cc lets.o addsome.c
cc lets.o addsome.o
```

The last choice would be the fastest, since both programs already are in object code. Note, too, that you could use the **addsome.o** file with any other program that you devised that would call the **addsome( )** function.

Normally, **cc** produces object files only when two or more files are compiled, but you can request an object file even if you compile only one file. The on-line manual will give you a complete outline of your options.

Summary: cc—C compiler

name	options	arguments
cc	[-c, -o]	file(s)

Description: cc compiles programs in the C language. If the input file is in C, its name should end in **.c**; if it is an object code file, its name should end in **.o**. The submitted files are compiled (if necessary) to create an executable program file called **a.out**. An object code file is created for each C file and is stored in a file whose name is the same as the original, except the **.c** is replaced by **.o**. (This step is skipped if only one program is submitted.)

Options: **-c**
      Suppresses the loading phase (creating **a.out**) and forces an object file to be produced.
-o filename
      Causes the executable program to be given the name **filename** instead of **a.out**.

Example: **cc -o poker straight.c flush.o**
      This command takes a C program from the file **straight.c** and the object code of a previously compiled C program from the file **flush.o**. The C program from **straight.c** is compiled and the object code is placed in a file called **straight.o**. The two object codes are combined along with required C routines to form an executable program called **poker**. Typing **poker** will run the program.

Object Files and *a.out*

When you submit a program to one of the UNIX compilers, it generally produces two types of output files: object files (identified by ending in **.o**) and a loaded and executable file (called **a.out** by default). Both contain machine-language versions of your programs, so you may wonder what the difference is. (If you don't wonder, you have our permission to skip this box.)

An object file contains the machine-language code for your program. It is, however, an incomplete file. First, your program will probably use one or more system functions. By that, we mean programs provided by the system. Examples would be print or write statements, trig functions, and the like. Your object file will not contain the code for these functions; it just has the code for the part of the program that you wrote. Secondly, you may have spread your program over two or more files. The object files wouldn't contain the instructions needed to tie the files together. Thirdly, an object file is not set up to run; it is just a passive storehouse of information.

The **a.out** file, on the other hand, *is* ready to run. It includes the code for system functions, it combines your files together if you have more than one, and it is set up to execute when you type its name. It contains the same sort of code as the **.o** files; it is just more complete.

Well, you may wonder, why bother with object code files if **a.out** is all you need to run a program? The answer is that object files become very handy if you modularize your programs. In FORTRAN, you should give each subroutine its own file. In Pascal and C, you should give individual procedures and functions their own files. In this manner, you can build up your personal library of little task-solvers and construct programs from various combinations of files. Even if you don't have such ambitions, this approach of separating programs into several files allows you to update individual files without having

BASIC SPOKEN HERE...

PASCAL SPOKEN HERE...

to recompile the entire program. Object files compile much more quickly than does the original code.

Can you mix together object code files from different compilers? You can to some extent, but not in a casual manner. It takes a special blend of information to do so; a blend that is beyond the scope of this modest book. The pamphlet, *A Portable FORTRAN 77 Compiler,* by S. I. Feldman and P. J. Weinberger (a Bell Labs publication) provides information on how to make C and FOR-TRAN programs compatible.

The FORTRAN Compiler: *f77*

The UNIX FORTRAN compiler is called **f77** to remind us that it can handle the latest version of FORTRAN (FORTRAN 77). A great mass of FORTRAN programming is in the preceding version (called FORTRAN IV or FORTRAN 66), and **f77** accepts programs in that version, too. In fact, it accepts all sorts of files; the on-line manual will document the limits of its appetite. We'll assume here that you are interested in running a standard FORTRAN program (either 77 or 66). (The **f77** compiler replaces the **fc** complier, which just did FORTRAN 66.)

The first step, once you have a FORTRAN program, is to place it in a file whose name ends in **.f.** This identifies the file as a FORTRAN file to the **f77** compiler. (Incidentally, the column spacing in the files should be set up the same way that they are on punched cards; i.e., columns 2-5 for line numbers, column 6 for the continuation mark, and columns 7-72 for statements.) Then, submit the file to the compiler by typing **f77** and the file name. For example, if your program is in a file called **sun.f,** you would type

```
f77 sun.f
```

If your program is acceptable, **f77** then produces two files. The first is called **a.out** and the second, **sun.o.** The **sun.o** file contains the object code for your program, and **a.out** has the executable version. (See the preceding box if you have forgotten the difference.) To run your program, just type

```
a.out
```

If your program is spread over more than one file (in subroutine files, for example), just enter all the file names after the **f77** command. These files can be FORTRAN files, object code files, or a mixture of the two. For example, suppose you had already compiled the three files **sun.f**, **moon.f**, and **earth.f**, and had saved the corresponding object code files. If you then changed **moon.f** and needed all three files for a complete program, you could type

```
f77 sun.o moon.f earth.o
```

to get a new **a.out** file. As we've mentioned earlier, it's a good idea to change the name of the **a.out** file if you plan to use the program again.

Summary: f77—compiles FORTRAN programs

name	options	arguments
f77	[-o, -c]	file(s)

Description: **f77** compiles programs written in FORTRAN. If the program is written in FORTRAN, it should be placed in a file whose name ends in **.f**. If the program is in object code form, it should be in a file whose name ends in **.o**. The compiler takes **.f** files, compiles them, and stores the object code in files of the same name, but with the **.f** replaced by a **.o**. The object code, along with required support routines, are loaded into an executable file called **a.out**.

Option: **-o filename**
This option causes the executable program to be called **filename** instead of **a.out**.
-c
This suppresses loading but still produces object files for each source.

Example: **f77 -o porker slop.f**
This command takes the FORTRAN program in the file **slop.f**, compiles it, and places the object code for it in a file named **slop.o**. It then takes the object code, combines it with the required FORTRAN support programs, and loads them into an executable file named **porker**. The program can be run by typing **porker**.

The Pascal Compiler: *pc*

The **cc** and **f77** compilers are standard components of the UNIX system, but there is no standard Pascal compiler. Many systems, however, have the Pascal **pc** compiler developed at Berkeley, and we will use it as a typical example. It is used in the same fashion as **cc** and **f77**. Pascal programs should be stored in files whose names end in **.p**. Suppose, for example, you have a Pascal program stored in a file called **rascal.p**. To compile your Pascal rascal, type:

```
pc rascal.p
```

If the compiler finds no major errors, **pc** will provide you with a file called **a.out**, which will contain the executable version of your program. To use it, type:

```
a.out
```

Again, we remind you that it is a good idea to change the name of the **a.out** file so that some new **a.out** doesn't come along and clobber it.

Like **cc** and **f77**, **pc** generates object code files in addition to **a.out**. Normally, it does so only if you compile two or more files at the same time, but you can request object code even for a single file. The UNIX on-line manual will outline your options.

Once you have object code versions of your Pascal procedures, you can combine them with Pascal files. There are some details of referencing that you'll have to attend to; you'll have to check with your system's manuals or staff to learn the specific requirements.

Summary: pc—compiles Pascal programs		
name	**options**	**arguments**
pc	[-c, -o]	file(s)

Description: **pc** compiles programs written in Pascal. Pascal file names should end in **.p**. The compiler also accepts object code programs contained in files whose names end in **.o**. The object code produced for a **.p** file is placed in a file of the same name but with the **.p** replaced by an **.o**. A complete program is assembled from all the files and is loaded along with the required system routines into an executable file named **a.out**. This file can be run by typing its name and [return].

Options:

-c

Suppresses the loading phase (creating **a.out**) and forces an object file to be produced, even if only one program is compiled.

-o filename

Causes the executable program to be given the name **filename** instead of **a.out**.

Example:

pc -o zorro mask.p sword.o

This command compiles the Pascal program in **mask.p** and places the object code for that program in the file **mask.o**. It then combines this object code with the code in **sword.o** and with the system code to produce a complete program which is loaded into the file **zorro**.

Compiler	Accepts* files names end with	Produces[†] .o files	Executable program[†] placed in file
cc	.c, .o	If more than one file is submitted.	a.out
f77	.f, .o	Yes	a.out
pc	.p, .o	If more than one file is submitted.	a.out

* partial list
† assuming no options specified

Compilers and files.

Compilers: Summing Up

As you probably noticed, the compilers **cc**, **f77**, and **pc** are all used much the same way. Each accepts language files (whose names should end in **.c**, **.f**, and **.p**, respectively) and object code files (whose names should end in **.o**). Each will accept several files simultaneously and will combine them into a complete program. Each can generate object code files from the language source files. Each loads the assembled program into a file called **a.out** which can then be run by typing its name. About the only point of caution that we might raise is that you cannot routinely feed object code files produced by one compiler to a compiler for a different language. (This task is not impossible, but it is definitely beyond the scope of this book.)

The compilers are easy to use and will produce efficient programs, so if you know one of these languages, get in there and write a great program!

Running a Program in Background

Has this happened to you? You start a program running at a terminal. Then you think of something else you want to do on the computer, but the program seems to take forever (i.e., more than 60 seconds) and you have to sit twiddling your thumbs until the program is done. If you enjoy that sort of situation, read no further. But if you think you deserve better, UNIX agrees. That's why UNIX offers the background job option, which lets the system work on a problem out of view, freeing the terminal for other tasks or games.

The way to run a program in background is simple. Suppose, for example, you have a program called **a.out** that reads information from one file, does a bunch of amazing things, and then prints brilliant results into a second file. To run this program in background, type:

```
a.out &
```

The **&** symbol following the command is the instruction that tells UNIX to run the program in background. Once you enter this command, you'll get a response but the response will depend on the system you are using. If you are using the C shell, the response you get will look like this:

```
[1] 6784
%
```

221

The first line assigns your line two numbers. The [1] means that this is your job number 1 in background. If you started another job in background before this one finished, it would be called [2]. The 6784 is a job identification number assigned by the system to this particular job. The actual number assigned will depend on what the computer is doing just then. (Every job running on the system, background or not, is assigned its individual job identification number.) Do these numbers have any uses? Yes, and we will tell you one of them before this chapter is done.

The second line, the usual UNIX prompt, tells you that UNIX is ready for your next command. Now you can continue your work while your program works away unseen by you. Neat! When the job finishes, you will get a message like

```
[1] Done    a.out
```

on the screen.

The Bourne shell version is a bit terser. It doesn't tell you when the job is done, and it reports back just the system job number. It doesn't assign a personal number, such as the one that the C shell gives in brackets.

There are some things you should know before doing background jobs. First, if the system is heavily loaded with tasks, background jobs will just bog it down further. Secondly, you can't give a background job any input from the terminal. If your job needs terminal input, it will just get stuck and stop when it reaches that point. Thirdly, if your program normally sends output to the screen, it still will when in background. This means that you could find yourself inundated by a string of numbers while you are editing one of your sensitive poems. There are remedies for these situations. If the system is heavily loaded, don't run background jobs. If your job normally takes input from the terminal, you can use redirection (see the next chapter) to get the program to take its input from a file. Just remember to put the right data in the file. Finally, you can use redirection to channel the output to a file instead of to the screen.

Sometimes, it can happen that your job gets stuck or is taking too long and you want to stop it. Here's where we get to use the identification numbers. For example, to end the job we mentioned previously, you can type:

```
kill 6784
```

and the job is "killed." Don't worry, the job doesn't feel a thing. (In the language of UNIX, "stopping" a job merely suspends it and it can be

resumed at a later time. "Killing" a job aborts it and gets it off the system. We will talk a little more about stopped jobs in Chapter 11.)

Those of you with a UNIX C shell could also kill the job with a

```
kill %1
```

command, where the **%1** identifies the job as the one labeled [1] earlier.

Additional Programming Features

UNIX has much more language support than we have described so far. Here, we would like to point out some additional options just so that you will know what's there.

Many UNIX systems carry one or more interactive languages such as BASIC or Logo. Several versions are available. One usually initiates an interactive language by typing in a key word, such as:

```
basic
bas
```

or

```
logo
```

The key word calls up the interpreter and changes the user prompt (perhaps to > or *) to remind you that you are working in that language now. Once this happens, you can then communicate with the computer in that language. When you are finished, typing another keyword (perhaps **goodbye** or **bye**) takes you back to the usual UNIX mode and returns the usual UNIX prompt.

Many UNIX systems carry a Pascal load-and-run interpreter (called **pix**) in addition to a Pascal compiler. This interpreter does not make Pascal an interactive language; you still have to submit a complete Pascal program in a file to it. The interpreter translates the program into an intermediate code line by line but without taking the overview of the program that the compiler does. The result is that the interpreter is quicker to produce a program, but the compiler gives a program that runs faster. This makes the interpreter good for developing programs and the compiler good for putting together the finished product.

Other programming aids include **lint** (which checks out C programs), **cb** (which beautifies C programs with proper indentations and the like), and **make** (which helps you maintain large programs). If you revise a subroutine, **make** puts together the whole program with minimum recompilation.

Two other languages commonly found on UNIX systems are APL and LISP. The former is handled by the interpreter **apl** while the latter is handled by the compiler **liszt** and the interpreter **lisp**.

There is one other language that you may wish to program in. UNIX, itself. Not only does UNIX have a large number of commands, but it also has some control statements that allow you to use UNIX programs to perform loops and make logical decisions. You can construct a program from a series of such commands, store them in a file, and, then, use the **chmod** command to make that file into a program that you can run just by typing the file name. We will give a simple example of this in Chapter 12.

A Final Word

Actually, there is no final word. UNIX is an open-ended system, and you can go as far as your knowledge and imagination can take you. If you obtain a compiler or interpreter (written in C) for some other language, you can install it in your directory and use it. If you want to create your own computer language, go ahead. Not only can you install it in your own directory, but UNIX supplies **yacc** (Yet Another Compiler Compiler) to help you put together a compiler for it!

Review Questions

A. Matching functions.

(This will be a tough one.) Match the compiler with the language it compiles:

1. cc   **a.** Pascal
2. f77   **b.** French
3. pc   **c.** FORTRAN
                            d. C

B. Questions

1. Which of the following is a proper name to give to a file containing a Pascal program?
   a. blaise.c
   b. blaise.p
   c. blaise.o
   d. blaise
2. What two files are produced by the following command: **f77 henry.f**?
3. You have the object code of a C program stored in a file named **red.o**. Will typing the file name cause this program to run?

Answers:

A. 1–d, 2–c, 3–a

B. **1.** b; **2. a.out** and **henry.o**; **3.** No; you type the name of the executable file (**a.out** by default), not the object code file, to run a program.

Exercises at the Terminal

If you know how to use FORTRAN, Pascal, or C, write a simple program in one of those languages. Then, try the following:

1. Make a programming error deliberately and see what the compiler says about it.
2. Correct the error and compile the program.
3. Run the program.
4. Obtain the object code file for the program.
5. Feed the object code to the compiler and see how that works.

9

File Management Commands: *wc, sort,* and *pr*

In this chapter, you will find:

9   FILE MANAGEMENT COMMANDS: *wc, sort,* and *pr*

Introduction: The Shell Command Line

When you sit down to a UNIX system, you have hundreds of UNIX commands at your call. Many will become indispensable to you, some you will use occasionally, and some you may never see. There are some basic commands that almost every user needs to know, and frequent use will burn them into your brain. The more you use the system, the more commands you'll know by heart, but with so many commands available, remembering the details can be a problem. Fortunately, most UNIX commands are used in a similar fashion. Unfortunately, there are many exceptions, but we can view this as a sign of the vibrant vitality of the UNIX system.

We've seen the main elements of a command in Chapter 3, but you probably would enjoy seeing them again. The elements are the command name, the options, and the arguments. (Technically, anything following the command name is an argument, but we will use the term "argument" to mean the file, the directory, or whatever it is that the command acts upon, and we will use the term "option" to indicate a modification of the command.) When put together on one line, these elements constitute the "command line." An example of a command line is:

    ls -l /usr

Here the command name is **ls**, the option is **-l** (i.e., the *l*ong form), and the argument is the directory name **/usr**.

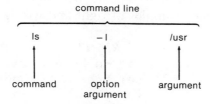

Command line structure.

Computers, being the simple-minded machines they are, require that you follow rules when typing in a command line. Here are some of them.

1. Each element should be separated from the others by at least one space. UNIX uses the spaces to tell when one element ends and another begins, so if you type:

```
ls-l /usr
```

UNIX will think you are looking for a command called **ls-l**, and if you type:

```
ls -l/usr
```

UNIX will think you are looking for an option called **-l/usr**. In either case, you will leave UNIX dumbfounded. Why can't UNIX figure out what you really meant? After all, there aren't any other command names beginning with **ls**, so UNIX should have known that **ls-l** must have been intended to be **ls -l**. Ah, but UNIX is so flexible that you *could* have *created* a new command called **ls-l**, so UNIX takes the safe route and doesn't try to second guess what you meant. Since many users forget to put a space between a command name and the option flag, we remind you once again: *put a space after the command name*. On the other hand, *don't* put spaces within an element.

RIGHT	WRONG
ls -l /usr	ls - l /usr
ls -s /bin	ls-s /bin

2. The proper order of elements is command name, options, and arguments. Often, you don't need any options and, sometimes, you don't need an argument; just omit the elements you don't need. Here are some examples of right and wrong command line orders.

RIGHT	WRONG
cat -n hobo	cat hobo -n
cat hobo	hobo cat
ls -a	-a ls

A few commands may violate this sequence.

3. Options usually are indicated with the "flag" notation, where one or more characters follow a hyphen. Typical examples are the **-n**, **-a**, and **-l** flags that we just saw. More than one option can be used at a time

(unless they contradict each other) and the order usually is not important. Multiple option flags may be separated from each other by spaces or, if they require no further input, may be strung together on the same hyphen. (In some instances, only one of these two approaches may work, depending on the particular command.) For example, if we wished to get a long listing (**-l**) of all files (**-a**) indicating file type (**-F**), we could type any of the following left-hand examples:

RIGHT	*WRONG*
ls -l -a -F	ls -l-a-F
ls -laF	ls -l a F
ls -Fla	
ls -F -la	

What's meant by "requiring no further input"? We mean an option that is called up just by giving a letter or symbol alone. For example, the **-l** and the **-a** options of **ls** need no further input. On the other hand, the **-o** option of **cc** (see Chapter 8) needs a file name to be supplied with it.

4. Some commands take, or can take, more than one argument. These should be separated from each other by spaces.

RIGHT	*WRONG*
cat cabbage king walrus	cat cabbagekingwalrus
	cat cabbage, king, walrus

5. You can combine several commands on one line by separating them by semicolons. For example, if you wanted to compile the FORTRAN program in the file **lulu.f** and, then, run the resulting **a.out** program, you could type:

```
f77 lulu.f; a.out
```

A command can be your own creation. For example, we saw in the last chapter that you can run a computer program simply by typing the name of the file in which the executable program is stored. Later, we will see other ways of producing your own commands.

We now would like to share some more commands with you. We'll try to keep the descriptions brief and will leave the clever uses to your imagination. Also, we will try to group the commands together by function instead of alphabetically. Also, to keep this section manageable, we will outline just the more common options. We'll start with commands relating to file management.

File Management Commands

Word counting: *wc*

The **wc** command tells you how many lines, words, and characters you have in a file. If you have a file called **gourd**, you find this information by typing:

```
wc gourd
```

and UNIX responds with, say,

```
79   378   2936 gourd
```

This response tells you that there are 79 lines, 378 words, and 2936 characters in the file **gourd**. You can have more than one file as an argument. For example, the command:

```
wc gourd mango
```

would produce a result like this:

```
 79   378   2936 gourd
132   310   2357 mango
211   688   5293 total
```

Not only does **wc** count the lines, words, and characters in each file, it also finds the totals for you!

The most commonly used options for **wc** are **-l**, **-w**, and **-c**. The first one counts lines only, the second counts words only, and the last option counts characters only. Of course, you can combine them as described in the preceding section. Hence:

```
wc -lw darkeyes
```

would count the number of lines and words in **darkeyes** but not the number of characters.

name	options	arguments
	Summary: wc—word count	
wc	[-l, -w, -c, -p]	[filename(s)]

Description: **wc** is a counting program; by default, it works in the **-lwc** option, counting the lines, words, and characters in the named files. If more that one file is given, **wc** gives the counts for each file plus the combined totals for all files. If no file is given, **wc** uses the standard input—the terminal. In this case, you should terminate the input with a [control-d]. Multiple options should be strung together on the same hyphen.

Options:
- **-l**   Counts lines
- **-w**   Counts words
- **-c**   Counts characters
- **-p**   Counts pages (66 lines) {BSD}

Example: **wc -w Essay**
This command would count the number of words in the file **Essay**.

File checking: *head* {BSD} and *tail*

These two commands give you a quick way to check the contents of a file with **head** showing you the first ten lines of a file, and **tail** showing you the last ten lines. To see the first ten lines of the file **overheels**, type:

```
head overheels
```

To see the last ten lines of the files **feathers** and **spin**, type:

```
tail feathers spin
```

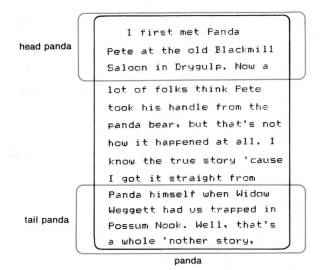

head panda

> I first met Panda
> Pete at the old Blackmill
> Saloon in Drygulp. Now a
> lot of folks think Pete
> took his handle from the
> panda bear, but that's not
> how it happened at all. I
> know the true story 'cause
> I got it straight from

tail panda

> Panda himself when Widow
> Weggett had us trapped in
> Possum Nook. Well, that's
> a whole 'nother story,

panda

A *head* and *tail* look at a file.

Summary: head—looks at the head of a file {BSD}

name	options	arguments
head	[-number]	filename(s)

Description: **head** shows the first 10 lines of the named files, unless the number option specifies a different number of lines.

Option: -number
For "number," substitute the number of lines you wish to have printed.

Example: **head -15 hunter**
This command prints out on the screen the first 15 lines of the file **hunter**.

Summary: `tail`—gives the last part of a file

name	options	arguments
`tail`	[+ / −**number**[**lbc**] [**r**]]	filename(s)

Description: **tail** shows the tail end of a file; by default, it delivers the last 10 lines. **tail** will only work with one file at a time.

Options: + number
Start "number" from the beginning.
− number
Start "number" from the end.
lbc
Indicates whether "number" is to be counted in lines (**l**), blocks (**b**), or characters (**c**). **l** is assumed if no letter is given.
r
Prints the lines in reverse order. A **-r** with no number option given prints the entire file in reverse order.

Examples: **tail -20 gate**
Prints the last 20 lines of the file **gate**.
tail +30c gate
Prints the file **gate** starting with the 30th character.
tail -15r gate
Prints the last 15 lines of the file **gate** in reverse order.

Note: Constructions of the form **tail -15 -r gate** are not allowed; all the options have to be strung after one **+** or **−**.

Sorting: *sort*

One of UNIX's great labor-saving commands is the **sort**, which can sort files numerically or alphabetically. The sorting function can be used simply or with some fancy options. We will just take a basic look this time and will save the fancy stuff for Chapter 12. The **sort** function, when used without options, sorts files alphabetically by line. Actually, the idea of "alphabetical" order has to be extended since a file may contain nonalphabetic characters. The basic order used is called the "machine-collating sequence," and it may be different on different machines. For UNIX, the following points are generally true:

1. Uppercase letters (capitals) are sorted separately from lowercase letters. Within each case, the standard alphabetical order is used.
2. Numbers are sorted by the first digit. The sorting order is 0,1,2,3,4,5,6,7,8,9.
3. The remaining symbols—ones like), %, +, and !—are not grouped together. Some may come between the numbers and the alphabet, and others before or after all numbers and letters.

Let's look at how a particular example might work. Suppose that the contents of **grabbag** are:

```
Here is a small
file with some
words in it
and also
some numbers like
1
23
and
102.

    The first line is blank; this one begins with a blank.
```

This is how the command

```
sort grabbag
```

would arrange them on one system:

```
    The first line is blank; this one begins with a blank.
1
102.
23
Here is a small
and
and also
```

```
file with some
some numbers like
words in it
```

Note that the line beginning "The first . . ." was not placed with the other alphabetical lines. The reason is that the first character of that line is a blank, not a "T," so the line was placed according to where blanks go. (The **-b** option will cause blanks to be ignored.) Also note that 102 is listed before 23! This is because **sort** treats numbers as words and sorts them by their first digit. (The **-n** option treats numbers as numbers and sorts them arithmetically; it would place the numbers in **file1** in the order 1, 23, 102.) Finally, notice that **sort** lists capital letters before lowercase letters.

If you feed more than one file to **sort**, it will sort them *and* merge the results. This is great for combining, say, inventory lists.

Normally, the **sort** function sends its output to the terminal. To save the results, you can use redirection. For example, to sort and merge the files **redsox** and **whitesox** and then store the results in a file called **pinksox**, type:

```
sort redsox whitesox > pinksox
```

Or, you can use the **-o** option described in the following summary.

Summary: `sort`—sorts and merges files

name	options	arguments
`sort`	[-b, -d, -f, -n, -o, -r]	filename(s)

Description: **sort** sorts and merges the lines from the named files and sends the result to the screen. In the default mode, lines are sorted by the machine-collating sequence, which is an extended alphabetical order encompassing letters, digits, and other symbols. Capital letters are sorted separately from small letters.

Options: **-b**
Ignore initial blanks when sorting.

-d

"Dictionary" order, using only letters, digits, and blanks to determine order.

-f

Ignore the distinction between capital and lowercase letters.

-n

Sort numbers by arithmetic value instead of by first digit.

-o filename

Place the output in a file called "filename" instead of on the screen. The name can be the same as one of the input names.

-r

Sort in reverse order.

Example: **sort -fr -o sortbag grabbag**

This command would sort the lines of the file **grabbag**. Capitalization will be ignored by the sorting process and the lines will be in reverse alphabetical order. The results will be stored in the file **sortbag**.

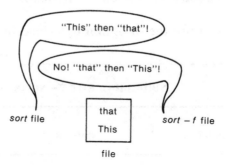

sort vs. *sort −f.*

File Comparison: *cmp, comm,* and *diff*

While cleaning up your filing system, you find two files with the same name but in different directories. Are they really the same? Or, let's say that you have two similarly named files. One is updated, but you don't remember which. Can you quickly compare the two? This is a small sample of the potential uses for some sort of system function that compares files. We will look at three UNIX possibilities.

The first is **cmp**; it is the simplest and tells you the least. It compares two files and finds the location (line and byte) of the first disagreement between the two. An interchange between you and UNIX might look like this:

```
% cmp rascal.p rascall.p
rascal.p rascall.p differ: char 48, line 21
```

The **comm** command tells you more, but it works successfully only with files sorted in the ASCII collating sequence. It prints out three columns. The first column lists lines found only in the first file; the second column lists lines found only in the second file, and the third column lists lines found in both files. Here is a typical user-UNIX dialogue:

```
% comm giftlist1 giftlist2
      Android, Arnold
            Falpha, Alpha
            Filename, Ronald
            Gossens, Waldo
            Goto, Dmitri
      Spumoni, Brunhilda
Spumoni, Hopalong
            Vlug, Merrimee
Yeti, Milo
            Zazzy, Quintus
```

The columns overlap, but you can see which lines are shared and which are not. In this case, only **giftlist1** contains "Spumoni, Hopalong" and "Yeti, Milo." Only **giftlist2** contains "Android, Arnold" and "Spumoni, Brunhilda." The rest of the names are in both lists. You can suppress the printing of any column you choose; the details for this are in the summary.

The **diff** command is the most powerful of the three. It finds the difference between two files and then tells you the most efficient way to make the first file identical to the second! It is a big help in updating files.

If we run **diff** on the same two files that we used **comm** on (i.e., we type **diff giftlist1 giftlist2**), we get this result:

```
0a1
> Android, Arnold
5c6
< Spumoni, Hopalong
---
```

```
> Spumoni, Brunhilda
7d7
< Yeti, Milo
```

This needs some interpretation. The **a**, **c**, and **d** stand for **append, change**, and **delete**. The numbers are line numbers, the "<" means a line from the first file, and the ">" means a line from the second file. We can paraphrase the output this way:

> Add to the beginning (line 0) of the first file, line 1 ("Android, Arnold") of the second file.
>
> Change line 5 of the first file ("Spumoni, Hopalong") to line 6 ("Spumoni, Brunhilda") of the second file.
>
> Delete line 7 ("Yeti, Milo") of the first file.

Keep in mind that the goal of **diff** is to show how to make the first file identical to the second; thus, all the changes listed by **diff** apply to the first file only. Of course, if all you wanted to do was make the two files identical, you could just use the **cp** command to make a second copy.

The BSD version of **diff** doesn't stop there, however. It also will compare two *directories*, tell you which filenames are not common to both, and then go ahead and compare the contents of the files whose names are common to both directories.

Summary: `cmp`—compares two files, finding location of difference		
name	**options**	**arguments**
cmp	−l	filename1 filename2

Description: **cmp** looks through the two input files and prints the byte and line number of the first difference between the two. You can use − for filename1 if you want one of the files to be the standard input.

Option: **-l**
    The long option prints the byte number (decimal) and the differing bytes (octal) for each and every difference.

Example: **cmp -l remember**
This will print out the location of the first difference between what you type on the terminal (terminated by a [control–d]) and what is in the file **remember**.

Summary: `comm`—find lines common to two sorted files

name	options	arguments
`comm`	`[ -1, -2, -3 ]`	filename1 filename2

Description: **comm** reads the two named files (which should be in ASCII collating sequence) and produces three columns of output. The first column contains lines found only in the first file, the second column contains lines found only in the second file, and the third column contains lines found in both files.

Options:
−1   Don't print the first column.
−2   Don't print the second column.
−3   Don't print the third column.

Example: **comm -12 listA listB**
This command will print only those lines found in both **listA** and **listB**.

Summary: `diff`—finds the difference between two files or directories

name	options	arguments
`diff`	`[-b, -e, -r]`	file1 file2 or

directory1 directory2
{BSD}

Description: **diff**, when the two arguments are text files, compares the files and produces output showing what changes to make in the first file in order to make it identical to the second file. When the two arguments are directories, **diff** lists files found only in one directory and applies itself to all file pairs found in both directories.

The output format uses "a" for *append,* "c" for *change,* and "d" for *delete.* The symbol "<" means a line from the first file, and ">" indicates a line from the second file. Numbers denote the lines affected. The following is an example:

```
8a10,12
 >Barth, Garth
 >Cuddles, Misty
 >Dollar, Petro
```

This means to append line 10 to line 12 of file2 after line 8 of file1. Then, the three lines from file2 are shown.

Options: **-b**
Ignores trailing blanks in a line; other blank strings are considered equal regardless of length. Thus, this option would consider the following two lines to be the same:

    eye of a newt
    eye of   a   newt

-e
Produces output in the form of **ed** editor commands.
-r
When using **diff** with directories, this option causes **diff** to be applied recursively to any subdirectories it encounters. (The word "recursively" here means that if the subdirectories have subdirectories, **diff** will be applied to them also.)

Example: **diff -e giftlist1 giftlist2**
This command causes the output to be expressed as **ed** commands. If the files are the same as the example in the text, then the output would be:

```
7d
5c
Spumoni, Brunhilda
.
0a
Android, Arnold
.
```

Notice that the commands include the period symbol that is needed to return to the command mode in **ed.**

Command	Operates on	Produces (if no options given)
cmp	Any two files (text or binary code).	Location of first difference, if any.
comm	Two sorted text files	Column 1: Lines only in first file. Column 2: Lines only in second file. Column 3: Lines in both files.
diff	Two text files.	Changes needed to make the first file just like the second file.

cmp, comm, **and** *diff.*

Redundancy Elimination: *uniq*

Suppose you have two mailing lists that you have sorted and merged together. You may have some addresses that are duplicated, and you might want to get rid of the repeated versions. You can do this with **uniq.** It will read a file, compare adjacent lines, reject repetitions, and print out the remaining lines on the terminal or into a file which you choose.

The file **weelist** has the following contents (we don't know why, it just does):

```
anchovies
apiaries
artichokes
```

```
artichokes
aviaries
```

The command:

```
uniq weelist
```

will produce the following output:

```
anchovies
apiaries
artichokes
aviaries
```

As you can see, **uniq** eliminated one copy of the word "artichokes" from the file. If you want to direct the output to a file, you need only to give the name of that file after the name of the file that is to be processed. Thus, the command:

```
uniq weelist newfile
```

would produce the same output, but would route it to the file **newfile** instead of to the screen.

Because **uniq** works by comparing adjacent lines, the duplicate lines must be next to the originals or else **uniq** won't spot them. Sorting the file first, using **sort**, will ensure that **uniq** works.

Summary: uniq—remove duplicated lines from a file		
name	**options**	**arguments**
uniq	[-u, -d, -c]	inputfile [outputfile]

Description: **uniq** reads the input file, compares adjacent lines, and prints out the file minus the repeated lines. If a second file name is given, the output is placed in that file instead of on the screen.

Options: **-u**
Prints out only those lines that have no duplicates. That is, a line that appears two or more times consecutively, in the original file, is not printed out at all.
-d
Prints out one copy each of just the lines with duplicates, i.e., unique lines are not printed.
-c
Prints the usual output, but precedes each line with the number of times which it occurs in the original file.

Example: **uniq -d ioulist urgent**
This command would scan the files **ioulist** for lines that appear more than once consecutively. One copy of each such line would be placed in the file **urgent**.

Making a Printed Copy

Video terminals are fun, but for some purposes (conducting inventories, wrapping fish, etc.), you really need printed paper output. You can use the commands in this section to give you a printed output.

lpr, lpq, and *lprm*

The **lpr** (for *l*ine *pr*inter) command sends one or more files to a line printer. To have the file **Fallreport** printed, type:

```
lpr Fallreport
```

Chaos would result, however, if this command sent your file directly to the printer, for other **lpr** commands might arrive in the middle of your print job and interrupt it. Instead, this command sends a copy of your file to a printer "queue," where it waits its turn to be printed.

The **lpq** command lets you check the contents of the line printer queue. For each file, it will print out (at the terminal, not on paper) the user name, an identification number, the file size, and the file name. Some systems will also print out how long the file has been in the queue. Here is a sample output from one system:

```
% lpq
Owner    Id     Chars   Filename
jowls    00217  31472   /usr/spool/lpd/cfa00217
```

Note that the file name is that of the copy in the queue, not of the original file.

Did you just send a 5000-word file to be printed and then realize it was the wrong file? The **lprm** command lets you remove a file (if it's yours) from the queue. Use the owner name (your login name) or the identification number or the filename as reported by **lpq** for the queue. Any of the following commands would remove the sample file that was just given.

```
lprm jowls
lprm 00217
lprm /usr/spool/lpd/cfa00217
```

To print several files, just list them all after the command:

```
lpr Winterreport Springreport Summerreport Fallreport
```

Each file will be separated from its neighbors by a banner page proclaiming your identity and by a blank page. If you want the files printed as one unit, you can do something like this:

```
cat Winterreport Springreport Summerreport Fallreport | lpr
```

(We will explain the "|" operator later in this chapter.)

Summary: `lpr`, `lpq`, and `lprm`—using the line printer

name	options	arguments
lpr lpq lprm	see below	[file names] file identification

Description: **lpr** sends the named files to the line printer queue from whence they are printed in an orderly fashion. If you omit a file name, **lpr** accepts input directly from your terminal; terminate the input with **[control–d]**.

lpq reports on the files in the line printer queue, assigning each file an owner name, an identification number, a file size, and a file name. The file name is that of the temporary queue file, not the original file name.

lprm removes files from the queue. It should be followed by one of the following identifications:

owner name (removes all queued files having an owner)
identification number (from the **lpq** command)
file name (from the **lpq** command)

Options: These vary wildly from system to system, so check your on-line manual or local guru. For example, on some systems, there is a **-r** option (for *r*eply) that informs you when the printing is finished. On other systems, there is a **-r** option (for *r*emove) that removes the file from your directory once it is printed!

Examples: **lpr some stuff**
                    This prints the contents of the files **some** and **stuff**; the files will be separated by a banner bearing your name.
                    lprm Ø3847
                    This removes the file Ø3847 (as identified by **lpq**) from the queue.

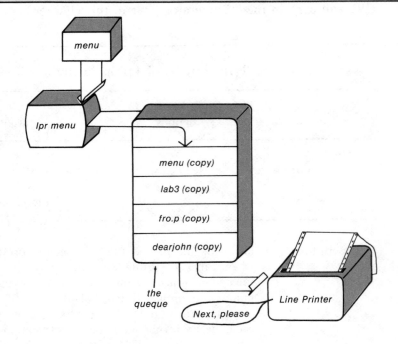

Using a line printer.

Simple Text Formatting: *pr*

The **lpr** command will print the files just as they are stored in the system. There are 66 lines to a printed page and **lpr** will use all 66 lines, leaving no space at the top or the bottom. The **pr** command lets you format your files to fit nicely on a page. When you use it, it puts 5 blank lines at the bottom of the page. At the top of the page, it puts two blank lines, a heading, and two more blank lines. The heading gives the date and time, the filename, and a page number. For instance, the command:

```
pr tale
```

might produce the following initial output:

```
Jul 27 19:34 1984 tale Page 1
```

Once upon a time in a distant kingdom, there lived a . . .

Normally this output is sent to the screen, so you need to use redirection to save the result; for example, we could have commanded:

```
pr tale > tale.pr
```

and had the results stored in a file called **tale.pr**.

If you like the paging but don't want the date, you can do some judicious editing on the file.

Summary: pr—prints partially formatted file onto standard output		
name	options	arguments
pr	[-n, -m, -t]	[file names]

Description: **pr** prints the named file onto the standard output. It divides the text into 66-line pages, placing five blank lines at the bottom of the page and a five-line heading at the top. The heading consists of two blank lines, a line bearing the date, file name, and page number, and two more blank lines.

Options: **-n**
Arranges text into *n* columns, where *n* is an integer.
-m
Prints two or more named files side by side. The first-named file goes into column 1, the second file into column 2, etc.
-t
Suppresses the five-line headings and tails.

Examples: **pr myths**
              This command prints out the file **myths** as just described;
              the heading would include a line like:

              May 1 12:29 1983 myths Page 1

              pr -4 words
              This command would print out the contents of the file
              words into four columns.
              pr -mt boys girls
              This command prints out the contents of **boys** in column
              1 and the contents of **girls** in column 2; there are no page
              headings or endings.

Well, that should be enough commands to help you get started. However, commands are not the only type of UNIX tool at hand. Another very important and useful type of tool is the redirection operator. Next, we look at some examples of this kind of aid.

Redirection

Redirection is one of those features that makes UNIX a joy to use. We've already seen one type of redirection in Chapter 4 when we discussed the > operator. Now we will trot out a full stable of redirection operators for your appreciation. They are >, >>, <, and |. (For good measure, we will throw in the **tee** command.) As you can see, they are fine looking operators, but what do they do? Read on, and see.

Redirecting Output to a File: >

This operator we have seen before. It allows us to redirect the output of a command or program to a file. An example is:

```
cat list1 list2 > list3
```

In this case, the output of **cat** is the joined contents of the files **list1** and **list2**. The file **list3** is created, and this file then is filled with the joined contents of **list1** and **list2**. For instance, if the contents of **file1** are:

```
milk 2 qt
bread 1 loaf
hamburger 2 lb
```

and, if **file2** contains

```
lettuce 1 hd
spaghetti 1 lb
garlic
basil
butter
```

then, the newly created **file3** will contain

```
milk 2 qt
bread 1 loaf
hamburger 2 lb
lettuce 1 hd
spaghetti 1 lb
garlic
basil
butter
```

The general form for using > is

```
COMMAND > filename
```

The command (which can include options and arguments and which can be an executable program of your own) should be one that produces some sort of output normally routed to the screen. It could be something like **ls**, but not something like **rm list1**, for this second command performs an action but doesn't produce an output to the screen.

Perhaps the most important point to remember is that the right-hand side of the command should be a file. (However, UNIX treats I/O devices as files, so the right-hand side of the command could represent a printer or another terminal. See the following box.) Using this command automatically causes a file to be created and be given the name you choose. If you already have a file by that name, it will be wiped out and replaced by the new one, so be careful or, else, use **noclobber** as described in Chapter 4. If you do have the **noclobber** option set, you can override it with the emphatic form:

```
COMMAND >! filename {BSD}
```

I/O Devices And Files

UNIX's marvelous redirection operators are made possible by the fact that UNIX treats I/O devices (input and output devices) as files. This means that each device is given a file name. These files usually are kept in the directory **/dev**. This directory contains a separate file for each terminal, printer, phone hook-up, tape drive, floppy disk, etc. For example, this is being typed on a terminal named **/dev/tty06**. (How can you tell what your terminal's file name is? Type in the command **tty** and UNIX will return you the device name.) If you **ls** the contents of **/dev**, you'll get to see all of the device file names.

How can you make use of these names? Normally, you don't have to. For instance, remember how we got the **cat** command to use the terminal for input? We typed:

```
cat
```

and UNIX interpreted the lack of a file name to mean that it could use the terminal as an input. However, we could also have used:

```
cat /dev/tty06
```

if we were using tty06. This would be using the filename directly, but omitting a file name is simpler in this case.

When we give a command like **ls**, this is really the same as

```
ls > /dev/tty06
```

if we are using tty06. Thus, when we use a command like

```
ls > save
```

we are just substituting one file for another as far as UNIX is concerned. This equivalence is what makes it simple to include the redirection feature.

When you use the redirection operators, you don't need to make use of device filenames. UNIX, itself, takes care of the bookkeeping, but it is the file system that makes redirection convenient.

Redirecting and Appending Output to a File: >>

Suppose you want to add information to an existing file. The >> operator was designed to do just that. To add the contents of file **newpigs** to the file **pigs**, just type:

```
cat newpigs >> pigs
```

The new material is appended to the end of the **pigs** file. Suppose there was no **pigs** file? Then, unless **noclobber** {BSD} was set, the file named **pigs** would be created to receive the contents of **newpigs**. If **noclobber** *is* set and **pigs** doesn't exist, you will be told so, and the command will not be executed. However, you can override the **noclobber** by being emphatic. Use:

```
cat newpigs >>! pigs
```

The general format for using >> is

```
COMMAND >> filename
```

where COMMAND is a command or sequence of commands that produces an output, and **filename** is the name of a file.

Redirecting Input From a File: <

The last two operators send data to files; this operator gets data out of files. You can use it with commands or programs that normally take input from the terminal. For example, you could use one of the editors to write a letter and store it in a file called **letter**. You could then mail it to another user (let's assume a login name of "hoppy") with the following command:

```
mail hoppy < letter
```

The < operator tells **mail** to take input from the file **letter** instead of from the terminal.

The general form for using this command is:

```
COMMAND < filename
```

The command should be one that would normally take input from the keyboard.

This form of redirection is particularly useful if you are running a program originally designed for punched cards. In FORTRAN, for example, a READ statement normally causes a punched card system to look for data on punched cards. (Where else!) The same program run on a UNIX system causes the system to expect *you* to type in that data from the keyboard when the program is run. You can get around this with the < operator. Suppose, for instance, that the executable program is in a file called **analyze**. You could place the data in a file called, say, **datafile**, and run the program this way:

```
analyze < datafile
```

When the program reaches the part where it reads data, it will read the data in **datafile**. The data should be entered in **datafile** in the same format used for the punched cards.

Combined Redirects

Suppose the program **analyze** produces some output that you want to save in a file called **results**. At the same time, you want **analyze** to get its input from the **datafile** file. You can do that with the command sequence:

```
analyze < datafile > results
```

This command causes the program **analyze** to look for input in the file **datafile** and to place its output into the file **results**. The redirection instructions can be in either order, but the command line or program name must come first. The next example would work also:

```
analyze > results < datafile
```

Don't use two or more inputs (or outputs) in the same command.

```
analyze < data1 < data2                    ◄———————————————— WRONG
```

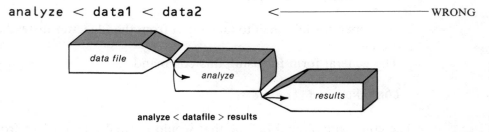

analyze < datafile > results

Combined redirects.

The Pipeline: |

Sam Nifty has lots of files in his directory. He wants to know how many, but he feels (rightly so) that the computer, not he, should do the counting. The **ls** command, he knows, lists the names of his files, and the **wc** command counts words. Can he use the > and < operators to somehow link these commands together? Not really, for these operators always link a command to a file, never a command to a command. He could create a temporary file and do it this way:

```
% ls > temp              <——————————— list files, store in temp
% wc -w temp             <——————————— count words in temp
% rm temp                <——————————— remove temp
```

However, this is a little awkward, and there is a real need for an operator that links a command to a command.

If there is a need, UNIX tries to fill it; for this particular need, UNIX provides the "pipeline" operator, which is represented by the symbol "|". (On some keyboards, this is a solid vertical line; on others, it is a vertical line with a small gap in the middle.) This operator **pipes** the output of one command into a second command. For example, Sam can solve his problem with this combined command:

```
ls | wc -w
```

In this case, the *output* of **ls** (i.e., a list of filenames) is accepted as the *input* of **wc -w**, which then counts the number of words. Because the list of filenames is shunted to **wc**, it does not appear on the screen; all that Sam will see is the final output of **wc**. Thus, this simple command that uses a pipe replaces three commands and counts the number of files that you have in your directory.

The general form for using the pipe is:

```
COMMAND | COMMAND
```

The output of the first command becomes the input of the second command. You can string together as many pipes as you need and you can use > and <, too. Suppose, for example, that you have written a program called **bigword** that selects words longer than 8 letters from its input and prints them out. What will the following compound command do?

```
bigword < MyLife | wc -w
```

This command causes **bigword** to search through the file **MyLife** for words longer than 8 letters; these words are then counted by **wc -w**, and the end result is the number of big words that you have in the file **MyLife**.

Here's an example with two pipes. Suppose you have a program **randomword** that chooses a hundred words at random from its input. (Perhaps you are an author who needs a few extra words to sprinkle through your work.) You want to sort these words alphabetically and process the list with **more** so that you can see them a page at a time. Here's how to do it.

```
randomword < MyLife | sort | more
```

In this example, the output of **randomword** is sent to **sort**, and the output of sort is then sent to **more**. Only the output of **more** is sent to the terminal, so the rest of the process is invisible to the user.

Split Output: *tee*

Suppose you are running a program and want to see the output as it is produced and want also to save the output in a file. One way is to run the

program twice; once without using $>$ and once using it. This is a bit wasteful and, thanks to **tee**, is unnecessary. Actually, **tee** is not an operator like $>$ or $|$ but is a command. It takes its input and routes it to two places: the terminal and the file of your choice. You can think of it as a tee-fitting to the pipeline. It is used this way:

```
ls | tee savels
```

The pipe relays the output of **ls** to **tee**; **tee** then sends the output to the terminal and to **savels**, the file that you choose for saving the output.

The output to the terminal can be piped further without affecting the contents of the file. For example, you can try this command:

```
ls | tee savels | sort -r
```

The file **savels** will contain a list of your files in alphabetical order (since that is what **ls** produces), but your terminal screen will show your files in reverse alphabetical order, for the other output of **tee** has been routed to **sort -r**, which sorts in reverse order.

The general form for using the **tee** command is this:

```
COMMAND | tee filename
```

Here the output of COMMAND is piped to **tee**, which routes copies of COMMAND's output to the terminal and to the file, **filename**. Actually, **tee** has a couple of options, which are described in the following summary.

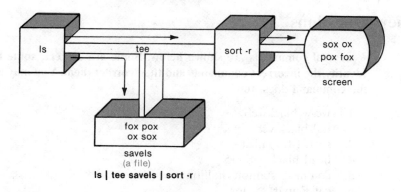

ls | tee savels | sort -r

The *tee.*

Summary: `tee`—splits output		
name	**options**	**argument**
`tee`	`[ -i, -a]`	filename(s)

Description: **tee** routes its input to the terminal and also to the named file or files.

Options: **-i**
This option ignores interrupts.
-a
This option causes the output to be added to the end of the named file.

Example: **ls -l /usr | tee -a clutter**
This command produces the long listing of the contents of the **/usr** directory. This listing is sent to the terminal screen and it also is added to the end of the file, **clutter**.

As you have seen, the redirection operators give you some very flexible means for routing data through the system. They are an important component of the design of UNIX, so make yourself familiar with them.

Review Questions

Several commands are shown below. Some are correct, some have errors in them. Identify the incorrect commands and then correct them. You may as well describe what the command does, too.

1. wc-w blackweb
2. tail blackweb
3. sort -f-b iou.list
4. head blackweb -15
5. comm -3 stallion Stallion
6. cat Rupart > lpr
7. blackweb > wc

Answers

1. **wc -w blackweb**; counts words in the file **blackweb**.
2. Correct; shows the last 10 lines of the file **blackweb**.
3. **sort -f -b iou.list** or **sort -fb iou.list**; sorts the contents of **iou.list** in machine-collating order, but ignores the difference between capital and small letters and ignores the initial blanks.
4. **head -15 blackweb**; shows the first 15 lines of **blackweb**. (The incorrect version given in Question 4 would show the first 10 lines of **blackweb** and would then look for a file called **-15**; of course, if you had a file by that name, then the original instruction would be correct.)
5. Correct; shows in column 1 those lines that are only in the file **stallion** and shows in column 2 those lines that are only in the file **Stallion**; both files, however, need to be sorted for this to work correctly.
6. **cat Rupart | lpr** or **lpr Rupart**; sends the file **Rupart** to be printed on the line printer. The original command given in Question 6 would create a *file* called **lpr** and would place a copy of the contents of **Rupart** there.
7. **wc < blackweb** or **wc blackweb**; counts the lines, words, and characters in the file **blackweb**. The < and > operators require a command or executable file on the left, and a filename on the right.

Exercises at the Terminal

1. While in your home directory, do the following:
   A. List the contents of your home directory.
   B. Count the number of files you have using the command sequence shown earlier in the chapter (with pipes).
   C. Find your longest file.
   D. Read the beginning of three files using **head** and pipe the results through **more**.
2. Create two new files using an editor as follows:
   A. file **AA** contains 1
                      2
                      3
                      4

      file **BB** contains 1
                      a
                      b
                      c
   B. Now try the following commands:
               head AA BB
               tail AA BB
               cmp AA BB
               comm AA BB
               diff AA BB

```
            cat AA >> BB
            head AA BB
            sort AA
            sort BB
            wc -l B*
3.   Try a few commands like:
            who | sort | more
            who | sort | tee CC
            head CC
```

10

Adjusting Your Environment:
chmod, at, and *mesg*

In this chapter, you will find:

- Introduction
- Permissions: *chmod*
- Messages: *biff* {BSD} and *mesg*
- Commands for Your Terminal: *tty* and *stty*
- Locking Your Terminal: *lock* {BSD}
- System Usage: *uptime* and *w* {BSD}
- Using the UNIX Clock: *time, calendar,* and *at*
  - *time*
  - *calendar*
  - The *at* Command
- Customizing UNIX for Advanced Users: *.login, .profile,* and *.cshrc* Files
- Review Questions

10 ADJUSTING YOUR ENVIRONMENT: *chmod, at, and mesg*

Introduction

With UNIX you have some control over your working environment. For example, you can choose whether or not you will receive messages while you work. You can choose which of your files are open to others for reading and writing and which files are closed. Where you don't have control, you still can get information; for example, you can check to see how heavy the work load is. So, without further ado, here are some useful UNIX commands for your consideration.

Permissions: *chmod*

The **chmod** (for "change mode") command gives you the final say on who can read and use your files and who can't. This command considers the UNIX users' world to be divided into three classes:

1. You, the user (**u**).
2. Your group (**g**).
3. Others (**o**).

What's this bit about a group? UNIX was developed at Bell Labs in order to be used in research there. So, originally, a "group" would correspond to a particular research group. What constitutes a "group" for you will depend on your system. Perhaps it might be students in the same class or workers in the same department, or it might be arbitrary. Whatever the system, users in the same group are assigned the same "group number," and this number is stored in the **/etc/passwd** file, which also contains your login name, your home directory assignment, and your encrypted password. So UNIX knows what group you are in and who else is in it (even if you don't).

In addition to three classes, there are three kinds of permissions that **chmod** considers.

1. Read permission (**r**)—this includes permission to **cat**, **more**, **lpr**, and **cp** a file.

2. Write permission (**w**)—this is permission to change a file, which includes editing a file and appending to a file.
3. Execute permission (**x**)—this is permission to run an executable file; for example, a program.

You can check to see what permissions are in effect by using the **-l** option for **ls** on the pertinent files. For example, the command:

```
ls -l a.out expgrow.f
```

could produce this output:

```
-rwxr-xr-x 1 doeman    25957 Jan 27 15:44 a.out
-rw-r--r-- 1 doeman      671 Jan 27 15:17 expgrow.f
```

The symbols on the left (-rwxr-xr-x) contain the information about permissions. There are ten columns. The first, which contains a hyphen for these examples, contains a "d" for directories and other letters for special kinds of files. Don't worry about that column.

The next 9 columns are actually 3 groups of 3 columns each. The first group of three reports on user permissions, the second group of three on group permissions, and the final group of three on other permissions. We can spread out the 3 groupings for **a.out** like this:

rwx	r-x	r-x
user	group	other users

Within each grouping, the first column shows an "r" for read permission, the second column a "w" for write permission, and the third column an "x" for execute permission. A "-" means no permission.

Thus, for the **a.out** file shown above, the user has read, write, and execute permissions (rwx) for the file **a.out**; members of the same group have read and execute permissions (r-x), but no write permission. Other users also have read and execute permissions (r-x) but no write permission. Permissions for the **expgrow.f** account are similar, except no one has execution permission.

What does this all mean? It means that anyone on the system could read or copy these two files. Only the user, however, could alter these two files in this directory. (However, if you copied this file into your directory, you would then be able to write as well as read and execute.) Finally, anyone who wanted to could run the program **a.out** by typing the name of the file. (If the other user were in a different directory, he would have to use the full pathname of the file.) In most systems, these particular permissions are established by default; **chmod** lets you change them.

The **chmod** command is used a bit differently from most other UNIX commands. The simplest way to use it is to type **chmod** and then type in a space. Then comes an "instruction segment" with three parts and no spaces. The first part of the segment consists of one or more letters identifying the classes to be affected, the next part is a "+" or "−" sign for adding or subtracting permissions, and the final part is one or more letters identifying the permissions to be affected. After the instruction segment is another space and the name(s) of the file(s) to be affected by the changes. This may sound a little confusing, but it is simple once you see a few examples. So, here are some examples:

```
chmod g+w growexp.f
chmod go-rx a.out
```

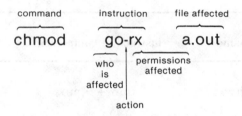

Parts of a *chmod* command.

The first example grants other members of your group (**g**) the right to write (**w**) in the file **growexp.f**. The second example takes away both read (**r**) and execute (**x**) privileges from members of your group (**g**) and from others (**o**). If we repeated the **ls -l** command now, the result would be:

```
-rwx------ 1 doeman   25957 Jan 27 15:44 a.out
-rw-rw-r-- 1 doeman     671 Jan 27 15:17 expgrow.f
```

You can include more than one permission instruction by separating them by commas. For instance:

```
chmod g+w,o-r project.big
```

would let other group members write in the **project.big** file and would deny other users permission to read that file. There should be no spaces within the instruction segment.

You can use **chmod** on your directories, also. Just use the directory name instead of the file name. Just what are the effects of these permissions on directories? Read permission for a directory lets one read (using **ls**, for example) the names of the files in the directory. Write permission lets one create new files in the directory and remove files from the directory. Finally, execute permission for a directory lets one **cd** to that directory.

Perhaps you wonder what the point is in changing permissions for yourself (**u**). First, you can create a file of UNIX commands. If you give that file "execute" status, then typing that file name will cause the commands in the file to be executed. We'll talk more about this in Chapter 12. Secondly, by removing write permission, you can protect yourself from accidentally changing a valuable file.

Summary: `chmod` — change modes or permissions on files

name	instruction components	argument
`chmod`	`ugo,+ -,rwx`	file name(s) or directory name(s)

Description: **chmod** grants or removes read, write, and execute permissions for three classes of users: user (you), group (your group), and others. A **chmod** command has three parts: the command name (**chmod**, of course), the instruction string, and the name of the file to be affected. The instruction string also has three parts: letter(s) indicating who is affected, a **+** or **−** symbol indicating the action to be taken, and letter(s) indicating which permissions are affected. The code is as follows:

who:
     u the user
     g the user's group
     o others (everyone other than **u** or **g**)
action:
     + add permission
     - remove permission
permission:

> **r** read
> **w** write
> **x** execute
>
> Example: Suppose you (login name booky) gave the command **ls -l** and found the following permissions for your **payroll** file:
>
> ```
> -rwxrwxrwx 1 booky    1776 Jan 4 9:33 payroll
> ```
>
> If you wanted to remove the write and execute permissions for your "group" and "other" users, type:
>
> ```
> chmod            go-wx              payroll
> ```
>
> The "g" refers to group, the "o" to others. The "-" means remove permissions "w" and "x".

Messages: *biff* {BSD} and *mesg*

Normally, accounts are set up so that if someone sends you mail or tries to write to you while you are on a terminal, you will get a message to that effect. This makes a UNIX system a friendly and neighborly environment. Sometimes, however, you may not want to be interrupted. For those times, UNIX gives you ways to turn off the messages; **biff** controls incoming mail and **mesg** controls attempts to **write** to you. To halt notification of incoming mail, type:

```
biff n
```

To prevent people from reaching you with **write**, type:

```
mesg n
```

When you feel more open to the world, you can reestablish your communication links with:

```
biff y
```

and

```
mesg y
```

If you forget your state, just type:

```
biff
```

and

```
mesg
```

and UNIX will let you know your current state. The command will endure until you log out.

Normally, **biff y** and **mesg y** are included in the standard **.login** and **.profile** files (see the end of the chapter). You can change that if you like, so that you can log in with **biff n** and/or **mesg n**.

Summary: `biff`—notification of mail {BSD}

name	options	arguments
`biff`		[y, n]

Description: The command **biff y** tells UNIX to inform you when mail arrives, tell you the sender, and give the first few lines.

The command **biff n** turns off this service. However, logging in or typing "mail" will still give you the usual messages.

Typing **biff** will cause UNIX to reply with "is y" or "is n," as the case may be.

Summary: `mesg`—permit or deny messages from `write`

name	options	arguments
`mesg`		[-y, -n]

Description: Typing **mesg y** allows other users to communicate with you using **write**.

Typing **mesg n** forbids other users from communicating with you using **write**.

Typing **mesg** will cause UNIX to reply with "is y" or "is n," as the case may be.

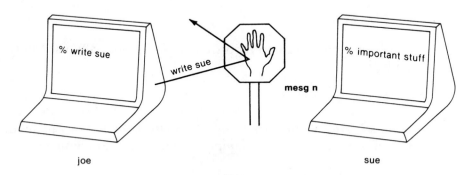

mesg **at work.**

Commands for Your Terminal: *tty* and *stty*

The **tty** command tells you the pathname of your terminal. For example, the command:

```
tty
```

might elicit the response

```
/dev/tty08
```

This means you are using terminal number 8 and the terminal is treated as a file in the **/dev** (for device) directory.

The **stty** command is used to set terminal options, such as the "baud rate" (transmission speed), parity, echo, and which key is the erase key. Much of **stty** concerns the interface between the terminal and the computer, but we will just look at some of the less technical aspects. Normally, the system takes care of these matters for you, but you might want to change some of the choices.

The first step is to determine the current situation. Type:

```
stty
```

and UNIX will report back the baud rate and option settings that are different from the default (standard) values. You can get more information by typing:

```
stty all                                                        {BSD}
```

which inspires UNIX to report on ALL the normally used options. Finally, typing:

```
stty everything                                                 {BSD}
```

tempts UNIX to print out *everything* **stty** knows. For our modest purpose, **stty all** suffices. Here is a sample response to that command:

```
speed 9600 baud;
erase   kill   intr   quit   stop      eof
#       @      ^C     ^\     ^S/^Q     ^D
```

This means that the communication rate is set at 9600 baud. The "erase" character is set to the "#" character, the "kill" character is set to the "@" character, the "interrupt" symbol is [control-c], the "quit" symbol is [control-\], the stop-and-start symbols are [control-s] and [control-q], and the End-of-File symbol is [control-d].

What does this all mean?

1. Typing the # symbol erases the last character typed.
2. Typing the @ symbol erases the entire current line typed.
3. Typing [control-c] interrupts and aborts your current job. (Some programs, such as the editors, possess some immunity to this command.)
4. Typing [control-\] causes UNIX to quit your current job. This command is stronger than the interrupt [control-c] command. For example, if you are in the **vi** text mode, an interrupt will put you in the **vi** command mode, but a quit [control-\] will dump you into the **ex** editor.
5. Typing [control-s] suspends the production of output, and typing [control-q] restarts it. You can use these commands if the output is going by on the screen too fast for you to read. You may get a burst of

output when you restart the flow, for there may be some output stored in a buffer, just waiting to rush out.

6. The End-of-File symbol identifies the end of a file. We used it, for example, when feeding **cat** input from the keyboard.

It is easy to change these assignments. Suppose you want to change the erase character to [control–h]. Then, you would type this:

```
stty erase [control-h]
```

More generally, you would type **stty**, then the function you wish to change, and then the key assignment you desire.

To make such a change permanent, place the instruction in your **.login** or **.profile** file, as described at the end of this chapter.

Locking Your Terminal: *lock* {BSD}

Occasionally, you may have to leave your terminal for a few minutes. You don't want to log out just yet, but, also, you don't want to leave your directories open to any passersby. The **lock** command lets you "lock up" the terminal while you are gone. It works like this. You type:

```
lock
```

UNIX then queries:

```
Key:
```

You type in a password of one or more characters. UNIX then says:

```
Again:
```

You repeat the password and the terminal is locked until you type the password in one final time. Until you do so, punching keys will seem to have no effect.

Caution! Do not forget your **lock** "password." If you do, you'll have to login on another terminal and use the **kill** command to terminate the **lock**. Also, do not abuse this command if you are sharing terminals in a terminal room!

Summary: lock—reserves your terminal {BSD}		
name	**options**	**arguments**
lock		
Description:	When you type **lock**, the system will request that you give it a password. It will ask you to repeat the password you gave it. Then, it will prevent any one from using the terminal until the password is given once more.	

System Usage: *uptime* and *w* {BSD}

Does the system seem sluggish? You can check out the current workload with the **uptime** command. Typing **uptime** elicits a response like:

```
3:01pm up 16:31, 20 users, load average: 3.99, 2.73, 2.45
```

This translates into the following information. The time is 3:01 P.M. and the system has been up for 16 hours, 31 minutes. Twenty users are on the system now. The load averages for the last 1, 5, and 15 minutes, respectively, are 3.99, 2.73, and 2.45.

The load average is the average number of jobs waiting to be run. Your jobs are delayed if this number is larger than 1.

If the load seems rather large, say 5 or 10, you may want to come back some other time since the system will delay some time (10–30 seconds or more; the time varies considerably from system to system) before responding to your command.

If you are curious about who is bogging the system down, you can run a **who** as described in Chapter 3. For a more detailed view, try the **w** command, which also tells what the users are doing. Here is a typical response to typing **w**:

```
3:13pm up 16:43, 7 users, load average: 3.74, 3.74, 3.20
User     tty     login@ idle    JCPU     PCPU     what
camus    tty03   12:40pm         4:55     16       vi assmt6.p
tolstoy  tty07   12:36pm         8:56     41       pc obj.p
```

```
mann      tty08    2:19pm   1     1:57       11      -csh
dickens   tty09    2:25pm         1:25      1:08     logo
plato     tty11    12:49pm        1:11       9       learn
mailer    tty18    1:54pm         2:37      2:06     old_rogue
wiseone   tty29    1:42pm         1:19       48      w
```

The first line is the same as the output to **uptime**. Next comes seven columns of information. The first three give the user name, terminal number, and time of login. "Idle" is the number of minutes since the user last typed anything. "JCPU" is the total CPU time (in minutes and seconds) used since the person logged in, and "PCPU" is the CPU timed for the user's current job. Finally, the last column identifies the user's current job. (CPU stands for "central processing unit"; these times indicate how much time you have actually been making use of the CPU.)

Summary: uptime—how long the system has been up and how heavily is it loaded		
name	**options**	**arguments**
uptime		
Description:	**uptime** prints the current time, the time the system has been up, and the average load for the last 1, 5, and 15 minutes. The load is defined in terms of the average number of jobs waiting to be run.	

Summary: w—who is on and what they are doing {BSD}		
name	**options**	**arguments**
w	[-h, -s]	[user]

Description: **w** first prints out a heading as described for **uptime**. Then, it prints out 7 columns. The first three are the user's login name, the user's terminal, and the user's login time. The next three are the idle time (minutes since last user typing), JCPU (total CPU time used since login), and PCPU (CPU time for current job). The final column gives the name and arguments for the current job. If you specify a particular user, this information is provided for that user only.

Options: **-h**
Suppresses the heading.
-s
Short form—abbreviate tty identification, omit login times and CPU times, and omit arguments to commands.

Example: **w -hs oafie**
This command would just list the user, terminal number, idle time, and job name. It might look like this:
oafie   16   2 vi

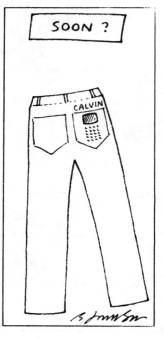

Using the UNIX clock: *time, calendar,* and *at*

Never let it be said that UNIX won't even give you the time of the day; it gladly informs you whenever you give the **date** command. UNIX can support the **date** command because it keeps track of the time internally. This ability helps it to perform such diverse tasks as timing commands (**time**), providing you with a reminder service (**calendar**), and running a command for you at some later time of your choice.

time

The **time** command tells you how long a simple command takes. Its general form is:

```
time COMMAND
```

After you give this instruction, the COMMAND (which can be any UNIX command or program execution) is run, and when it is finished, you are given a breakdown of how much time was used. The standard output of **time** looks like this:

```
15.0 real        5.2 user        2.1 sys
```

These times are in seconds. The time labeled "real" is the elapsed time from when you first give the command until the command is completed. Because UNIX is a time-sharing system, it may have been doing some other tasks during that time period, so "real" time doesn't really represent how much time was devoted to your needs. The next two times relate just to the CPU time spent on your command. The "user" time is time spent executing the command, and "system" time is the additional time spent in the system as a result of the command.

The Berkeley C shell gives the results in a slightly different order:

```
4.9u 2.2s 0:16 44%
```

First comes user time, then system time, then real (total elapsed) time, and, then, a percentage that expresses the ratio of user + system time to real time. Also, with the C shell, the **time** command with no argument will total these times for your current login period.

These "time" commands are very important when you are renting CPU time which can cost $180 per hour or more.

calendar

The **calendar** command provides a built-in reminder service. (Don't confuse it with the **cal** command, which generates monthly and yearly calendars.) Actually, you don't even execute the **calendar** command. Your responsibility is to create a *file* named **calendar** in your login directory. In this file, you place dated reminders such as:

```
September 22          Dentist at 2:30
9/24          dinner at Antoine's, 8pm
PAY AUTO INSURANCE Sept 28
```

Early each morning, UNIX will look through all the login directories for files named **calendar**. Whenever it finds one, it will read the file and look for lines containing the date for today or tomorrow. The lines that it finds, it will mail to the directory's owner. Thus, you receive a reminder via **mail** the day before the date and, then, on the day itself.

The date can be anywhere on the line, and you can use abbreviations as above. However, **calendar** does not recognize dates where the day precedes the month. Thus, you won't be reminded of lines containing dates such as "25 December" or "25/12."

The *at* Command

With this command, you can put together a list of commands and tell UNIX when to run them. Suppose, for example, you want to know who will be logged in at 10:00 A.M. but you have to leave at 9:00 A.M. You could create a file called **curiosity** and put this line in it:

```
who > whosave
```

This is the command you would like to run at 10:00 A.M. am. To make it run then, type:

```
at 10 curiosity
```

When 10:00 A.M. rolls around, UNIX will check to see what commands are in the file **curiosity** and will then execute them for you! Note, however, that UNIX doesn't check the time all that often for **at** commands. Instead, it checks periodically every 10–30 minutes, depending on the system. So **at** may miss your target time by a bit.

You can give a date in addition to a time if you like; see the following summary for details.

Summary: `time`—time a command

name	option	argument
`time`		command name

Description: **time**, when followed by a command name, runs the named command and gives you a breakdown of the time used. Three times are given.

"Real" or elapsed time—This is the actual time that passes from the moment you initiate the command until the command is finished. If UNIX is switching back and forth between your demands and those of other users, all that time is included, too.

"User" time—This is the CPU time used solely for the execution of your command.

"System" time—This is additional CPU time spent in the system in the course of setting up and servicing the command.

The C-shell version gives the times in a different sequence; it also gives a percentage that expresses the ratio of user + system time to real time. This version, when given without an argument, gives you the totals of these times since you logged in.

Example: **time cc woo.c**

This command will cause the command **cc woo.c** to run. When execution of the command is finished, UNIX will print out the time summary for **cc woo.c**:

```
6.0 real   1.1 user   0.9 sys
```

1.1 sec was used to execute the command; another 0.9 sec was spent in the system supporting the command execution, and 4.0 (i.e., 6.0 − 1.1 − 0.9) seconds were spent time-sharing.

Summary: calendar—a reminder service

Description: To use this service, create in your login directory a file called **calendar**. Put notes to yourself in this file. Every line in this file containing a recognizable date is mailed by UNIX to you twice: (1) on the day before the date listed and (2) on the date itself. The date can be anywhere on the line. It should include the month and the day *in that order*, and you can use reasonable abbreviations.

Examples: The **calendar** file can contain entries such as:
```
Buy goose March 19
call gus mar. 20 at 3 pm
3/23 Report due
```

Summary: at—execute commands at a later time

name	arguments
at	time [day] [file name]

Description: **at** causes the commands contained in the named file to be run at the given time. If no file is given, the commands are taken from the terminal. (In this mode, hit [return] after the time, type in the commands, then hit a [control–d] to close off the command.) UNIX checks periodically, usually every 10–20 minutes, for **at** programs to run. If the time you choose falls between two check times, your command is run the second check time.

The time parameter is specified by 1 to 4 digits; 1 to 2 digits are interpreted as hours; 3 to 4 digits are interpreted as hours and minutes. A 24-hour clock is assumed, but you can follow the digits with an **A**, **P**, **N**, or **M** to indicate AM, PM, Noon, or Midnight, respectively.

The optional day argument can have either of two forms:
1. A month name (or abbreviation) followed by a day number; e.g., **June 7** or **aug 23**.
2. A day of the week; e.g., **Monday** or **fr**. This form can be followed by the word **week** to indicate a date a week later.

Examples:

at 23 cmdlist
Runs the commands in the file **cmdlist** at 23 hrs; i.e., 11:00 P.M.
at 1115P cmdlist
Runs at 11:15 P.M.
at 1 feb 3 cmdlist
Runs at 1:00 A.M., Feb. 3.
at 2 mon week cmdlist
Runs at 2:00 P.M., a week after next Monday.

Customizing UNIX for Advanced Users: *.login, .profile,* and *.cshrc* Files

When you log in on a UNIX system, the system peeks into your home directory and reads information used to set up your working environment. Because this information is contained in files that you own, you can change the files and nudge UNIX to fit your own needs and desires.

You may not have noticed these files, for they don't show up when you give a **ls** command unless you use the **-a** (for *a*ll) option. (The reason they don't show up is that their names begin with a ".", and any name beginning with a "." is ignored by the **ls** command.) The names and numbers of these "dot" files will depend on the system.

A user who habitually uses the Bourne shell will have one login file, the **.profile** file. The C-shell user will have two login files, **.login** and **.cshrc**. Both the **.login** file and the **.profile** file contain information that initiates your environment whenever you log in. The **.cshrc** file contains information used in setting up the C shell for you. In the following discussion, we will use the Berkeley system as a specific example.

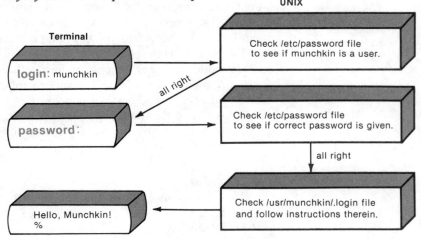

Condensed login procedure.

Just what kind of information is in these files? Mostly, there are commands to the system. When UNIX reads the file, it executes the commands it finds there. Here's an example of what might be found in a **.login** file, which you can see by using **cat** as follows:

```
% cat .login
set path=(. /usr/new /usr/ucb /bin /usr/bin /usr/local)
set ignoreeof
stty dec; biff n
mesg n
%
```

Some of these entries you won't want to fool with until you are pretty familiar with the system, but let's see what is meant. The first line (the one with "set path") tells UNIX where to search for commands. If, for instance, you give the command **blorg**, UNIX first looks through a select list of shell commands for **blorg**; if it doesn't find it, UNIX then looks through the directories named in the **set path** command. (The first one on this list is ".", which is short for your current working directory.) The **path** variable may prove useful to you if you develop your own library of programs and shell scripts (see Chapter 12). Then, you can create a directory to store all these programs. If you then add this directory to the **set** list, you can use them just as you do standard UNIX commands.

The **set ignoreeof** line instructs UNIX to ignore any use of a [control–d] as a way of logging out. If this were not set and you were, say, leaving **mail** by typing [control–d], the accidental typing of the key again would log you off of the system. With **ignoreeof** set, you have to use **logout** to logout.

The **stty dec** command tells UNIX that the user prefers to use DEC software standard control characters (for example, erase is [delete] and kill is [control–u]). So, UNIX sets up the appropriate interface. The **biff n** and the **mesg n** commands have the same meanings that we discussed earlier.

What about, say, the **.cshrc** file? The basic file usually looks quite simple, containing lines like:

```
set history=15
alias lf 'ls -Fla'
```

Both the history command and the alias command are discussed in detail in the next chapter.

The usual practice is to use **.cshrc** for stuff specifically involving the C shell. The history and alias functions, for example, work just in the C shell. Information to set up terminal conditions, on the other hand, is placed in **.login**. One reason for this division of labor is that it is possible to create new C shells while you work. If you do so, the information in **.cshrc** is used to set up the new shell, but since you are still on the same terminal, UNIX doesn't need to run through the information in **.login** again. The shell-changing business is of more concern to system programs than to the typical user, so you probably don't have to worry too much about these matters.

What else can you do with these "dot" files? You could change what is there (for instance, replacing **mesg n** with **mesg y**). More interestingly, you can add new commands to the list. For example, if you would like to know the state of the system when you log in, you can add a line with the command:

```
uptime
```

and that command will be automatically executed every time you log in. If you want to keep a record of your login times, you could add this command:

```
date >> logrecord
```

281

Each time you log in, the date and time will be added to a new file called **logrecord**.

You can make use of the **echo** command, which repeats on the screen (or "echoes") the words that follow it. For example, the command:

```
echo Howdy there, you old neuron box.
```

when placed in the **.login** file, would cause that phrase to be printed each time you log in.

The C-shell user has other opportunities to use these "dot" files. For example, the **noclobber** option that we discussed in Chapter 4 (it protects your files from being accidentally overwritten by redirection commands) is a C-shell option. To make it a permanent choice, place this line in the **.cshrc** file:

```
set noclobber
```

There are many options that can be set in the C shell; the on-line manual will have a run-down of them in the **csh** entry.

When you change one of the dot files, the change is not actuated until the next time that the system reads the file. Normally that would occur the next

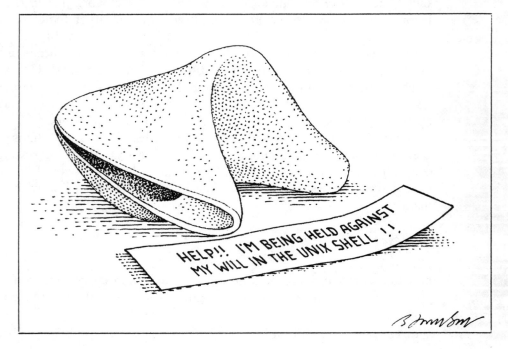

time you log in. If, however, you have changed, say, **.cshrc**, you can make the change effective immediately by giving the command:

```
source .cshrc
```

If you like playing around with the system, you will be pleased to know that there is also a **.logout** file that is read when you log out. You can construct your own distinctive logout pattern and, perhaps, leave a parting message.

Some systems have a program called **fortune**; it yields random sayings such as:

```
"When God endowed human beings with brains, He did not
intend to guarantee them."
```

or

```
"Death is nature's way of telling you to slow down."
```

Putting the line **fortune** in your **.login** or **.logout** file will ensure you of getting a small dose of such wisdom each time you use the system.

These are some examples of the useful or frivolous uses you can make of the UNIX system of login files. Don't be afraid to experiment, but *don't mess with these files until you are competent in using a UNIX editor.* If you accidentally remove one of the original lines, you may find the system behaving strangely the next time you log in. One safeguard is to make back-up copies of the original files before you try to make modifications.

Review Questions

Explain what each of the following commands are used for.

1. chmod
2. biff
3. mesg
4. lock
5. w
6. time
7. calendar
8. at

Answers:

1. Change modes or permissions on files. **2.** Notification of mail. **3.** Permit or deny messages from **write**. **4.** Reserves your terminal. **5.** Who are on and what they are doing. **6.** Time a command. **7.** A reminder service. **8.** Execute commands at a later time.

11

Special C-Shell Features:
history, alias, and *jobs* {BSD}

In this chapter, you will find:

11 SPECIAL C-SHELL FEATURES: *history, alias,* and *jobs* {BSD}

The C Shell

The folks at Berkeley (more officially, the University of California, Berkeley Campus) have made several major additions to the original Bell UNIX. These additions have been incorporated into the C shell, which is used in place of the Bell shell (also known as the Bourne shell, or sh, for short).

The Berkeley releases of UNIX are called BSD 4.2 (Berkeley Software Distribution 4.2), BSD 2.7, etc., depending on the computer used and on the number of the latest release.

Some of the changes consist of adding new commands or command options; other changes give UNIX important new facilities. We will use the rest of this chapter to look at three major extensions: *history, aliasing,* and *job control.*

These new UNIX abilities are important in their own right, but they also illustrate one of the major strengths of UNIX. UNIX is an open-ended system that can grow and incorporate new ideas. What we describe in this book is not the last word on UNIX. UNIX will continue to grow more amazing and more diversified every year.

History: A System That Remembers

The first remarkable new feature that we will investigate is the ability of the C shell to keep a history of the commands that you issue to it. The number of commands it remembers is usually around 20, but you can change that number if you like. The history function makes it easy to repeat earlier commands; it also makes it possible to modify them before repeating them.

Repeating an Earlier Command: Event Identifiers

We will look at an example to see how the history function lets us easily repeat commands. Hilary Dale, after doing a few things on the system, types the command:

```
history
```

UNIX responds with the following list:

```
1 mail
2 cd energy
3 vi walls.f
4 f77 walls.f floors.o windows.o roof.o temp.o
5 a.out
6 vi checkfile
7 vi walls.f
8 history
```

This, obviously, is a list of the commands that she has executed. (UNIX refers to each command line as an "event.")

Apparently (starting at command 3), she modified part of a FORTRAN program, compiled it along with the unchanged portions, ran the new version, checked it, found something wrong, and, then, fixed up the **walls.f** program. Her next step will be to repeat command 4. She can, of course, retype the entire command, or she can use some nifty history features. She can type any of the following entries to rerun that command:

```
!4
```
(identification by command number)

or
```
!f
```
(identification by command name)

or
```
!-5
```
(identification by relative position)

or
```
!?77?
```
(identification by pattern)

Each of these commands (which we will call "event identifiers") will repeat command 4, by first printing out what the command was. The !-character alerts UNIX that the command uses the history list.

The first form means, "Run the fourth command from the history list."

The second form means, "Run the most recent command from the history list beginning with the character 'f'."

The third form means, "Look back 5 commands and run that command."

The fourth form means, "Find the most recent command line with the pattern '77' in it, and run that command." The question marks on either side identify the pattern.

The two commands that use patterns, **!f** and **!?77?**, have the advantage that you probably won't have to look up the history list numbers to use them.

The second form of event identifier need not be limited to one character after the **!**. If a history list had a **mkdir** command followed by a **more** command, since it was most recently executed, then **!m** would rerun the **more** command, and a **!mk** command would run the **mkdir** command. You can use as many letters as you need to identify your chosen command unambiguously.

The fourth form can use a pattern from anywhere in the line; the commands **!?oof?** or **!?wind?** would have worked just as well. The command **?wall?**, however, would have rerun command 7 instead of command 5, since it was the most recent command line containing that pattern.

A special case of a history repeat command is:

```
!!
```

Not only does it look very assertive, it repeats the previous command. Thus, it is the same as **!-l**, but it is typed more quickly.

Adding to a History Command

History substitutions (that's the official term for translating event identifiers into ordinary commands) do a lot more for you than just repeat earlier commands. For one thing, they can be incorporated into longer commands. Suppose, for example, you have just run the following command:

```
sort namelist1 namelist2 namelist3 namelist4
```

As the output begins pouring down the screen, you realize that you forgot to redirect the output. You can hit the [control–c] key or whatever key generates an interrupt signal for your system; this doesn't count as a command and doesn't go on the history list. Then, you can type:

```
!! > finallist
```

UNIX translates this as:

```
sort namelist1 namelist2 namelist3 namelist4 > finallist
```

and you are in business!

Similarly, the command:

```
!5 | more
```

would rerun your fifth command and pipe its output through **more**.

The history reference needn't be the first part of your command line. For example, if you wanted to time a command that you had just run, you can give the command:

```
time !!
```

You can also make **!!** part of a single command string. For example, suppose your last command were:

```
ls -F /usr/doc
```

and that you next wanted to see what was in the directory **/usr/doc/csh**. You can type:

```
!!/csh
```

and the history facility will interpret this as:

```
ls -F /usr/doc/csh
```

Whenever UNIX sees the special character **!** in a command line (with some exceptions, such as in >>!), it checks the history list and makes the appropriate substitution, putting spaces where you put them and omitting spaces where you omitted them.

Simple Command Line Editing

You are putting a Pascal program together and have just typed:

```
pv peter.p piper.p picked.p a.p peck.p of.p pickled.p
```

You hit the return key, and UNIX replies:

```
pv: not found
```

Then, you realized that you typed **pv** instead of **pc**. Cheer up, you don't have to retype the whole line. This next command line will patch it up:

```
^pv^pc
```

The caret character ∧ at the beginning of a command line tells UNIX that you wish to make a correction in the preceding command. (On some terminals, the ∧ character is represented by a vertical arrow.) The characters between the first and second ∧ are then replaced by the characters following the second ∧. UNIX will print out the corrected line,

```
pc peter.p piper.p picked.p a.p peck.p of.p pickled.p
```

and, then, will execute it.

Substitution occurs at the first instance of the pattern, so make your pattern unambiguous. Suppose, for example, you enter:

```
pc that.p old.p black.l magic.p
```

You want to correct **black.l** to **black.p**. The command:

```
^l^p
```

is no good, because it will change the first **l** to a **p**; i.e., the "corrected" version will read:

```
pc that.p opd.p black.l magic.p
```

The correct solution is to type in:

```
^.l^.p or ^k.l^k.p
```

which identifies the "l" as being the one that is at the end of "black.l".

Selecting Parts of a Command Line: Word Identifiers

Sometimes you may want to use just part of an earlier command; for instance, you may want to **vi** a file that you **cat**ted earlier. (That's UNIX lingo.) The history system has a way for you to specify not only the command line but, also, individual words from the line. The words are numbered from left to right, and the first word (the command name) is number 0. To avoid confusion with command line numbers, the word numbers are preceded by a ":", a colon. There also are some special symbols used: ∧ is word number one, $ is the last word, and * stands for all the words after word 0. The : can be omitted with these last three symbols. A word identifier, then, is a construction such as **:2** or **$**. A word identifier is not used alone but is appended to an event identifier so that UNIX will know which command to look at.

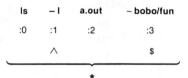

History representation of words of an event.

Structure of a complete word specification.

Suppose, for example, your fourth command was:

```
cat that.c doormat.c hat.c pat.c
```

Here's how different history references would be translated:

Reference	*Meaning*	
!4	cat that.c doormat.c hat.c pat.c	
!4:0	cat	(0th word of 4th command)
!4:1	that.c	
!4^	that.c	
vi !4:2	vi doormat.c	
edit !4$	edit pat.c	
more !4:2-4	more doormat.c hat.c pat.c	
lpr !4*	lpr that.c doormat.c hat.c pat.c	

Notice that you can use the hyphen (-) to give a range of words. The special symbol * means much the same as ^-$. The difference is that ^-$ can represent one or more arguments while * can represent 0 or more arguments. Let's clarify that. Suppose that this is part of your history list:

1. cat dwarf giant
2. cd dungeon
3. ls

Then these are some history substitutions:

Reference	Meaning	
more !1:^-$	more dwarf giant	
more !1*	more dwarf giant	
cat !3*	cat	(with no argument)
cat !3^-$	error	(looks for at least one argument for **ls** and finds none)

There is one other convention that can simplify life a bit. If you are referring to the immediately preceding command, you can omit the line identifier. For example, if the last command were number 5, then the following would be equivalent:

```
cat !5:2
cat !!:2
cat !:2
```

However, a solitary **!** without following characters means nothing.

Initiating Your History Service

The command that starts up the history service is

```
set history=n
```

where "n" stands for the number of command lines that will be remembered. Normally, this command will be found in your **.cshrc** file; thus, it is activated each time you log in. You can use a UNIX editor to change the value of "n." There should be no spaces on either side of the "=" sign.

RIGHT   *WRONG*
set history=20   set history = 20

The UNIX history service may not tell you when Hannibal crossed the Alps or the essential features of feudalism, but it can cut down on the amount of typing that you do and, thus, reduce the number of keyboard errors. It also can be used in UNIX programming and, in the next section, we will see how it can enhance the "alias" system.

Summary: `history`—prints a list of last commands given

name	option	arguments
`history`		

Description: **history** prints out a list of the last "n" commands or events run by the C shell. "n" can be set in the **.cshrc** file by adding the line

    `set history=n`

The history list can also be used to substitute for commands using the "!" symbol as shown next.

A. Identifying commands or "events."

!n	Command number "n" from the history list.
!-n	The "nth" command before the present one.
!c	The most recent command beginning with the character "c."
!?pat?	The most recent command containing the pattern "pat."

B. Identifying words within an event: the first word is number 0.

:n	The "nth" word in the event.
:^ or ^	Same as **:1**.
:$ or $	The last word in an event.
:n1-n2	The "n1" through "n2" words.
^-$	Words 1 through the last word.
*	Words 1 through the last, or no word at all if there is no word 1.

C. Special notations.

!!	The preceding command line.
!	The preceding command line (must be followed by a word identifier).
!*	The options and arguments, if any, of the preceding command.

Example: Typing:

!! will repeat the previous command.

!5 will run event No. 5 on the history list.

^ls^ls -l will run the previous command by substituting **ls -l** for **ls**.

> **more !5:3-$** will run the command **more** on history event
> No. 5, from word No. 3 to the end of event
> No. 5.
>
> There are several modifiers that you can add to history substitutions.
> They consist of letters or symbols preceded by a colon. We'll leave it to
> you to investigate the on-line manual for details; see the sections on **csh**
> and **newcsh**. Most of the modifiers are more useful as components of
> UNIX programming than as casual aids.

Customizing UNIX: The Alias

The C shell offers you a marvelous opportunity to rename, redefine, and
rearrange commands in a way that suits your needs. The method is easy and
is called making "aliases." We will get you started with a few examples, and
you can take it from there.

Establishing a Simple Alias

Perhaps you have a combination of command and options that you use
often. For example, you may like using:

```
ls -Fla
```

when you list your files in order to mark your directories (**-F**), see your permissions (**-l**), and to make sure that you list "dot" files (**-a**). The "alias" facility lets you create your own abbreviations for such commands. To make, say,
l an abbreviation for **ls -Fla**, you can evoke the aliasing ability by typing:

```
alias l ls -Fla
```

Henceforth, until you log out, whenever you type "l", UNIX will interpret it
to mean **ls -Fla**.

A command with an *alias*.

The alias name can be a standard UNIX name. For example, if you type:

```
alias cp cp -i
```

then, UNIX will use *your* definition of **cp** rather than its own.

The usual form for an alias command is:

```
alias USER ABBREVIATION COMMAND
```

You can use aliases for commands and executable files but not for directory or nonexecutable file names. (The **ln** command provides a similar service for these files.)

To get rid of an alias, use the **unalias** command:

```
unalias ABBREVIATION
```

This removes the named abbreviation from your current alias list. To see what your alias list is, just type:

```
alias
```

and UNIX will show the aliases currently in effect in your account. Some may have been set up by the people who set up your account.

Permanent Aliases

Once you develop an alias that you like, you can let UNIX remember it for you and can establish it automatically every time you log in. The trick is to store the alias (or aliases) in the **.cshrc** file. Just use an editor to enter that file and add a new line consisting of the alias. Type the line just as you would if you were giving UNIX an alias command directly.

Aliases With Arguments

Suppose you wish to use the **l** alias (stands for **ls -Fla**) shown earlier on the **/dev** directory. Just type:

```
l /dev
```

UNIX will recognize your alias whether it is the only command on a line or if it is part of a larger command. Therefore, UNIX will interpret your command to be:

```
ls -Fla /dev
```

Aliases for Compound Commands

An alias can stand for more than one command. Suppose, for example, you have a subdirectory **neatstuff** that you often switch to and which you normally do a **ls** to once you are there. Thus, your normal sequence of commands is:

```
cd neatstuff
ls
```

You can make the following alias do the same thing:

```
alias ns 'cd neatstuff; ls'
```

Then, you need just type:

```
ns
```

instead of the other stuff. The single quotation marks were used so that UNIX would know that the whole phrase, consisting of 2 commands separated by a ";", was part of the alias.

Making Aliases for Complex Commands by Advance Users: \!*

Of course, the **l** alias may be troublesome if you have a long list of files. Perhaps you want to pipe the listing through the **more** command so that you can see the output a page at a time. You could try this:

```
alias L 'ls -Fla | more'
```

(The quote marks ensure that the whole list of commands is included in the alias.) This alias works fine as long as you use it in your working directory, but it messes up if you try to apply it to another directory. If, for instance, you type:

```
L /dev
```

the command is interpreted as:

```
ls -Fla | more /dev
```

which is meaningless. What you need is an alias that would translate to:

```
ls -Fla /dev | more
```

The problem is that we have to get the **/dev** argument into the middle of the command instead of at the end.

The answer to this problem is to combine the powers of the history service with the alias procedure. We will show you the answer, and then explain it. The answer is:

```
alias L 'ls -Fla \!* | more'
```

Here we see a new construction: \!*. The !* symbolism is straight from *history*, and it stands for the arguments, if any, of the preceding command. The \ (backslash) is what is known as an "escape." In this case, it inactivates the history symbol (!) while you type in the alias. Otherwise, UNIX would look at the command which you made just before defining the alias and would insert its arguments in the definition. Here is an example of what we mean. Suppose you typed the following two lines (leaving out the backslash):

```
cc pat.c wat.c
alias Ls 'ls -Fla !* | more'
```

Then, UNIX would set up this alias for you:

```
alias Ls 'ls -Fla pat.c wat.c | more'
```

This is not too useful, for then **Ls** will list only those two named files. *With* the backslash, we escape this problem; history substitution will take place when the alias is *used*, not when it is *defined*. Thus, the command:

```
L /dev
```

causes UNIX to execute the following command:

```
ls -Fla /dev | more
```

(First, UNIX reads the line **L /dev**. Next, it substitutes for **L**; this makes the **L /dev** command the one that precedes the use of the alias, so **!*** is interpreted as **/dev**.)

This was just one specific example, but you can use the \!*construction whenever you create an alias that needs to place arguments within the defining expression. Here is one more example:

```
alias cd 'cd \!*; ls
```

This alias will cause UNIX to give you a listing of the new directory whenever you change directories. That is, the command:

```
cd ~lola
```

will be translated to

```
cd ~lola; ls
```

ALIAS COMMAND...

Aliases in Aliases

Yes, you read right. Once you have defined an alias, you can use it as part of a definition of a new alias. In this manner, you can build up a little empire of aliases. Aliases needn't be confined to UNIX procedures, either. They can be defined in terms of programs or procedures that you have written. By using aliases, you can program in UNIX without really knowing how to program. No wonder thousands of UNIX users never go anywhere without their aliases.

The Bourne shell does not have aliasing. However, you can accomplish many of the same things by using shell scripts, which we will describe briefly in the next chapter. Compared to the alias, the shell script is a little more awkward to use but it is more versatile.

Summary: `alias`—list aliases or make aliases

name	arguments

```
alias
alias Abbreviation Command
unalias Abbreviation
```

Description:	`alias` prints out a list of aliases.
	To make new aliases, use the second form given above. Permanent aliases can be kept in the **.cshrc** file.
	To remove aliases, use the third form.
Example:	**alias list ls**
	Teaches UNIX a new name for the **ls** command.
	alias pp cat /usr/poopsie/phone
	Giving the command **pp** is the same as causing the typing of **cat /usr/poopsie/phone**.
	For more details on using **alias**, see the text examples or the on-line manual discussion under "csh." (This section of the manual is about 20 pages long with less than one page discussing **alias**.)

Job Control

A job is a task that you have the computer do for you. Editing a file is a job, compiling a program is a job, creating a directory is a job, and listing your files is a job. Job control gives you the option of suspending a job and resuming it later and, also, of switching a job back and forth between foreground and background.

Stopping and Restarting a Job: *[control–z]* and *fg*

You are in the midst of editing a large file or of running an interactive program and you receive mail that you want to reply to immediately. You can stop your current job by typing:

```
[control-z]
```

and, then, attend to your mail. When you want to start the job up again, type:

```
fg
```

(for "foreground"), and your job resumes where you left off. If you were editing a file in **vi**, you would be returned to the line you were working on.

Simple? Simple! Type **[control–z]** to stop the job and **fg** to resume it. What if you stop a job and forget about it? If you do, you will be given a warning when you try to log off. UNIX will say

```
Stopped jobs
```

and not let you log out. However, if you persistently try to log out, UNIX will eventually let you, and will kill your stopped jobs. A better idea is to bring the job to foreground and terminate it properly.

Incidentally, with some keyboards, many people accidentally hit a [control–z] instead of **ZZ** when attempting to leave **vi**. This leads to some mysterious "Stopped jobs" messages. Of course, once they read this section, those users won't find the messages so mysterious.

Background Jobs: *&* and *fg*

In Chapter 8, we showed how to run a program in background, freeing the terminal for other work. If you don't remember or didn't read that section,

301

we will remind you that the method is to follow the command with the **&** symbol. For example, to get a listing of your files in background, you could type:

```
ls -la > Listing &
```

UNIX will place the job in background and give you a message like:

```
[1] 1492
```

The first number is a personal job control number that we will show you how to use in the next section. The second is the process ID (identification) number, which is a system number assigned uniquely to your job. Meanwhile, you could do another job while the background task is being executed. Eventually, UNIX would notify you that the task was done, and you would find that the file **Listing** had been added to your directory. Remember, though, that if a job normally sends output to the screen, it will do so even if running in background.

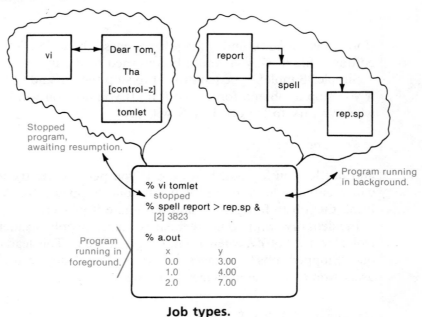

Job types.

If you want to bring the background job back into the foreground, i.e., on your terminal, just type:

```
fg
```

Background is a good place for slow, low-priority jobs; running a **spell** or **nroff** program (as discussed in Chapter 12) on a large file provides some good candidates for background jobs.

Multiple Jobs : *jobs* and *bg*

You are a blur of activity. You've stopped a job, started up two jobs in background, started and stopped another job, and, then, started up yet another job. But, what was that first job you started? And, what job is going to come into foreground the next time you type **fg**? You need some way to check on what you've done and to identify the various tasks you have underway. Perhaps you also need a vacation. Well, UNIX may not help with the vacation, but it can deal with the other problems.

The simplest, quickest way to review what you are doing is to type:

```
jobs
```

This command will then list and label the jobs that you have initiated at your terminal. (If you are using two terminals simultaneously, each will have its own job list.) Here is a sample response:

```
[2]     Stopped         vi whatamess
[3]     Stopped         vi *7
[4]   - Stopped         f77 ~wiseone/bigprograms/begin.f
[5]   + Stopped         vi fing
[6]     Running         ls -R / | sort -o jnk
```

The first column identifies the job with a number in brackets; we will call this the "job number." The "+" in the fourth line indicates the "current" job, and the "-" in the third line is the next most current job. (**Jobs** has an interesting conception of "current." All stopped jobs are more current than running jobs. The most recently stopped job is the most current. Of running jobs, the least recently initiated job is the most current.) Jobs labeled "Stopped" are, indeed, stopped. A job labeled "Running" is running in background. The final column gives the name of the job.

How do you use this information? Suppose you want to resume work on job [2]. One way is to type:

```
fg %2
```

The % character is used to introduce a job number, so this instruction means to bring job [2] into foreground. More simply, you can omit the **fg** and just type:

```
%2
```

What happens if you just type **fg** with no further information? Then, the job labeled with the **+** sign will be brought into foreground.

You can also take a stopped job and start it up in background, and you can stop a job already running in background. You actually have two choices for putting a stopped job in background. The first just uses the **&** operator. For example, to start job [4] in background, you can type:

```
%4 &
```

Or, you can use the **bg** (for "background") command:

```
bg %4
```

The result is the same in either case. The job is placed in background and you receive a message such as:

```
[4] f77 ~wiseone/bigprograms/begin.f &
```

telling you the name of job [4] and that it now is running in background.

To stop, say, job [6] running in background, just type:

```
stop %6
```

Job Numbers and Process ID Numbers

Earlier, we mentioned that each job you stop or put into background is given a job number (in brackets) and, also, a process ID number. Why two numbers? And what are their uses?

First, the job numbers assigned by **job** are personal to you and your terminal. The first job you stop or put in background after logging in on a given terminal is called [1], the next one [2], . . .; the sequence is fairly predictable. They are small integers that are easily typed, and they are the labels recognized by the C-shell job control system. However, these numbers are not unique; your neighbor could very well also have a job [1] and a job [2]. To keep things straight, the computing system needs a method to assign each job a unique identification; that is the purpose of the process ID number.

Another difference is that only jobs that you stop or place in background are given job numbers, but every job you run is assigned an ID number. In short, the job number is a local, useful-to-you label, and the process ID number is a system-wide, useful-to-UNIX label.

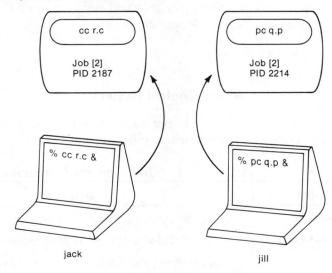

Job numbers and PIDs.

You can get both labels displayed by using the **-l** option on **jobs**; see the **job** summary given below. The **ps** (for "process status") will give you the ID number (among other things), but not the job number. However, **ps** works in both the Bourne shell and the C shell, while **jobs** is purely a C-shell command.

Terminating Unruly Jobs: *kill*

Into every computer user's life comes the program that just won't quit. The computer insists on taking some trivial error seriously and expends considerable time doing useless things with great speed and accuracy. If a program is doing this in background, you can't stop it with a simple **interrupt** (using [control–c] or [break]). You need a special tool, and that tool is **kill**. To use **kill**, you need to know either the job number or the process ID number. Suppose these numbers are [3] and 3456, respectively. Then, either of the following commands will terminate the troublesome job:

```
kill %3
```

or

```
kill 3456
```

Occasionally, a complex process will not succumb to this command. In that case, try the potent **-9** option, as in:

```
kill -9 %3
```

A Summary of the Job Control System

Table 11-1 is a list of the operations that we have discussed; following it are more complete summaries of **jobs**, **ps**, and **kill**.

Table 11-1. Job Control Commands

Command	Definition
[control–z]	Stops the job you are working on.
COMMAND &	Makes COMMAND run in background.
jobs	Lists stopped and background jobs, assigning them job numbers given in brackets, as [1]. The "current" job is identified with a "+" and the next most current with a "-". Since one can go back and forth between jobs, the current job may not be the last one on the list.
fg	Brings the "+" marked job from the **jobs** list into the foreground, starting it if stopped.
fg %n	Brings job [n] from the **jobs** list into the foreground, starting it if stopped.
%n	Short for **fg** %n.
%n &	Restarts job [n], placing it in background.
bg	Puts the "+" marked job from the **jobs** list into background, starting it if stopped.
bg %n	Puts job [n] from the **jobs** list into background, starting it if stopped.
stop %n	Stops the specified background job.
kill %n	Kills job [n]; that is, terminates the job rather than merely suspending it.

Summary: jobs—list and identify stopped and background jobs

name	option	arguments
jobs	[-l]	

Description: **jobs** prints out a list of stopped jobs and jobs running in background. The format is as follows:

```
[1] + Stopped    vi whatamess
[2] - Stopped    vi fing
[3]   Running    ls -R / | sort -o jnk
```

The first column is the assigned job number enclosed in brackets. The second column contains a + for the "current" job and a - for the next most current job. The third column states whether the job is stopped or running in background. The final column gives the name of the job.

The "currency" order for from-most-to-least is stopped jobs (most recently stopped to least recently stopped) and, then, jobs running in background (from first initiated job to last initiated job). In the example given above, the user went back to [1] after stopping [2], and, then, stopped [1] again.

The job numbers are assigned for a given terminal; if you use two terminals simultaneously, each will have its own list of job numbers.

Option: **-l**
This option gives a long listing that also includes the process identification number (PID). This is a unique system-wide number. Different users may have jobs with the same job number, but no two jobs have the same process ID number.

Summary: ps—process status report

name	option	arguments
ps	[a]	

Description: ps prints information about processes, i.e., jobs, currently in the system. The output consists of the process identification number (PID), the terminal (TT), CPU time used (TIME), the state of the process (STAT), and the command (COMMAND). The PID is a number uniquely assigned to the process. The state is described by a four-letter sequence. The first letter can be R (for running), T (for stopped), P, D, or S (for various states of temporary inactivity), or I (for idle). The other three letters relate to more technical matters; the interested user should refer to the on-line manual.

Option: a
This option displays **ps** information for all terminals, not just the user's.

Summary: kill—terminate jobs

name	options	arguments
kill	[-9]	job number or process ID

Description: **kill** terminates the specified job. You can specify the job either by the job number assigned by **jobs** or with the process identification number (PID) given by **ps** or **jobs -l**. The form when using a job number given as [n] is:
kill %n

The form when using the PID number is:
kill number

Option: **-9**
This is a "sure kill" which can be used if the ordinary kill fails. This actually is a special case of a more general option.

Example: Suppose the job **spell Essay > err &** has job number [3] and a PID of 3492. You can terminate the job with either:
kill %3
or
kill 3492

COMPUTER ENHANCED AGRICULTURAL PRODUCTION

Job Control in the Bourne Shell

Of the operations that we have discussed in this section, the only one available in the Bourne shell is the putting of a job in background with the **&** operator. If you need to terminate a job there, use the **ps** command to find the process ID number, and use **kill** with that PID number as just described.

Review Questions

A. Here is the result of a history command:

```
1 cd English
2 head My.Summer Faulkner Tragedy
3 cd /usr/nerkie/project.c
4 ls
5 history
```

Translate each of the following history references, assuming each is typed as the sixth command.

```
1.  !1
2.  !c
3.  !?erk?
4.  !2 | more
5.  vi !he:2
6.  wc !2*
7.  more !3^/guesses
```

B. Suppose all the following aliases are in effect:

```
alias rm rm -i
alias c 'cd; ls'
alias cr 'cd \!*; rm *'
```

How, then, would the following commands be interpreted?

```
1.  rm junkfile
2.  c
3.  c junkdirectory
4.  cr junkdirectory
```

C. Here is the result of a jobs command:

```
[1]  +Stopped    edit lice
[2]   Running    spell sports > error.sp
[3]  -Stopped    spell chess > error.ck
```

What would each of the following commands accomplish?

```
1.  %3
2.  fg
3.  stop %2
4.  bg %3
5.  kill %1
```

Answers

A. **1.** cd English
  2. cd /usr/nerkie/project.c
  3. cd /usr/nerkie/project.c
  4. head My.Summer Faulkner Tragedy | more
  5. vi Faulkner
  6. wc My.Summer Faulkner Tragedy
  7. more /usr/nerkie/project.c/guesses

B. **1.** `rm -i junkfile`   (UNIX asks you to confirm your **rm** order before acting.)
  2. `cd; ls`   (Change to home directory, list the files and directories there.)
  3. `cd; ls junkdirectory`   (Change to home directory, but list the contents of **junkdirectory**—will fail unless **junkdirectory** is a subdirectory of the home directory.)
  4. `cd junkdirectory; rm -i *`   (Change to **junkdirectory**, then remove all files there, asking for confirmation.)

Notes:

  1. In Question 3, **junkdirectory** is attached to **ls** rather than **cd** because **ls** is the command immediately preceding the directory name.
  2. In Question 4, **junkdirectory** is attached to **cd** rather than **rm** because of the *history* substitution.
  3. In Question 4, the **rm -i** option is used because **rm** was redefined in another alias to mean that.

C. **1.** Resumes job [3], running it in foreground.
  2. Resumes job [1], since it is the "current" (+) job.
  3. Stops (suspends) job [2].
  4. Restarts job [3], running it in background.
  5. Terminates job [1].

12

Information Processing: *grep, find,* and *spell*

In this chapter, you will find:

- Introduction
- Finding Stuff: *grep* and *find*
- File Searching: *grep*
  - File Names
  - Patterns
  - Forms of Regular Expression
  - Options
- Finding Files: *find*
  - Search Criteria
  - Actions
- For Advanced Users: More Complex Forms of *find*
  - The Directory Pathname
  - The Search Criterion
- Revisiting Sort: Using Fields
  - Fields and Field Separators
  - Using Fields With *sort*
  - Multiple Fields
  - Subdividing a Field
  - Flag Options and Fields
- Word Processing
  - Checking Your Spelling: *spell*
  - Simple Formatting: *fmt* {BSD}
  - Text Formatters: A Brief Introduction to *nroff* and *troff*
- Other Aids for the Writer
- A Quick Peek at *awk*

- An Introduction to Shell Scripts
- Other UNIX Utilities
- Graphics Utilities
    - Using *graph* and *plot*
    - Using *plot2d*
    - The "S" Package
- Where Do We Go From Here?
- Review Questions
- Exercises at the Terminal

12 INFORMATION PROCESSING: *grep, find, and spell*

In the cool confines of the Programming Division of Dray Conglomerate, Delia Delphond took off her softball cap and shook her auburn curls loose. She had just finished updating the statistical files for her softball team, the Byte Boomers. Now she copied the files for the other teams in the company league; it was her turn to put together the league stats. First, she used **sort** to put together a league masterfile of batting statistics arranged alphabetically by player. Then, using the field-specification option of **sort**, she created a file listing the players in descending order of batting averages. Next, again using the field-specification **sort** option and piping it through **head**, she created files giving the top ten players for each of several categories: home runs, RBIs, hits, runs, triples, doubles, walks, stolen bases, and strike-outs. Curious about how her team was doing, she used **grep** to find Byte Boomers on the top ten lists. Good, they were making a fine showing. The name D. Delphond, in particular, appeared in several lists. Smiling, she turned her attention to the team statistics. Using **awk**, she had UNIX sum up the "at bats," the hits, etc., for each team and calculate the team averages. Then, she went on to handle the pitching stats.

Delia enjoyed going through the statistics, but she didn't care much for her next task, preparing a press summary for the company paper, *Draybits*. She'd much rather bat than write. However, with the help of a UNIX editor, she put together a blurb of rather irregular line length. She ran the file through **spell** and corrected the errors that had shown up—words such as "avarage" and "notewordy." Next she invoked a shell script of hers that first sent the file through **fmt** to tidy it up and, then, forwarded the result through **mail** to the *Draybit's* newspaper editor.

She leaned back in her chair and relaxed for a few moments. Not for too long, however, for she had her regular work to do, too. Besides being a nifty shortstop, Delia was a prolific Pascal programmer (a ppp, for short). She had scattered her program files through several subdirectories, and now, she decided to gather them together in one place. She created a directory for that purpose and then set up a **find** command that would locate all her files whose names ended in **.p** and move them to the new directory.

Delia checked the time (using **date**, of course). It was time for her next project, the long-awaited salary raise! She put her cap back on at a jaunty angle, picked up the analysis she had prepared using the UNIX system, and set off for the President's office; Dray wouldn't have a chance.

*   *   *   *

Introduction

There is more to be said of UNIX than can be squeezed into a book this size. So far, we have concentrated on the more basic operations. Now we will turn to a few UNIX commands and utilities that take you beyond the basics. Many of them are really useful only when you deal with large numbers of files and directories. (Both "commands" and "utilities" are programs run by UNIX; we are using the word "utility" to indicate a program more elaborate than a "command.") We will describe some of the simpler examples, such as **grep**, in fair detail. Others, such as the powerful **awk**, are rather extensive in scope and rules, and we will give them just a brief introduction.

Finding Stuff: *grep* and *find*

These commands are useful when you have to look through several files or directories to find a particular file entry or file. The **grep** command lets you find which files contain a particular word, name, phrase, etc. The **find** command lets you find files that satisfy some criterion of yours (having a certain name, not used for two months, having a certain suffix, etc.) and, then, have something done to those files (print the names, move them to another directory, remove them, etc.). We introduced **grep** in Chapter 7; now let's take a more complete look.

File Searching: *grep*

Sometimes, through necessity or curiosity, you may want to search through one or more files for some form of information. For example, you may want to know which of several letter files contain references to the Wapoo Fruit Company. Or you may have a set of files constituting a large C program and you want to know which ones use a certain function. Let's look at a simpler example using just one file. On most systems, there is a file called **/etc/passwd** that contains information about the system users. (See the following box.) Suppose you want to find out more about someone using the login name of "physh" and your system does not have the **finger** command. Then, you can have the **/etc/passwd** file searched for the word "physh" and the line(s) containing that word will be printed out. To do this, give the command:

```
grep physh /etc/passwd
```

The response might look like this:

```
physh:xMTyUrR:201:10:Jon Foreman:/usr/physh:/bin/csh
```

This line from the **/etc/passwd** file is interpreted in the following box; the important point is that the pattern of the command was:

```
grep pattern filename
```

Thus, the basic manner of using **grep** is pretty simple. On the other hand, the following explanation will be a little lengthy. That's because we will describe some additional features of **grep** that you may want to use.

The */etc/passwd* File

The UNIX system has to keep track of who is allowed to use the system, of login names, group memberships, passwords, and user identification numbers. UNIX may want to know your phone number and, on multiple shell systems, which shell you use. All this information is kept in the **/etc/passwd** file. Let's look at the sample line we used in the section on **grep** and see how such a file can be set up.

```
physh:xMTyUrR:201:10:Jon Foreman:/usr/physh:/bin/csh
```

The line is broken up into seven "fields," with each separated from the adjoining fields by a colon (:). (We will discuss fields again when we revisit **sort**.)

1. The first field contains the user's login name; (physh).
2. The second field contains the user's password; (xMTyUrR).
   Don't panic—the password is encrypted into a secret code.
3. The third field contains the user identification number; (201).
4. Next comes the user's group number; (10).
5. Then, the personal information; (Jon Foreman).
6. The sixth field contains the user's home directory; (/usr/physh).
7. The final field gives the user's login shell; (csh).

If a user has not set up a password, the field will be empty, but the colons will be left as place keepers; thus the line would look like this:

```
luscious::1313:24:Lucy, ext. 777:/usr/luscious:/bin/csh
```

More generally, **grep** is used this way:

`grep` option(s) pattern filename(s)

Let's look at each part of this form, starting with "filename(s)" and working backwards.

File Names

You can give one file name or several for **grep** to search. When you use more than one file name, **grep** will tag each line that it finds with the name of the file that the line was in. For example, if we type:

```
grep dentistry boyd carson douglass ernst
```

the response might look like this:

```
boyd:without which the undoubted charms of dentistry would be
boyd:unless, of course, you are speaking of dentistry.
boyd: I would rather suffer the agonies of amateur dentistry
douglass:in dentistry. Aside from that, he was in no way
```

Here, three lines containing "dentistry" were found in the **boyd** file, while one was found in the **douglass** file, and none were found in the remaining files.

You can use "wild-card" substitution for file names when using **grep**. Consider the commands:

```
grep reverse *.c
```

and

```
grep Renaldo /usr/phoebe/*
```

The first would search for "reverse" in all files ending in **.c** (i.e., C-language files) in your current working directory. The second would search all the files in the **/usr/phoebe** directory for "Renaldo."

Patterns

So far, we have used single words for the pattern. In general, the pattern can be a "string" or, else, a limited form of "regular expression." A "string" is just a sequence of ordinary characters. All the examples that we have used so far for **grep** patterns are strings. A "regular expression," on the other hand, may include characters with special meanings. For example, we will see that **grep** recognizes the pattern "b.g" as representing any three-character string beginning in "b" and ending in "g." The pattern "b.g" is a regular expression, and the "." in it is a special character playing much the same role that a "?" does when used in a shell command. Like the shell, **grep** recognizes certain regular expressions for patterns, but the rules it uses, as we shall see later, are not the ones used by the shell.

Strings merit a closer look since most of the time that you use **grep**, you probably will use strings. If the string is just a single word, you can use it just as in the previous examples. But, what if you want to find something like "Los Angeles"? The command:

```
grep Los Angeles cityfile
```

will not work, for **grep** will think that the pattern sought was "Los" and that "Angeles" was the name of the first file to be searched. To avoid this confusion, you can place the pattern in single quotes; that is, use:

```
grep 'Los Angeles' cityfile
```

and all will be well.

When **grep** looks for a string, it doesn't care whether it finds the string by itself or embedded in a larger string. For example, the command:

```
grep man moon
```

will not only find the word "man" in the **moon** file, it will also find such words as "woman," "mantra," and "command," for they all contain the string "man" within them. Some implementations of **grep** have a **-w** option (whole words only) that picks up only lines that contain the pattern as an isolated word. If your system lacks that option, you might try putting spaces in the pattern, as in ' man ', but that will fail to pick up lines in which "man" is the first or last word and, also, those constructions such as "man." or "man," because these all lack one of the specified spaces. (Remember, a space is a character, too.)

You may run into problems if the pattern *string* you use contains some of the special characters used by UNIX (e.g., * or ?) or by **grep** regular expressions (e.g., . or |).

Sometimes, it is sufficient to enclose the pattern in single quotes. For instance, the command:

```
grep * froggy
```

will confuse UNIX, but the command:

```
grep '*' froggy
```

will cause the system to search the **froggy** file for lines containing the symbol "*".

Some characters, such as the C-shell **history** character (!) or those described in the following section on regular expressions, will also need to be preceded by a backslash (\) to *turn off* their special meanings. (The backslash is a special character that says to ignore any special properties possessed by the following character. Thus, **cat** * will print out all the files in a directory, while **cat** * will only print a file with the literal name *.) Therefore, the command:

```
grep '!' dinnerreview
```

will confuse the C shell (**history** will look for a command beginning with a quote mark), but the command:

```
grep '\!' dinnerreview
```

will seek lines containing exclamation marks.

Forms of Regular Expression

Now we can take a look at the forms of regular expressions recognized by **grep**. Basically, these forms (with some omissions) are the same as those used by **ed** and **ex**. Here's a rundown of the most important rules:

1. A period (.) in a pattern stands for any one character; it plays the same role in **grep** patterns as the **?** does in UNIX shell wild-card substitution. Thus, the command:

    ```
    grep 'c.n' horply
    ```

    will find such strings as "can" and "con," but not "coin," since "coin" has two characters, not one, between the "c" and the "n."

2. A string in brackets (i.e., enclosed in **[]**) matches any one character in the string. (This is the same as the UNIX shell's use of brackets.) Thus, the pattern:

    ```
    [wW]easel
    ```

    will match "weasel," or "Weasel," but not "wWeasel." You can use a hyphen to indicate a range of characters. For example,

    ```
    [m-t]ap
    ```

    would match the strings "map," "nap," etc., up to "tap."

3. Preceding a string in brackets with a caret (^) causes **grep** to make matches using the characters *not* in the list. For instance,

    ```
    [^m-t]ap
    ```

    would match strings like "cap" and "zap" but not strings like "map" and "tap."

4. A regular expression preceded by a ∧ will match only those lines that begin with the expression. Thus, the command:

    ```
    grep '^James' slist
    ```

    would find the first of the following lines and would skip the second:

    James Watt
    Henry James

5. Similarly, a regular expression followed by a $ will match only those lines with the expression at the end. Therefore,

    ```
    grep 'James$' slist
    ```

    would find "Henry James" but not "James Watt" in the preceding example.

    You can use both the ∧ and the $ if you want to find only lines that match the pattern in their entirety. For example, the command:

```
grep '^The King of Red Gulch$' oddfile
```

would find the line

"The King of Red Gulch"

and skip over the line:

"The King of Red Gulch sauntered over to Doc Buzzard's table."

6.   A backslash (\) followed by any character other than a digit or parenthe-sis matches that character, turning off any special meaning that character might have. For instance, suppose you wanted to search a file for men-tions of Pascal files, which have names ending in ".p". You can type:

```
grep '\.p' Pasctext
```

If you omitted the \, **grep** would interpret the period as described in rule 1.

Options

Grep options are indicated in the usual way, using flags. Here are some that you may find useful:

1.   The **-n** option precedes each found line with its line number in the file. Here is a sample command and the response:

```
grep -n PASCAL Johnletter

237: wanted to search a file for mentions of PASCAL files,
```

2.   The **-i** option ignores the case of letters. Ordinarily, the string "twits" will not be matched to "Twits" or "TWITS," but it will be if the **-i** option is in effect.
3.   The **-c** option prints a count of the number of lines that match, but doesn't print the lines themselves. If you are searching several files, it prints the name of each file followed by the number of matching lines in that file.
4.   The **-w** option, if available, causes **grep** to choose only lines that con-tain the pattern as an isolated word, not as part of a longer word.

Summary: `grep`—search a file for a pattern

name	options	arguments
`grep`	`[-n, -i, -c, -w]`	pattern [filename(s)]

Description: **grep** searches the named files for lines containing the given pattern and then prints out the matching lines. If more than one file is searched, the name of the file containing each line is printed, too. If no file name is given, **grep** looks to the standard input; thus, **grep** can be used with pipes. The pattern can be a single string, or it can be a limited form of regular expression as described in the text. A pattern containing spaces or special characters such as "*" should be set off by single quotes. Normally, **grep** will match any string containing the pattern; for example, "whose" matches "hose."

Options:	-n	Precedes each matching line with its line number.
	-i	Ignores the case of letters when making comparisons.
	-c	Prints only a count of matching lines.
	-w	Matches only complete words with the pattern; "whose" does not match "hose."

| Example: | **grep -iw hop peter bugs** |
| | This command searches the files **peter** and **bugs** for occurrences of the words "hop," "HOP," "Hop," etc. It ignores words such as "hope" or "shop." |

Finding Files: *find*

The **find** command searches for files that meet some criterion. You can search for files that have a certain name or are a certain size or files not accessed for a certain number of days or having a certain number of links; and this is just a partial list. Once the files are found, you can have the pathnames printed out, you can have the files themselves printed or removed or otherwise acted upon. The search will begin at the directory you specify and will then descend down all its subdirectories and all their subdirectories, etc., leaving no nook or cranny unexplored (except, of course, for forbidden nooks and crannies like those in some English muffins). A branching search such as this is termed "recursive."

It would be difficult to fit the capabilities of the **find** command into the usual format for commands, so **find** has its own unique structure. The basic sequence goes like this:

```
find directory pathname      search criterion      action
```

The "directory pathname" is the pathname of the directory that will be recursively searched (all subdirectories, etc.) for the desired files. The "search criterion" identifies the files that are sought. The "action" tells what to do with the files once they are found. The criterion and the action are identified with special flags, which we will discuss soon. Here is an example of a **find** command:

```
find /usr -name calendar -print
```

The directory pathname is **/usr**, so the search starts here and proceeds recursively through all directories branching off this directory. The search criterion is **-name calendar**; this means UNIX will search for files bearing the name **calendar**. Finally, the action is **-print**, meaning that each time a file is found that meets the search criterion, its pathname is displayed. The output might look like this:

```
/usr/flossie/calendar
/usr/nerkie/calendar
/usr/sluggo/calendar
```

This would tell us which users were using UNIX's **calendar** feature.

Naming the directory is straightforward, but the search criterion and action sections need further discussion.

Search Criteria

Find recognizes several search criteria. They take the form of an identifying flag word (a hyphen joined to a word, e.g., **-name**) followed by a space and a word or number. Here are the more common ones.

A. Finding a file by name:

Use the **-name** flag followed by the desired name. The name can be a simple word as in the preceding example, or it can use the shell wild-card substitutions: **[]**, **?**, and *****. If you use these special symbols, place the name in single quotes. Here are some examples of acceptable uses.

Criterion	Files sought
`-name nail`	Files named "nail".
`-name '*.c'`	All files whose names end in ".c".
`-name '*.?'`	All files for which the next to last character is a period.

B. Finding a file by last access:

Use the **-atime** flag followed by the number of days since the file was last accessed. Plus and minus signs may be used to indicate greater than or less than.

Criterion	Files sought
`-atime 7`	Files last accessed exactly 7 days ago.
`-atime -14`	Files accessed more recently than 14 days ago.

C. Finding a file by last modification:

Use the **-mtime** flag followed by the number of days since the file was last modified. Plus and minus signs may be used to indicate greater than or less than.

Criterion	Files sought
`-mtime 20`	Files last modified 20 days ago.
`-mtime +45`	Files modified more than 45 days ago.

D. Finding files modified more recently than a given file.

Use the **-newer** flag followed by the name of a file.

Criterion	Files sought
`-newer slopware`	Files modified more recently than **slopware** was.

Actions

You have three flag options to choose from for the action section of the command: **-print**, **-exec**, and **-ok**.

A. The **-print** option.

This option prints the pathname for every file found that matches the criterion.

B. The **-exec** option.

This option lets you give a command to be applied to the found files. The command should follow the flag and should be terminated with a space, a backslash, and then a semicolon. A set of braces, i.e., { }, can be used to represent the name of the files found. For example,

```
find . -atime +100 -exec rm {} \;
```

This command would find and remove all files in your current directory (and its offshoots) that haven't been used in over 100 days.

C. The **ok** option.

This option is just like the **-exec** option except that it asks for your "ok" for each file found before it executes the command. For instance, if you gave the command:

```
find . -atime +100 -ok rm {} \;
```

and the system found a file called **first.prog** that satisfied the criterion, the system would then query you:

```
<rm ... ./first.prog> ?
```

If you reply with the letter **y**, the command is executed; otherwise it is not. A command along the lines of this example is a handy aid in cleaning up your file systems.

For Advanced Users: More Complex Forms of *find*

You can expand each of the basic sections of the **find** command to pinpoint more exactly what you want done.

The Directory Pathname

You actually can give a list of directories to be searched. For instance,

```
find ~lester ~festus . -name '*.p' -print
```

would search lester's home directory, festus's home directory, and your current directory for files whose names end in ".p" and would then print the pathnames of those files.

The Search Criterion

The search criteria we have given are called "primaries." You can combine them or act upon them in the following three basic ways.

1. The **!** operator negates a primary. It should precede the primary and would be isolated by spaces on either side. If you use the C shell, use **\!** instead of **!** in order not to invoke **history**.

Criterion	Meaning
`-newer fops`	Files revised more recently than **fops**.
`\! -newer fops`	Files not revised more recently than **fops**.
`\! -name '*.f'`	Files whose names do not end in ".f".

327

2. Listing two or more criteria in a row causes **find** to seek those files that simultaneously satisfy all criteria.

Criteria	*Meaning*
`-name calendar -size +2`	Files named **calendar** having a size greater than 2 blocks.
`-size +2 -size -6`	Files whose size is greater than 2 blocks and less than 6 blocks.

3. Separating two criteria with a **-o** flag (a space on either side) causes **find** to search for files that satisfy one or the other criterion.

Criteria	*Meaning*
`-name turk -o -name terk`	Files named **turk** or **terk**.
`-atime +7 -o -mtime +14`	Files that haven't been accessed within 7 days or modified within 14 days.

Summary: find—find designated files and act upon them

name	arguments
find	directory pathname(s) search criteria action(s)

Description: **find** searches the named directories recursively for files matching the specified criteria. It then performs the specified actions on the files.

Search Criteria: In the following, "n" represents a decimal integer. It can be given with or without a sign. With no sign, it means n exactly; +n means greater than n; -n means less than n.

-name filename	Files named "filename."
-size n	Files of size n blocks (one block is 512 bytes).
-links n	Files with n links.
-atime n	Files accessed n days ago.

	-mtime n	Files modified n days ago.
	-newer filename	Files modified more recently than the file "filename".

Actions: **-print**
Print the pathnames of the found files.
-exec command \;
Executes the given command upon finding a file; the symbolism {} represents the found file.
-ok command \;
Same as **-exec**, except your approval is requested before each execution; reply with a **y** to have the command executed.

Note: There is a procedure for combining criteria. A **!** or a **\!** (isolated by spaces) before a criterion negates it. Giving two or more criteria means that all must be satisfied by the file. Separating two criteria by an **-o** (isolated by spaces) means one *or* the other. Escaped parentheses, i.e., **\ (** and **\)**, can be used to clarify groupings.

Examples: **find . -name boobtube -print**
This command searches through the current directory and all its offshoots for a file named **boobtube**.
find . -atime +30 -atime -60 -exec mv {} ./old \;
This command finds all files in the current working directory (and its offshoots, and their offshoots, etc.) that have been used within 60 days but not within 30 days. These files then are moved to the directory *./old*.

Revisiting Sort: Using Fields

When we discussed **sort** in Chapter 9, we saw that it sorted files on the basis of the beginning of each line. This is useful, for example, if you have a mailing list in which people are listed last name first. But you might want to sort that same list on the basis of city or state. You *can* do that, too, providing you have set up your file accordingly. The key is to break up each line into "fields." As will be shown, you can instruct **sort** to look only at certain fields when sorting. Thus, you can set up the file so that last names are in the first field and states in, say, the sixth field. Having the **file** sorted by the sixth field would then sort the file by state.

Fields and Field Separators

What makes up a field? That is a matter of definition. If you don't specify differently, fields are non-empty, non-blank strings separated by blanks. For example, in the line:

```
McHaggis, Jamie 33883 Sea Drive, Tuna Gap, California 94888
```

line	McHaggis,	Jamie	33883	Sea	Drive,	Tuna	Gap,	California	94889
Field number	1	2	3	4	5	6	7	8	9

Fields in a line.

the first field is "McHaggis," the fifth field is "Drive," and the last field is "94888." For some types of files, the blank is a fine field separator, but not for a mailing list. The reason is that a metropolis such as "Hogback" uses one field but a town like "San Luis Obispo" uses three fields, and this would throw off the numbering of the field containing the state.

line	Blugston,	Eve	13	Jowl	Drive,	Hogback,	AR	72777		
Field Number	1	2	3	4	5	6	7	8		
Field Number	1	2	3	4	5	6	7	8	9	10
line	Blugstone,	Frappo	896	Jewel	Road,	San	Luis	Obispo,	CA	93401

A problem with using a blank as a field separator.

To get around this sort of problem, you can choose your own field separator. A common choice is the colon. You could make a file entry look like this:

```
McHaggis:Jamie::33883 Sea Drive:Tuna Gap:California:94888
```

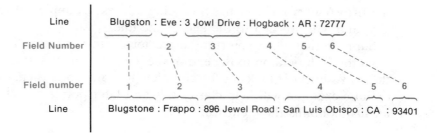

Using a colon as a field separator.

In this case, the first field is the last name, the second field is the first name, the third field (empty, in this case) is the middle name or initial, the fourth field is the street address, the fifth field is the city, etc. Note that a field now can have spaces within it, as the fourth field does, or it can be completely empty, as is the third field. The value of the empty field is that it is a place keeper; even though a middle name is missing in this case, the address is still in the fourth field. Also notice that we haven't left any spaces at the beginning or ends of the fields. This, as you may remember, is because a space itself is a character. Therefore ": Wickley :" is a field containing 9 characters (the first and last being the space character), and it would be sorted differently from the 7-character field ":Wickley:". The **-b** option of **sort** would ignore leading blanks but not the trailing blanks in a field, so it is simpler to just leave out extra blanks in the first place. Of course, you also could carefully use the exact same number of blanks for each entry.

Using Fields With *sort*

But, how does **sort** know to use a colon instead of a blank as a field separator? You have to use the **-t** option to tell it so. When you use this option, you follow the **-t** with the symbol that is to be the field separator; the symbol follows the "t" directly with no spaces. Thus, to use the colon as a separator, you would use **-t:** as the flag.

Next, how do you tell **sort** which fields to use? You include a flag consisting of a plus sign followed by a number. This tells **sort** how many fields to *skip*. For example, the command:

```
sort -t: +4 maillist
```

tells **sort** to recognize colons as a field separator and to skip 4 fields before comparing lines in the **maillist** file. This means the comparison will start with the fifth field, which, in the preceding address example, corresponds to the city, and will proceed to the end of the line.

Suppose that when you run the previous command, two lines are identical from the fifth field on to the end of the line. How does **sort** decide to arrange these two lines? It looks at the complete line and sorts them on that basis. A definite example will help clarify this and later points, so let's suppose that **maillist** contains these entries:

```
Morgan:Joe::315 Second Street:Riesenstadt:CA:94707
Vegetable:Joe:Fritz:1002 Market Pl.:Riesenstadt:CA:94707
Morgan:Joe::315 Second Street:Redville:OH:40817
Morgan:Joe::315 Second Street:Hot'n'wet:TX:72727
Antibody:Aristotle:Asis:26 Furtz Way:Redville:OH:40822
Zircon:Bilbo:Nagy:1313 Ratgut Blvd.:Hot'n'wet:TX:72702
```

Then, the result of **sort -t: +4 maillist** is:

```
Zircon:Bilbo:Nagy:1313 Ratgut Blvd.:Hot'n'wet:TX:72702
Morgan:Joe::315 Second Street:Hot'n'wet:TX:72727
Morgan:Joe::315 Second Street:Redville:OH:40817
Antibody:Aristotle:Asis:26 Furtz Way:Redville:OH:40822
Morgan:Joe::315 Second Street:Riesenstadt:CA:94707
Vegetable:Joe:Fritz:1002 Market Pl.:Riesenstadt:CA:94707
```

The last two lines in the sorted list have the same city, state, and zip code, so the tie was decided by looking at the rest of line and, alphabetically, "Morgan" precedes "Vegetable."

You also can tell **sort** where to stop the comparison by using a flag consisting of a minus sign followed by a number. This tells **sort** to stop at the end of the numbered field. Thus,

```
sort -t: +4 -6 maillist
```

would mean to sort the file on the basis of the fifth and sixth fields. If two or more lines have identical fifth and sixth fields, they are then sorted further on the basis of the whole line as before.

Multiple Fields

With **sort**, you can create your own sorting scheme by using multiple fields. **Sort** will first sort the file using the first field pattern you give it. Then, within a block of lines that are identical for those fields, it will sort further using the next field pattern you give. For example, consider the command:

```
sort -t: +0 -1 +5 maillist
```

The first field pattern is "**+0 -1**", which is simply the first field; in this case, the last name. So, first, the file is sorted by last name. The second field pattern is "**+5**", which means field 6 to the end of the line. (Whenever a "plus" field option is given without a "minus" field option, the pattern comparison goes to the end of the line.) In this case, the second pattern corresponds to state and zip code. Thus, all those address lines containing the same last name are further sorted on the basis of state and zip code. This command would yield:

```
Antibody:Aristotle:Asis:26 Furtz Way:Redville:OH:40822
Morgan:Joe::315 Second Street:Riesenstadt:CA:94707
Morgan:Joe::315 Second Street:Redville:OH:40817
Morgan:Joe::315 Second Street:Hot'n'wet:TX:72727
Vegetable:Joe:Fritz:1002 Market Pl.:Riesenstadt:CA:94707
Zircon:Bilbo:Nagy:1313 Ratgut Blvd.:Hot'n'wet:TX:72702
```

Note how the various Morgans are arranged in order of state, not city.

On the other hand, the command:

```
sort -t: +5 -6 +1 maillist
```

would sort the file first by state. Then, those with the same state would be sorted by field 2 (first name) to the end.

To repeat the main point of this section, when you give a series of field ranges by which to sort, the sorting is done first by the first range and, then, ties are resolved by the next range, and so on. Any remaining ties are resolved by looking at the whole line; **sort** always has a reason for putting lines where it does.

Subdividing a Field

You can refine the sorting process even further. Within each field, you can have **sort** skip over a certain number of characters. This is done by adding a decimal point to the field number and following it with the number of characters to be skipped. For instance,

```
sort +2.3 inventory
```

would skip the first two fields and three characters when sorting the file **inventory**; that is, it would start at the fourth character of the third field.

Flag Options and Fields

Several of the **sort** options we discussed in Chapter 7 can be applied globally or just for certain fields. The choice is controlled by the placement of the option letter. Consider the following two commands:

```
sort -r +4 -5 somefile
sort +4r -5 somefile
```

In the first command, the **r** (reverse) option is invoked universally. Lines will be in reverse order on the basis of field 5, and ties will be resolved by applying reverse order to the whole line. In the second command, the **r** option applies only to the initial ordering using field 5; ties are resolved by applying normal order to the whole line. If a field locator option has any additional options appended, then all global options are overridden for that field. That is, if the instruction is:

```
sort -n +4 -5 +6r somefile
```

then, the **-n** option will apply to field 5 but not to field 7. (Remember, the +6 means skip 6 fields, so the **-r** option will begin with field 7.

Summary: sort—sorts files		
name	**options**	**arguments**
sort	[-tc, +n.m, -n.m]	[filename(s)]

Description: **sort** options allow you to sort files on the basis of chosen fields within a line.

Options: **-tc**
              This option sets the field separator to be the character "c". (A blank is the default.)
              +n.m
              sort skips n fields and, then, m characters before beginning comparisons. A "+n" is the same as "+n.0".
              -n.m
              sort stops comparison after skipping n fields from the beginning plus m characters. A "-n" is the same as "-n.m".

Notes: The **b**, **d**, **f**, **n**, and **r** options can be appended to the field locator flags; this causes the option to apply to just that field. Options appearing before the field locators apply globally except that all global flags are turned off for fields with a local flag.

              If multiple fields are specified, sorting is first done by the first field given. Lines having that field identical are then sorted by the second specified field, etc. Remaining ties are resolved by looking at the whole line.

Example: **sort -t: -r +2 -3 +5n sauerbrot**
              The field separator is declared to be a colon. The file **sauerbrot** is sorted in reverse order by field 3. Lines having the same field 3 are further sorted numerically by the sixth field to the end of the line; the numerical sorting is not in reverse order. Lines identical to this point are then sorted on the basis of the whole line, again using reverse order.

Of the **sort** options we discussed in Chapter 7, the following can also be used but limited to a field: **b**, **d**, **f**, **n**, and **r**. The method is (as in the preceding discussion) to append the letter to the field number.

Sort is so flexible and has so many options that you should be able to tackle about any sorting problem that comes up except, perhaps, multiple-line records (where the information for each entry is spread over more than one line) and your laundry.

Word Processing

The phrase "word processing" represents a variety of computer abilities designed to help you prepare written documents. One of the most important

aspects of word processing is the editor, a facility that lets you create and revise files of text. We already have looked at some of the UNIX editors in Chapters 5 and 6 and have seen how they can ease the writer's burden. Now we will look at a few more writer's aids.

Checking Your Spelling: *spell*

You have just completed an important letter, but you are worried about your spelling. You could sit down and check out each word with a dictionary, or you can let UNIX do that for you. Suppose your letter is in the file **sendcash**. You can give the command:

```
spell sendcash
```

and UNIX will then compare each word in your file with words in a spelling list it maintains. If one of your words is not on the list or is not derivable from some standard rules (adding an "s" or an "ing", etc.), that word is printed out on the terminal. (If you make gobs of spelling errors, you may need to use redirection to save all your errors in a file.)

Suppose **sendcash** looks like this:

```
Dear Ruggles,


   I'm at a real nice place. It's the sub-basement of
Mildew Hall at Forkney College; have you ever been their?
If you have, you will knoe that I need mony bad! Please,
please send some soon! The autochthons here are spooky.
I'm looking forward to recieving your next letter.
                                        Love,
                                        Buffy
```

The output of the **spell** command would look like this:

```
autochthons
Buffy
Forkney
knoe
mony
recieving
Ruggles
```

This example points out some of the pitfalls of **spell**. First, it may not recognize some proper names. Secondly, although it caught "knoe," "mony," and "recieving," it didn't catch the fact that "their" should have been spelled "there." **Spell** can check to see if a word is on its list, but it can't tell whether you used it correctly. Thirdly, **spell** doesn't tell you the correct spelling. Finally, you may know some words, such as "autochthons" and certain four-letter words, that are not on **spell**'s list. Nonetheless, **spell** is a big help, especially with long files.

Simple Formatting: *fmt* {BSD}

You have prepared some text and have then gone back and edited it a bit. Now, it says what you want to say, but the physical form is a bit ragged. Suppose, for instance, that part of your file **jimbo** looks like this:

```
     There's nothing wrong with Big Jim's
proposal that a little elbow grease below and a little
monetary grease above won't fix.
Also, I think you should look into Shifty Seth's counter-
offer before Dopey gets wind of it.
I
```

337

```
doubt much will come of it, but we got to be a little
careful right now.
```

You would like to even out the lines a bit. (This task is part of the process called "formatting.") Give the command:

```
fmt jimbo
```

and the above text will be reformed (or formatted) into:

```
     There's nothing wrong with Big Jim's proposal that a
little elbow grease below and a little monetary grease
above won't fix. Also, I think you should look into Shifty
Seth's counter-offer before Dopey gets wind of it. I doubt
much will come of it, but we got to be a little careful
right now.
```

Notice how the complete lines are now *about* the same length; this process of filling up lines with words is called "filling."

To save the output of **fmt**, use redirection.

The **fmt** command is a quick but simple-minded formatter. It preserves initial spaces in a line, such as the initial indentation of a paragraph, and it preserves blank lines. But something like a mailing address would be formatted into one line. If you have text with trickier formatting requirements, you may want to look into a full-blown formatting utility such as **nroff**.

Text Formatters: A Brief Introduction to *nroff* and *troff*

Nroff and **troff** are quite similar to each other. The chief difference is that **nroff** produces output suited to line printers while **troff** produces output intended for a phototypesetter. For simplicity, we will refer just to **nroff** for the rest of this section. A complete explanation of **nroff** would take many, many pages, so we will confine ourselves to a brief examination of how **nroff** is used and what it can do. The operating scheme of **nroff** is this:

1. *Embedded commands* are placed in the text.
2. The text is submitted to the **nroff** processor.
3. The processor rearranges the text as indicated by the embedded commands.
4. The resulting text is sent to the standard output.

For this scheme to work, **nroff** must have some way to tell the difference between embedded commands and text. This is accomplished through the appearance and placement of the embedded commands. Each embedded command consists of a period in column one followed by two letters (and occasionally, by some additional characters). Each command is placed at the far left of the line and each command is the sole inhabitant of the line.

The commands themselves do such things as set the size of the top, bottom, left, and right margins. Also, they set line spacing, set paragraph forms, set up footnotes, generate line shifts and underlining, create multiple column output, set type size, number pages, and the like. There are nearly a hundred embedded commands and there is also a facility for defining "macros," which are combinations of the basic commands. Here, so you can see what they look like, are a few **nroff** commands.

Command	*Meaning*
`.pl`	Set page length to default of 11 inches.
`.br`	Break, start a new line.
`.ll +0.5`	Increase line length by 0.5 inch.
`.ce 10`	Center next 10 lines.

A text prepared for **nroff** would start with several lines of such instructions setting up the general format of the text. Additional commands would be scattered through the text to identify paragraphs, mark section headings, isolate lines, and the like.

If you want to learn more about **nroff** but don't wish to plunge into several score new commands, check to see if your on-line manual has information about the **nroff -ms** option. The **-ms** option is a simplified (but less flexible) version of **nroff** using preset values for parameters, such as margins and page size, and it uses convenient macro definitions for setting up paragraphs. For example, the embedded instruction **.PP** produces a standard paragraph that is indented, set off by blank lines, filled (as many words as fit are placed in each line), and right justified (extra spaces added to even up the right margin). Here is an example of a short text with embedded **-ms** commands. (Note that in any file to be treated by **nroff**, the first line should be an embedded instruction.)

```
.PP
First, remove the skin from the chicken breasts.
Next, use a deboning knife to remove the flesh from the
bones; this may be done more easily if the breasts are half-thawed.
```

```
Now cut up the breasts into bite-sized chunks and dredge
them in a mixture of flour, salt, pepper, and spices.
 .PP
After readying the chicken, take a bunch of green onions,
cut off the tips, wash the onions, and chop them up into small bits.
Place them
into a bowl so that you can quickly dump them in with the
chicken at the proper time.
 .PP
Now heat up the olive oil and the butter.
As it reaches cooking temperature, dump in the garlic.
When the garlic browns, add the chicken breasts.
```

It is recommended that you start each sentence on a new line to make editing easier. If this is in a file called **chicken**, the command:

```
nroff -ms chicken
```

will produce the following output:

```
    First, remove the skin from the chicken breasts. Next, use a
deboning knife to remove the flesh from the bones; this may be
done more easily if the breasts are half-thawed. Now cut up the
breasts into bite-sized chunks and dredge them in a mixture of
flour, salt, pepper, and spices.

    After readying the chicken, take a bunch of green onions, cut
off the tips, wash the onions, and chop them up into small bits.
Place them into a bowl so that you can quickly dump them in with
the chicken at the proper time.

    Now heat up the olive oil and the butter. As it reaches cooking
temperature, dump in the garlic. When the garlic browns, add the
chicken breasts.
```

Note that a top margin was put in. (A bottom margin was, too, but we suppressed it to save space.)

To save the output of **nroff**, use redirection.

When using **nroff**, you can put in the commands as you write, or you can go back and put them in at a later time; but it is easier to insert them as you write.

Other Aids for the Writer

Your system may have other programs to help you with your writing. The current distribution of the Berkeley version of UNIX, for example, has **diction**, **explain**, and **style**. These programs analyze your prose; of course, you don't have to follow their advice if you don't like it.

Diction ("diction" means good word choice) searches the file you give it for words and phrases on its "hit list" of undesirables. When it finds a sentence of yours containing something from the list, it prints out the sentence with the offending word or phrase in brackets. Not all "hits" (as **diction** calls its discoveries) are genuine, for some of the entries on the list are words that are often, but not always, misused.

As an example, we used **diction** on the first paragraph of the **sort** section— the one that starts with:

"When we discussed **sort** in . . ."

by giving the command:

```
diction sortparag
```

Here is the response from **diction**:

```
    when we discussed sort in chapter 7 we saw that it sorted
files[ on the basis of ]the beginning of each line.

  but you might want to sort that same list[ on the basis of ]
  city or state.


number of sentences 8 number of hits 2
```

Here we see that **diction** scored two hits. It does not like the phrase "on the basis of." Why not? Ask **explain**.

Explain tells you what **diction** doesn't like about the words and phrases it picked out. **Explain** is used after you have collected a list of cast-outs from diction. Then, when you have your usual prompt and you type **explain**, the program asks you for the word or phrase you want analyzed. You give it a phrase that **diction** had bracketed, and **explain** tells you what it doesn't like about the phrase and it suggests better alternatives as shown by the following.

```
% explain
phrase?
on the basis of
use "by, from, because" for "on the basis of"
phrase?
[control-d]
%
```

Another program to help you with your word processing is **style**. **Style** analyzes the readability of text submitted to it. It looks at word length, sentence length, and sentence complexity and assigns a grade level equivalent to the text. It also compiles statistics on several other matters such as relative use-frequency of verb types and of parts of speech. We will not go into the details here, but its use is similar to that of **diction**.

A Quick Peek at *awk*

Suppose you have a file in which the first column is the name of an item, the second column is its price, and the third column is the number sold. You want to add a fourth column giving the money value of the sales, but you don't want to make the calculation yourself. (Why get a computer if you have to do the work yourself?) Can you get UNIX to help? You have a file of names, debts, and last payment dates. You want to create a file containing information about everyone who owes more than $50.00 and hasn't paid in two months. Can UNIX help you? The answer to both questions (surprise!) is yes, providing you know how to use **awk**.

Awk is one of the most interesting of the UNIX utilities, and although we don't have space here to explain it completely, we wanted to give you an idea of what it can do and how it works. In UNIX-speak, **awk** is a "pattern scanning and processing language." By pattern scanning, we mean that **awk** can look through a file for certain patterns. In this, it is like **grep** except that **awk** is both more general (the patterns can be rather sophisticated) and more specific (the patterns can be limited to particular fields within a line). Processing

means that once **awk** finds an appropriate line, it can do something with it, e.g., print it, change it, or sum numbers in it.

One important type of use of **awk** is as a file processor. Given a file consisting of three columns of numbers, for example, **awk** can produce a new file consisting of the original three columns plus a fourth that is the arithmetic product of, say, the first two columns. Indeed, **awk** can do many of the same things that the popular Visicalc program can. **Awk** works with text as well as numbers. For example, a simple **awk** program can scan an address list and print out those people who live on a certain street. (**Grep** could do something similar, but **grep** would be fooled by entries containing people with the same name as the desired street.)

Awk was created by Alfred Aho, Brian Kernighan, and Peter Weinberger of Bell Labs. Some suspect a connection between the name of the utility and the names of the authors, but this is at best an awkward conjecture.

There are two methods of using **awk**. One method is to type something in the form:

```
awk program filename
```

where "program" consists of the instructions and "filename" is the name of the file **awk** is to act upon. The second method is to type:

```
awk -f file filename
```

where "file" is the name of the file containing the program instructions. This second method is, perhaps, a bit more difficult, but is much less likely to produce syntax error messages when you use symbols in the program that also have special meaning to the shell. We will confine our examples to the second method.

A program consists of one or more program lines. A program line consists in general of two parts, a pattern and an action; the action is enclosed in braces. Here's one possible line:

```
/rotate/ { print }
```

The pattern is "rotate" (simple string patterns are enclosed in slashes) and the action is "print." Using this, the **awk** program finds lines containing the string "rotate" and prints them; it is equivalent to using **grep rotate** filename.

Learning to use **awk** consists of learning the many possibilities for defining patterns and learning the possible actions. (Actually, the "print" action is not needed here, for a line that matches a pattern is printed automatically if you omit giving any action. Also, if you give an action without a pattern, that action is performed on all lines.)

We won't go into the many pattern-defining options, but we will let you in on the secret of using fields. Fields are defined as they are for **sort**; that is, fields are strings separated by blanks. Again, as in **sort**, you can choose some other character to be a field separator, but the method of doing so is different. (One way is to use the **-F** option followed immediately—no spaces—by the chosen character.) **Awk** has a labeling system for fields; $1 is the first field, $2 is the second field, and so forth. $0 has a special meaning; it stands for the entire line. These field labels can be used in patterns and actions both. Here are some examples.

Pattern	Meaning
/fish/	Any line containing the string "fish."
$1 ~ /fish/	Any line whose first field contains the string "fish."
$3 ~ /fish/	Any line whose third field contains the string "fish."
$1 !~ /fish/	Any line whose first field does not contain the string "fish."

Action	*Meaning*
`{print $2}`	Print only the second field.
`{print $4, $2}`	Print the contents of the fourth field, then of the second field.
`{print $2, $2+$4}`	Print the second field, then the sum of the second and fourth fields.
`{s=$2+$4;print s}`	Add the second and fourth fields, and print the sum.

Note the use of "∼" and "!" in the patterns. The tilde (∼) means the pattern to the right is contained in the field to the left. The !∼ combination means the pattern to the right is not contained in the field to the left. Also note that the **print** instruction can be used with individual fields and with combinations of fields.

You can do arithmetic in the action parts: + is addition, - is subtraction, * is multiplication, and \ is division. You can include more than one action by separating them by a semicolon, as in the preceding example.

Let's look at a simple example using some of these ideas. Let's take a file called **sales** that contains six columns of information. The first column is the name of an item, the second column is the selling price of the item, and the next four columns are quarterly sales figures for the item. (This is such a simple example that the prices remain constant for a year.) The file looks like this:

```
carts      29.99    45   13   55    22
corks       0.02    30   20   25    93
doors      49.99    40   15   20    25
geese      15.00     2    8    1   128
nighties   50.00    11   23   15    82
```

We would like to add two more columns: total items sold, and total cash sales. We create a file called, say, **addup** that looks like this:

```
{total=$3+$4+$5+$6; print $0, total, total*$2}
```

This action contains two parts separated by a semicolon. The first part sums the sales and cleverly calls the total "total." The second part prints the original line ($0), followed by the total, and, then, the total*$2, which means "total" times the second column.

The command:

```
awk -f addup sales
```

produces this output:

```
carts      29.99    45    13    55    22    135    4048.65
corks       0.02    30    20    25    93    168    3.36
doors      49.99    40    15    20    25    100    4999
geese      15.00     2     8     1   128    139    2085
nighties   50.00    11    23    15    82    131    6550
```

You could save the output in a file called **sumsales** by using redirection:

```
awk -f addup sales > sumsales
```

This introduction just scratches the surface of **awk**. The on-line manual has a concise summary of **awk**, but the Bell Labs publication, *Awk—a pattern scanning and processing language,* by A. V. Aho, B. W. Kernighan, and P. J. Weinberger, is easier to read and is much more informative. It also is much longer.

An Introduction to Shell Scripts

You (yes, you!) can create your own UNIX commands even if you don't know a programming language. Instead of using C or some other language, you can use the standard UNIX commands as building blocks for new commands. The shell makes all this possible.

The shell (whether the Bourne shell, the C shell, or some other version) is a program. Normally, it takes its input from the terminal but, like other UNIX programs, it can also take input from a file. Suppose, for instance, you create a file called **checkup** with the following lines:

```
date
who | wc -l
```

If you are using the **sh** shell (the command name of the Bourne shell), you can type:

```
sh < checkup
```

and the UNIX instructions in the file will be run! To your immense delight, you will learn the time and date and see how many people are on the system. If you are in the C shell, use:

```
csh < checkup
```

If you like, you can use **chmod** to declare **checkup** executable. Then, all you need to do (as long as you are in the same directory) is to type:

```
checkup
```

and it will be interpreted as a command. If you really wish to be classy, you can create a directory just to store such commands. Then add the name of that directory to the list of directories in the "set path" line of your **.login** file. Then, no matter what directory you change to, UNIX will check your command directory for command names.

A file containing UNIX instructions is called a "shell script." The example we gave was pretty simple. For one thing, the **checkup** command doesn't need any input. We can, however, create shell scripts that do accept input. Suppose we have another command called **porky**. (We'll give the specifics of the command soon.) If we type the command **porky** and follow it by a series of words, UNIX, when spotting the following special symbols in a shell script, will then recognize **$0** to be the command name, **$1** to be the first word, **$2** to be the second word, etc. In addition, **$*** represents all the words after (but not including) **$0**. Here is an example you may not have thought of. Suppose the executable **porky** file contains this line:

```
mv $1 $1.$0
```

What will the command:

```
porky pig
```

do, assuming you have a file **pig**? UNIX will substitute **pig** for $1 and **porky** for $0. Thus, the command becomes:

```
mv pig pig.porky
```

You now have a command that will add **.porky** to the name of any file!
Here's another example. The shell script:

```
cat $* | lpr
```

would concatenate a list of files together before sending them to the line printer.

Since this is just an introduction, we won't go beyond this, except that we can't resist mentioning that UNIX has control statements that will let a shell script make logical decisions and set up loops. Those of you who have programming blood have the opportunity to create some rather sophisticated shell scripts.

Shell scripts are another example which shows that UNIX is an open-ended system. You can change things you don't like and add what you do like. No wonder that UNIX's popularity has grown so wildly!

Other Unix Utilities

Here is a partial list of other utilities that come with or can be acquired for UNIX systems. This list is intended to indicate the range of such options rather than to be exhaustive. New extensions will continue to pop up.

sed: **Sed** is a stream editor. The user creates a script of editing commands. **Sed** then acts upon input files, following the script instructions.
lex: **Lex** is a "lexical analyzer generator." It reads files, recognizes patterns, and performs actions. It can be used to generate programs, and it requires a knowledge of the C language.
eqn: This is a preprocessor for **troff**. It lets you set up equations and formulae for typesetting.
ingres: This is a powerful relational data-base management system.
ar: This maintains archives and libraries and combines several files into one for housekeeping efficiency.

Graphics Utilities

A picture is worth 10,000 words! And, until recently, a computer picture would cost about $10,000. However, the price of computer graphics is dropping significantly as more people value its use. *If* you have a graphics terminal connected to UNIX, there are several graphics utilities that might be available to you including the following:

A. **graph** and **plot**—The standard UNIX version 7 graphing commands.
B. **graphics**—A graphics utility added to UNIX System III.
C. **plot2d**—An alternative to the above commands, that was created at UC-Berkeley.
D. **qdp**—Short for "Quick and Dirty Plotter" from Lincoln Labs at MIT.
E. **plot 10**—A standard plotting package from Tektronix.
F. **S**—A sophisticated statistical and graphing package from Bell Labs.
G. Custom packages—Computer companies have produced many graphing utilities for their own use.

Since no single graphing utility is likely to become the standard for UNIX users, we will only give a very brief sample of three of these programs.

Using *graph* and *plot*

Suppose that you have a file called **data4** that contains the following numbers:

```
1   100
2   200
3   300
4   400
```

If you give the command

```
graph < data4 | plot
```

you would see a graph like the one shown in the following drawing.

There are several options available in **graph** that allow you to change the graph size, label axis and points, and so on. The on-line manual gives the details.

Using *plot2d*

Suppose that you have a file called **data6** that contains the following information:

```
1   10   100   1000
2   20   200   2000
3   30   300   3000
4   40   400   4000
5   50   500   5000
```

```
graph -s -h .50 < data4 | /usr/bin/plot
```

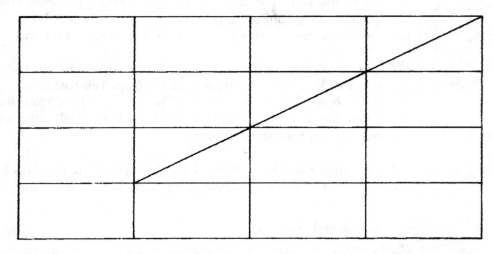

Graph using *greph* and *plot* commands.

If you give the following command:

```
plot2d data6 1 3 1 4
```

the resulting graph would look like the one in the following drawing.

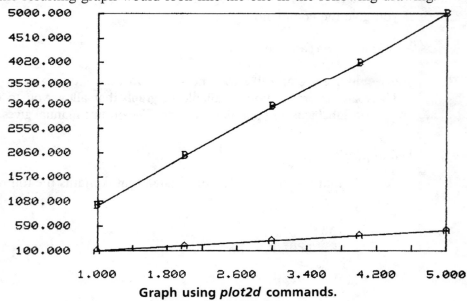

Graph using *plot2d* commands.

plot2d is considerably more versatile than **graph** and **plot**. In this simple example, we plotted column 1 along the X-axis versus column 3 along the Y-axis (shown with label "A"). In addition, we asked for a graph of column 1 versus column 4 on the same screen (shown with label "B"). A 40-page manual titled, *Plot2d User's Guide,* adds a few more options.

The "S" Package

S is an interactive system developed at Bell Labs for handling complex data. The graphics package can generate scatter plots, contour plots, and three-dimensional perspective plots. Some of its extensive graphics capability is shown in the two graphs in the following illustration.

These two graphs show the same data but from different perspectives. The summer months indicate that California is indeed a land of sunshine and opportunity.

Where Do We Go From Here?

If you have read through this book diligently and have mastered UNIX so far, then you have finished the book! Congratulations on your accomplishments and a hearty "thank you" from the authors for your intelligence and understanding.

However, you have not finished learning UNIX. In this book, we have discussed about 40% of UNIX's commands and, maybe, 20% of UNIX's utilities. We have chosen those commands and utilities that should change the least over the next few years. (The major utilities that we have *not* mentioned are those written for the programmer.) In addition, new software is constantly being developed. However, as we mentioned in Chapter 1, UNIX software is designed to work well and to lead a long and useful life. New programs generally will not replace old ones, but will add to them to give you more computing power, without making your past skills obsolete. And, in a similar manner, revisions to this book will be primarily to correct the author's errors (if there are any!) and to add new material, rather than to change the UNIX commands.

If you have any suggestions to make concerning this book, please write to us in care of the publisher.

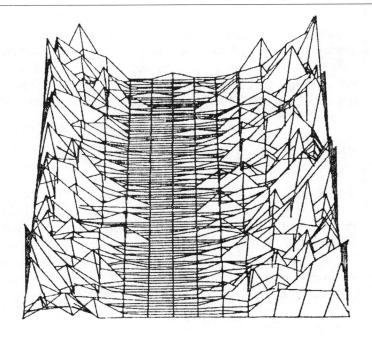

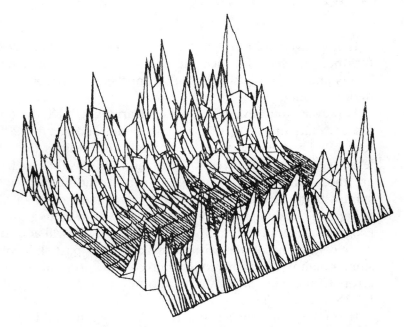

The 100-year rainfall patterns for San Rafael, California.

Review Questions

A. For each *grep* pattern on the left, indicate which pattern(s) following it would be matched.

1. 'to'	**a.** hot	**b.** to	**c.** toad	**d.** stool	**e.** To
2. -w 'to'	**a.** hot	**b.** to	**c.** toad	**d.** stool	**e.** To
3. -iw 'to'	**a.** hot	**b.** to	**c.** toad	**d.** stool	**e.** To
4. 't.n'	**a.** tin	**b.** stun	**c.** nation	**d.** stony	**e.** tnuch
5. 'a[o-t].'	**a.** art	**b.** act	**c.** task	**d.** tort	**e.** at

B. Describe what each of the following *find* commands would do.

1. find ~ -name '*.c' -exec mv { } ~/cdirect \;
2. find . -name '*.c' -size +3 -ok rm { } \;
3. find /usr \(-size +10 -atime +20 \) -o -size +30 -print

C. The questions in this section refer to a file named *maillist* whose contents are as follows:

```
Morgan:Joe::315 Second Street:Riesenstadt:CA:94707
Vegetable:Joe:Fritz:1002 Market Pl.:Riesenstadt:CA:94707
Morgan:Joe::315 Second Street:Redville:OH:40817
Morgan:Joe::315 Second Street:Hot'n'wet:TX:72727
Antibody:Aristotle:Asis:26 Furtz Way:Redville:OH:40822
Zircon:Bilbo:Nagy:1313 Ratgut Blvd.:Hot'n'wet:TX:72702
```

1. What order would each of the following commands produce?
   a. sort -t: +3n -4 +6n maillist
   b. sort -t: +3n -4 +6nr maillist
   c. sort -t: +6.3n maillist
2. Create an instruction that would sort **maillist** by state, and then by city within state, and then by name within city.

Answers:

A. 1. b,c,d; **2.** b; **3.** b,e; **4.** a,b,d; **5.** a,c.
B. 1. Search your home directory recursively for files whose names end in ".c" and move them to the directory ~/**cdirect**.
   2. Search your current working directory recursively for files whose names end in ".c" and have a size in excess of 3 blocks. Then for each found file, ask user if it should be removed.
   3. Search the /**usr** directory recursively for all files that either are bigger than ten blocks and haven't been used in over 20 days or else are bigger than 30 blocks. Print the pathnames of these files.

C. 1.a.

```
Antibody:Aristotle:Asis:26 Furtz Way:Redville:OH:40822
Morgan:Joe::315 Second Street:Redville:OH:40817
Morgan:Joe::315 Second Street:Hot'n'wet:TX:72727
Morgan:Joe::315 Second Street:Riesenstadt:CA:94707
Vegetable:Joe:Fritz:1002 Market Pl.:Riesenstadt:CA:94707
Zircon:Bilbo:Nagy:1313 Ratgut Blvd.:Hot'n'wet:TX:72702
```

C. 1.b.

```
Antibody:Aristotle:Asis:26 Furtz Way:Redville:OH:40822
Morgan:Joe::315 Second Street:Riesenstadt:CA:94707
Morgan:Joe::315 Second Street:Hot'n'wet:TX:72727
Morgan:Joe::315 Second Street:Redville:OH:40817
Vegetable:Joe:Fritz:1002 Market Pl.:Riesenstadt:CA:94707
Zircon:Bilbo:Nagy:1313 Ratgut Blvd.:Hot'n'wet:TX:72702
```

C. 1.c.

```
Zircon:Bilbo:Nagy:1313 Ratgut Blvd.:Hot'n'wet:TX:72702
Morgan:Joe::315 Second Street:Riesenstadt:CA:94707
Vegetable:Joe:Fritz:1002 Market Pl.:Riesenstadt:CA:94707
Morgan:Joe::315 Second Street:Redville:OH:40817
Antibody:Aristotle:Asis:26 Furtz Way:Redville:OH:40822
Morgan:Joe::315 Second Street:Hot'n'wet:TX:72727
```

C. 2.   **sort -t: +5 -6 +4 -5 +0 maillist**

Exercises at the Terminal

Duplicate as many features as you can of those described in the introductory story.

Appendices

List of Appendices

In this section, you will find:

- A Quick Index to Commands
- Bibliography
  - The Bell System Technical Journal
  - UNIX Manuals
  - Other Documentation
- CP/M and UNIX
- ASCII Table
  - Numerical Conversion
  - ASCII Definitions
- Glossary
- A Summary of UNIX Abbreviations
  - Shell Abbreviations for Files and Directories
  - Abbreviations Used by *grep, ed, edit,* and *ex*
  - Abbreviations Used by the C-Shell History Function
- UNIX Command Reference
  - Starting Up
  - Manipulating Files and Directories
  - Communication
  - Housekeeping Utilities
  - On-Line Help
  - Text Processing and Formatting
  - Information Handling
  - Running Jobs and Programs
  - Adjusting Your Environment
  - Graphics
- *ed/vi* Command Reference
  - The *ed* Line Editor—A Quick Summary
  - The *vi* Screen Editor—A Quick Summary
- Entering and Exiting the UNIX Shell

A   A Quick Index to Commands

B   Bibliography

This bibliography is divided into three parts that cover the following items:

1. Selected list of articles from the Bell System Journal.
2. The UNIX Programmer's Manual.
3. Selected articles and books about UNIX.

The Bell System Technical Journal

One issue of the Bell Journal (Vol. 57, No. 6, Part 2) has become a UNIX classic. Published in July–August 1978, it contains several articles by the principal founders of UNIX. All of the articles are written at a technical level.

Here is a partial selection from the Contents page.

1. The UNIX Time-Sharing System by D. M. Ritchie and K. Thompson.
2. UNIX Implementation by K. Thompson.
3. A Retrospective by D. M. Ritchie.
4. The UNIX Shell by S. R. Bourne.
5. The C Programming Language by D. M. Ritchie, S. C. Johnson, M. E. Lesk, and B. W. Kernighan.
6. Document Preparation by B. W. Kernighan, M. E. Lesk, and J. F. Ossanna, Jr.
7. The Programmer's Workbench by T. A. Dolotta, R. C. Haight, and J. R. Mashey.
8. The UNIX Operating System as a Base for Applications by G. W. R. Luderer, J. F. Maranzano, and B. A. Tague.

UNIX Manuals

As with UNIX systems, the UNIX manuals may vary from system to system. The manuals are organized in two parts, with Volume 1 being of most interest to the new user. Volume 1 of the manual contains a complete, terse description of all UNIX commands. It is the same document as the on-line manual described in Chapter 3. Volume 2 of the manual may vary and we have described one common version here.

Volume 1

Volume 1 of the UNIX Programmer's Manual contains a list of all available UNIX commands. Volume 1 is divided into eight sections as follows:

1. Common commands: ~ 200 commands.
2. System calls: ~ 50 commands.
3. Subroutines: ~ 60 commands.
4. Special files: ~ 25 commands.
5. File format and conventions: ~ 25 commands.
6. Games: ~ 25 commands.
7. Macro packages and language conventions: ~ 10 commands.
8. Maintenance commands and procedures: ~ 40 commands.

About 60 of these commands from section 1 are presented in this book.

Volume 2

This volume is divided into three parts. Parts A and B of this volume contain thirty-eight articles (in this example) that supplement Volume 1. The articles are grouped into six areas as follows:

1. General works—This is two articles that summarize UNIX in general and UNIX version 7 specifically.
2. Getting started—These five articles introduce the newcomer to the UNIX shell, to editing, and to "learn." These articles supplement the material in UNIX Primer Plus.
3. Document Preparation—Six articles describe document preparation, including the utilities, NROFF, TROFF, MS, TBL, and EQN.
4. Programming—These five articles focus on the C language and the program support tools.
5. Supporting tools and languages—This contains ten articles describing a variety of UNIX tools, including AWK and SED, as mentioned in Chapter 12.
6. Implementation and maintenance—This has ten articles on how to set up a UNIX system.

Part C contains several articles describing UC Berkeley's enhancements to UNIX. The most important articles for the newcomer include:

1. "An Introduction to the C shell," by William Joy.
2. "An Introduction to Display Editing with Vi (Revised)," by William Joy and Mark Horton.
3. "A Tutorial Introduction To Ex and Vi," by Bill Tuthill.
4. "Mail Reference Manual," by Kurt Shoens.

Other Documentation

Additional articles are constantly being added to the UNIX library. Furthermore, computer manufacturers using the UNIX system and UNIX look-alikes often supply more information.

Selected articles and books about UNIX.

Chace, Susan, "AT&T's UNIX, a Computer's Traffic Cop, Starts Selling Fast, May Enhance Bell's Role," *Wall Street Journal,* November 8, 1982.

Cherlin, E., "The UNIX Operating System: Portability a Plus," *Mini-Micro Systems*, April 1981.

Johnson, R. Colin, "Major Firms Join The UNIX Parade," *Electronics*, April 1981.

Johnson, R. Colin, "A Short History of UNIX," *Electronics,* March 1981.

Kernighan, Brian W. and Morgan, Samual P., "The UNIX Operating System: A Model for Software Design," *Science*, February 12, 1982.

Kernighan, Brian W. and Plauger, P.J., "Software Tools," Addision-Wesley, 1976.

Kernighan, Brian W. and Ritchie, Dennis M., "The C Programming Language," Prentice-Hall, 1978.

Nowitz, D.A. and Lesk, M.E., "Implementation of a UNIX Network," *Comput Commun*, February 1982.

Rosenblatt, Alfred, "1982 Award For Achievement," (Dennis Ritchie and Ken Thompson for Creating UNIX and C), *Electronics,* October 1982.

C   CP/M and UNIX

Someone who knows both UNIX and CP/M might object to comparing them since it is like comparing a Mercedes and a Vespa. UNIX generally runs on 16-bit or larger CPUs while CP/M runs on 8-bit CPUs. Also, UNIX is a multiuser, time-sharing system, while CP/M is primarily a single-user, single-task operating system. Finally, a UNIX computer system costs considerably more than a CP/M system, although the gap is narrowing.

So why bother to compare them?

The reason we discuss CP/M is that more people have used CP/M than any other operating system in the world. Over 1/2-million CP/M systems are being used today. It is the de facto standard operating system for 8-bit CPUs, and it has spawned an enormous amount of software development.

Since UNIX is emerging as a strong candidate as the most popular 16-bit operating system, new computer users and potential microcomputer buyers alike might like a brief overview summarizing the features of these two popular operating systems.

Comparing UNIX and CP/M

	UNIX	CP/M
I. Standard version available?	No; there are several versions and look-a-likes. However, Bell Labs Version 7, Bell Labs System III, and UC Berkeley distributions do set some standards.	Yes; Version 3.0 is the latest version.

UNIX will have more versions and more look-a-likes since it is more adaptable. Two systems that run standard UNIX are *Xenix* and *Onyx.* Unix look-alikes include *Coherent, Zeus, Idris, Cromix* and *Isis.* Many more such operating systems will be emerging in the near future.

CP/M-86 is an almost identical version of CP/M-80, but is written for 16-bit CPUs.

MP/M-86 is a multiuser version of CP/M.

Other 16-bit operating systems include MP/M-86, MP/MII, MS/DOS, MSP, UCSD Pascal P System, Oasis, etc.

This table compares the Berkeley version of UNIX with CP/M-80.

II. Primary Description.	Multiuser Multitasking Interactive	Single-user Single-task Interactive

The multiuser, multitasking features versus single-user, single-task operating system is the major descriptive difference between these two operating systems.

The hardware for a UNIX system can be purchased to support from one to more than 60 users simultaneously. Of course, depending on the number of users, there will be a tremendous difference in hardware costs.

III. Typical minimum configuration and estimated cost.	16-bit CPU
	128K–256K RAM
	800K floppy disk
	   10M hard disk single-user system costs $8,000 and up.
	   40M hard disk, small, multiple-user system costs $12,000 and up.
		8-bit CPU
		32K-64K RAM
		800K floppy disk
		   Single-user system costs $4,000 and up.

Comparing costs between dissimilar systems is very tricky at best. These cost figures should not be used for serious planning. They are only meant to be a very rough guide.

However, we should point out that UNIX comes with considerable software as part of the system, whereas, CP/M requires the purchase of most of its software.

IV. User interface.	Command line interpreter called the "Shell."	Console Command Processor called the "CCP."
1. Number of commands.	About 200.	16, counting utility programs.
2. Use of "wildcards."	Yes.	Yes.
3. Flexibility.	Shell is replaceable or can be customized.	CCP replaced with much difficulty.
4. Redirectable I/O.	Yes.	Not simple.
5. Command linking.	Yes with Pipes.	No.
6. Command language.	Yes, language includes control flow and variable usage.	No.

The biggest difference between CP/M and UNIX from the user's point of view would be the interface or link between the computer and the user.

The UNIX shell, with all of the features shown above, is one of the most versatile, flexible, and powerful command line interpreters available anywhere. Its extensive tools, including electronic mail and networking, bring together in one package all of the services that were listed and discussed under Electronic Office and Programming Support in Chapter 1.

Probably one-half of these shell "commands" could be purchased for a CP/M system as separate software packages. However, they would still not have the shell capabilities listed as Items 4, 5, and 6, above.

However, new variations of CP/M, such as MPM-86 or MP/NET-86, that are written for 16-bit CPUs, are incorporating some features similar to the UNIX shell, such as pipes and redirectable input/output.

V. File system.		
1. Structure.	Hierarchical or tree-structure with unlimited levels.	Dual level, as described below.
2. User file types.	Ordinary files and directories.	Yes, see below.
3. File name syntax requirement.	None; all files are treated equally.	Yes, see below.
4. File linking.	Yes.	Not easily.

The UNIX file system allows a more extensive organization of files than does CP/M. UNIX lets you create subdirectories to any level you wish. This was illustrated with several drawings in Chapter 4.

The CP/M file system essentially has two levels. The first level is called the user area, which provides a way to categorize files. The files themselves become the second level. However, in CP/M, the user area does not have the feature of a directory system; whereby, directories contain the _names_ of files.

The syntax used for naming files is slightly simpler on UNIX than CP/M. In UNIX, the file name for storing information can be whatever you want and 14 characters long. In CP/M, filenames are limited to 11 characters (including 3 for filetype) and should include a "file type" designator. For example, if you are drafting a letter to send to your state senator, you might call it "senletter" in UNIX or "seletter.txt" in CP/M. The .txt indicates that this is an editor file.

Both file systems require special syntax for files containing programs. CP/M uses the extension .COM after all programs that run, while UNIX use a .f after Fortran program file names, and a .p after Pascal program file names, and so on for other languages.

VI. Input/Output device compatibility.	Files contain device drivers to handle all I/O peripherals. If files are available, I/O add-on is easy.	BIOS (Basic Input/Output System) must be modified by user for each interface device. This is complex for CP/M.

Since UNIX is a multiuser system, large UNIX systems might have several different kinds of terminals, three or four printers, various disks drives, magnetic tape drives and plotters connected to the CPU. UNIX solves a potential large-scale incompatibility problem by using software or programs stored in "special" files for each "brand" of I/O device. These files already have been written for most common peripheral devices, so adding new I/O devices is easy.

CP/M requires modification of its BIOS. Generally, I/O manufacturers try to make their equipment compatible with CP/M installations.

UNIX's use of files to handle I/O has a valuable side benefit. Both the input to the CPU and the output from the CPU can be directed to any I/O device, printer, tape, disk, terminal, etc., or to a file, with just one or two keystrokes.

VII. Editing Facilities	Line-oriented editor called "ed." For some UNIX versions, a screen editor "vi" is available. Other screen editors, such as EMACS, are also available.	Line-oriented editor called "ED." WordStar, Electric Pencil, Select, etc., can be purchased.

Also, see the next section describing Word Processing Add-ons.

Generally speaking, most people prefer a screen editor over a line editor. The screen editor lets you move around and make changes anywhere you want on a screen filled with words or numbers. The line editor primarily restricts your activities to one or more lines at a time.

VIII. Word-processing add-on tools and utilities.	Yes; generally considered part of UNIX. Includes Formatters, Table Processor, Math Expressions, Spelling Check, Pattern Scanning	Extensive word-processing tools, including Indexers, Spellers, Grammar Checkers, Thesaurus, Word Counters, etc., can be purchased separately.

UNIX probably has one of the most powerful word-processing capabilities available for a general-purpose computer system. Any document, including scientific publications with specialized formatting requirements, such as tables, mathematical formulas, etc., can be prepared for typesetting using UNIX programs.

Similarly, the numerous word-processing packages mentioned above can give CP/M systems equal quality and much sophistication.

IX. Data base software.	Simple data base software is available in Shell commands. Some sophisticated software, like INGRES is available, but not easy to use.	Extensive software available, including dBaseII, Visicalc, Supercalc, Multiplan, Context MBA, etc.; just to mention a few.
X. Languages.	C, Fortran 77, BASIC, Pascal, APL, SNOBOL, Logo, and others.	BASIC, Fortran IV, Pascal, Pilot, and many others.

When you get a UNIX system, you get C and usually two or three other languages, such as BASIC, Pascal, FORTRAN, or COBOL.

However, you can purchase most common languages to add to either system.

XI. Other application software.	Limited at present, especially in business applications.	The most extensive software selection in the world can be purchased.

CP/M software selection is head and shoulders above any other system.

However, much CP/M software, such as Wordstar, is being rewritten in the C language and will be available for UNIX systems. And, in the next few years, we should see software translators available that will take CP/M software and rewrite it in the C language (or vice versa).

The trend in application software today is clearly towards what is called "menu-driven" programs. These types of programs provide the user with a selection of choices rather than requiring that specific commands be remembered. These menus, like the waiter's questions, "What kind of soup?", "What kind of salad dressing?", etc., are now available for almost every type of application program used, from word processing to accounting, especially for CP/M systems. The Berkeley version of the UNIX shell can easily be programmed using the "alias" command to provide simple menu-type programs.

To sum up, CP/M and UNIX were created in the early 1970s and have evolved to the point where they provide significant service to their users. They both present proven performance in their respective areas, primarily in the single-user and multiuser arenas.

However, another very clear trend for the near future is networking. Since UNIX is already a multiuser system, it can be relatively easily adapted to provide local area networking capabilities.

As we mentioned in Chapter 1, this ability of UNIX to adapt and the ability of UNIX to provide all of the Electronic Office features in one operating system guarantees that UNIX will be a favorite system for many users for a long time to come.

D   ASCII Table

Numerical Conversion

DECIMAL-HEXADECIMAL-OCTAL-BINARY-ASCII
NUMERICAL CONVERSION

DEC X_{10}	HEX X_{16}	OCT X_8	Binary $P\ X_2$	ASCII	Key*
0	00	00	0 000 0000	NUL	CTRL/1
1	01	01	1 000 0001	SOH	CTRL/A
2	02	02	1 000 0010	STX	CTRL/B
3	03	03	0 000 0011	ETX	CTRL/C
4	04	04	1 000 0100	EOT	CTRL/D
5	05	05	0 000 0101	ENQ	CTRL/E
6	06	06	0 000 0110	ACK	CTRL/F
7	07	07	1 000 0111	BEL	CTRL/G
8	08	10	1 000 1000	BS	CTRL/H, BACKSPACE
9	09	11	0 000 1001	HT	CTRL/I, TAB
10	0A	12	0 000 1010	LF	CTRL/J, LINE FEED
11	0B	13	1 000 1011	VT	CTRL/K
12	0C	14	0 000 1100	FF	CTRL/L
13	0D	15	1 000 1101	CR	CTRL/M, RETURN
14	0E	16	1 000 1110	SO	CTRL/N
15	0F	17	0 000 1111	SI	CTRL/O
16	10	20	1 001 0000	DLE	CTRL/P
17	11	21	0 001 0001	DC1	CTRL/Q
18	12	22	0 001 0010	DC2	CTRL/R
19	13	23	1 001 0011	DC3	CTRL/S
20	14	24	0 001 0100	DC4	CTRL/T
21	15	25	1 001 0101	NAK	CTRL/U
22	16	26	1 001 0110	SYN	CTRL/V
23	17	27	0 001 0111	ETB	CTRL/W
24	18	30	0 001 1000	CAN	CTRL/X
25	19	31	1 001 1001	EM	CTRL/Y
26	1A	32	1 001 1010	SUB	CTRL/Z
27	1B	33	0 001 1011	ESC	ESC, ESCAPE
28	1C	34	1 001 1100	FS	CTRL <
29	1D	35	0 001 1101	GS	CTRL/
30	1E	36	0 001 1110	RS	CTRL/ =
31	1F	37	1 001 1111	US	CTRL/-

DEC X_{10}	HEX X_{16}	OCT X_8	Binary P X_2	ASCII	Key*
32	20	40	1 010 0000	SP	SPACEBAR
33	21	41	0 010 0001	!	!
34	22	42	0 010 0010	"	"
35	23	43	1 010 0011	#	#
36	24	44	0 010 0100	$	$
37	25	45	1 010 0101	½	½
38	26	46	1 010 0110	&	&
39	27	47	0 010 0111	'	'
40	28	50	0 010 1000	(	(
41	29	51	1 010 1001	)	)
42	2A	52	1 010 1010	*	*
43	2B	53	0 010 1011	+	+
44	2C	54	1 010 1100	,	,
45	2D	55	0 010 1101	-	-
46	2E	56	0 010 1110	.	.
47	2F	57	1 010 1111	/	/
48	30	60	0 011 0000	0	0
49	31	61	1 011 0001	1	1
50	32	62	1 011 0010	2	2
51	33	63	0 011 0011	3	3
52	34	64	1 011 0100	4	4
53	35	65	0 011 0101	5	5
54	36	66	0 011 0110	6	6
55	37	67	1 011 0111	7	7
56	38	70	1 011 1000	8	8
57	39	71	0 011 1001	9	9
58	3A	72	0 011 1010	:	:
59	3B	73	1 011 1011	;	;
60	3C	74	0 011 1100	<	<
61	3D	75	1 011 1101	=	=
62	3E	76	1 011 1110	>	>
63	3F	77	0 011 1111	?	?
64	40	100	1 100 0000	@	@
65	41	101	0 100 0001	A	A
66	42	102	0 100 0010	B	B
67	43	103	1 100 0011	C	C
68	44	104	0 100 0100	D	D
69	45	105	1 100 0101	E	E
70	46	106	1 100 0110	F	F
71	47	107	0 100 0111	G	G

DEC X_{10}	HEX X_{16}	OCT X_8	Binary P X_2	ASCII	Key*
72	48	110	0 100 1000	H	H
73	49	111	1 100 1001	I	I
74	4A	112	1 100 1010	J	J
75	4B	113	0 100 1011	K	K
76	4C	114	1 100 1100	L	L
77	4D	115	0 100 1101	M	M
78	4E	116	0 100 1110	N	N
79	4F	117	1 100 1111	O	O
80	50	120	0 101 0000	P	P
81	51	121	1 101 0001	Q	Q
82	52	122	1 101 0010	R	R
83	53	123	0 101 0011	S	S
84	54	124	1 101 0100	T	T
85	55	125	0 101 0101	U	U
86	56	126	0 101 0110	V	V
87	57	127	1 101 0111	W	W
88	58	130	1 101 1000	X	X
89	59	131	0 101 1001	Y	Y
90	5A	132	0 101 1010	Z	Z
91	5B	133	1 101 1011	[	[
92	5C	134	0 101 1100	/	/
93	5D	135	1 101 1101	]	]
94	5E	136	1 101 1110	$\wedge$	$\wedge$
95	5F	137	0 101 1111	—	—
96	60	140	0 110 0000	`	`
97	61	141	1 110 0001	a	a
98	62	142	1 110 0010	b	b
99	63	143	0 110 0011	c	c
100	64	144	1 110 0100	d	d
101	65	145	0 110 0101	e	e
102	66	146	0 110 0110	f	f
103	67	147	1 110 0111	g	g
104	68	150	1 110 1000	h	h
105	69	151	0 110 1001	i	i
106	6A	152	0 110 1010	j	j
107	6B	153	1 110 1011	k	k
108	6C	154	0 110 1100	l	l
109	6D	155	1 110 1101	m	m
110	6E	156	1 110 1110	n	n
111	6F	157	0 110 1111	o	o

DEC X_{10}	HEX X_{16}	OCT X_8	Binary P X_2	ASCII	Key*
112	70	160	1 111 0000	p	p
113	71	161	0 111 0001	q	q
114	72	162	0 111 0010	r	r
115	73	163	1 111 0011	s	s
116	74	164	0 111 0100	t	t
117	75	165	1 111 0101	u	u
118	76	166	1 111 0110	v	v
119	77	167	0 111 0111	w	w
120	78	170	0 111 1000	x	x
121	79	171	1 111 1001	y	y
122	7A	172	1 111 1010	z	z
123	7B	173	0 111 1011	R	R
124	7C	174	1 111 1100	/	/
125	7D	175	0 111 1101	T	T
126	7E	176	0 111 1110	~	~
127	7F	177	1 111 1111	DEL	DEL, RUBOUT

P = Parity bit; "1" for odd number of 1's, "0" for even number of 1's.

*Those key sequences consisting of "CTRL/ " are typed in by simultaneously pressing the CTRL key and the key indicated. These sequences are based on those defined for the Diablo 1640 keyboard. These key sequences may be defined differently on other keyboards.

ASCII Definitions

ACK (Acknowledgment)—Used as a general "yes" answer to various queries, but it also sometimes indicates "I received your last transmission and I'm ready for your next."

ASCII—American Standard Code for Information Interchange.

BEL (Bell)—Activates a bell, beeper, or other audible alarm.

BS (Backspace)—Moves the carriage, print head, or cursor back one space or position.

CAN (Cancel)—Indicates that the material in the previous transmission is to be disregarded. The amount of material is decided by the user.

CR (Carriage Return, or Return)—Moves carriage, print head, or cursor back to beginning of line. On most terminals, the RETURN key causes both a CR and an FF (Form Feed).

DC1–DC4 (Device Controls)—These are used to control the user's terminal or similar devices. There are no standard functions assigned, except that DC4 frequently means "stop." The CCITT suggests a number of possible assignments; in general, they prefer using the first two controls for "on," and the last two for "off," and DC2 and DC4 to refer to the more important device. In some systems, these codes are labeled XON, TAPE, XOFF, and $\overline{\text{TAPE}}$, respectively. X means "transmitter," and TAPE and $\overline{\text{TAPE}}$ means "tape on" and "tape off." These labels are found on the keytops of some terminals.

DEL (Delete)—Used to delete a character. It is called RUBOUT on some terminals. It is not strictly a control character since it is not grouped with the other ASCII control characters. The DEL function has a binary all-ones bit pattern ($1111\ 1111_2$), and the reason for this is historic: the only way to erase a bit pattern punched into paper tape was to punch out all the holes so that the resulting pattern was equivalent to a null. ASCII still considers DEL equivalent to a null, although many operating systems use it to erase the preceding character.

DLE (Data Link Escape)—This control function uses a special type of escape sequence specifically used for controlling the data line and transmission facilities.

EM (End of Medium)—This is used to indicate the end of paper tape (or other storage medium) or that this is the end of the material on the medium.

ENQ (Enquiry)—This is usually used for requesting identification or status information. In some systems, this code is called WRU—"Who are you?"

EOT (End of Transmission)—Code used to mark end of transmission after one or more messages.

ESC (Escape)—This code marks the beginning of an escape sequence. An escape sequence consists of a series of codes which, as a group, have a special meaning, usually a control function. On some terminals, ESC is called ALT MODE.

ETB (End of Transmission Block)—This code is used when it is desired to break up a long message into blocks. ETB is used to mark block boundaries. The blocks usually have nothing to do with the format of the message being transmitted.

ETX (End of Text)—This code is used to mark the end of a text. See SOH. This code was originally called EOM, "End Of Message," and may be labeled as such on some terminals.

FF (Form Feed)—Advance to the top of next page.

FS, GS, RS, US (File, Group, Record and Unit Separator)—These are a set of codes that are used as "information separators" for delimiting portions of information. There is no standard usage, except that FS is expected to refer to the largest division, and US to the smallest.

HT (Horizontal Tab)—Used to tab carriage, print wheel, or cursor to the next predetermined stop on the same line. It is usually up to the user to decide where the horizontal tab stops are to be positioned.

LF (Line Feed)—This code moves the carriage, print head, or cursor down one line. Most systems combine CR (carriage return) with LF, and a new line is then called new line (NL).

NAK (Negative Acknowledgment)—Used to indicate "no" in answer to various queries. It is sometimes defined as "I received your last transmission, but it had errors and I'm awaiting a retransmission."

NUL (Null)—This code is used mainly as a space filler. See also SYN.

SI (Shift In)—Used after an SO code to indicate that codes revert to normal ASCII meaning.

SO (Shift Out)—Indicates that bit patterns to follow will have meanings outside the standard ASCII set and will continue to do so until SI is entered.

SOH (Start Of Heading)—This code is used to mark the beginning of a heading, when headings are used in messages along with text. Headings usually state the name and location of an addressee. This code was originally called SOM, "Start Of Message."

STX (Start of Text)—Used as a marker for beginning of text and end of heading (if used). Was originally called EOA, "End Of Address."

SUB (Substitute)—Indicates a character that is to be used to take the place of a character known to be wrong.

SYN (Synchronous Idle)—Some high-speed data communications systems use synchronized clocks at the transmitter and receiver ends. During idle periods, when there are no bit patterns to enable the receiver's clock to track the transmitter's, the receiver may drift out of sync. Every transmission following an idle period is therefore replaced by three or four SYN characters. The SYN code has a bit pattern that enables the receiver not only to lock onto the transmitter's clock, but also to determine the beginning and end points of each character. SYN characters may also be used to fill short idle periods to maintain synchronization, hence the name.

VT (Vertical Tab)—Used to tab the carriage, print head, or cursor to the next predetermined stop (usually a line).

E   Glossary

alias—A user-supplied name interpreted by the system to represent a command or program or some combination thereof.

aliasing—The process of creating an alias.

argument—An item of information following a command. It may, for example, modify the command or identify a file to be affected.

assembly language—A mnemonic code representing the basic instructions understood by a particular computer.

background—Running of system so that the terminal is left free for other uses.

backup—A file copy set aside as insurance in case something happens to the original.

baud rate—The rate at which information is transmitted between devices; for example, between a terminal and the computer. One baud is one unit of information (a bit) per second. A hundred baud is about 9 characters a second or 110 words a minute.

Berkeley Software Distribution—UNIX versions developed at the University of California, Berkeley. They bear names such as BSD 2.7 and BSD 4.2.

bit—The smallest unit of information or memory for a computer. A bit can have the value "0" or the value "1," and it forms the basis of the binary coding used internally by computers.

block—A standard chunk of memory used as a unit by the computer; a block typically consists of 512 bytes.

Bourne Shell—The UNIX shell used by the standard Bell Labs UNIX, Version 7.

BSD—Berkeley Software Distribution.

buffer—A temporary work area or storage area set up within the system memory. Buffers are often used by programs, such as editors, that access and alter text or data frequently.

bug—A design error in the hardware or software of a computer system.

byte—A unit of information or memory consisting of eight bits. A byte of memory will hold one character.

call—To summon a program into action.

change mode—To alter a set of parameters that describe a file, telling who can use it and how it can be used. The **chmod** command is used to do this.

character—A letter, numeral, punctuation mark, control character, blank, or other such symbol.

character string—A series of characters; for example, "gofats" and "hot&#$&23".

chip—A small chunk of silicon bearing the equivalent of a large number of electrical components; an integrated circuit.

clobber—To wipe out a file.

command—An instruction to the computer. A command typically is a character string that is typed in at a keyboard and is interpreted by the computer as a demand for a particular action.

command interpreter—A program that accepts commands from the keyboard and causes the commands to be executed. The shell is the UNIX command interpreter.

command line—A line consisting of one or more commands, each followed by its arguments, if any.

compiler—A master program that converts a high-level computer language (such as FORTRAN) into machine language.

concatenate—To string together two or more sequences, such as files, into one longer sequence. The **cat** command, for example, concatenates files.

control characters—Characters that are typed by pressing a key down while the [control] key is depressed. For instance, a [control–h] is typed by pressing the [h] key while the [control] key is depressed.

CPU—Abbreviation for Central Processing Unit. This is the part of the computer in which calculations and manipulations take place.

C Shell—The standard shell provided with Berkeley Standard versions of UNIX.

cursor—A marker on the screen, which is usually a rectangle of light or an underline mark.

directory—A file containing a list of associated files and subdirectories.

directory pathname—The complete name by which the directory is known; the pathname gives the sequence of directories by which the directory is linked to the root directory.

echo—To repeat a stream of characters. For example, the commands you type to the computer are echoed on the screen.

editor—A program to assist you in writing material to be stored in files. Editors allow you to modify existing files and create new ones.

EOF—Abbreviation for End of File. Files are terminated with a particular "end of file" character, usually a [control–d], that tells the system it has reached the end of the file.

escape—To divest a special character of its special meaning by preceding it with a backslash character. For example, the UNIX shell interprets a **?** to represent any single character, but a \? (an "escaped" question mark) is interpreted to be just a question-mark character.

event–A previous line of input from the terminal; usually either a command line or an attempted command line. The **history** function maintains a numbered list of the last several events that you have entered.

event identifier–A shorthand code used by you to identify earlier events on the history list.

execute–To run a command or program. (Not to be confused with "kill.")

field–A subsection of a line. Programs such as **sort** and **awk** can look at individual fields within a line.

field separator–The character used to separate one field from the next; a string of one or more spaces is the usual field separator.

file–A sequence of bytes constituting a unit of text, data, or program. A file can be stored in the system memory or on an external medium such as tape or disk.

filename expansion–The process by which UNIX matches filenames with metacharacters to actual file names; for example, matching **?oo?** to **foot** and **loop.**

filling–Adjusting the line lengths in text so that all lines have about the same length.

flag–An argument to a command indicating a particular option or modification. UNIX flags usually are indicated by a leading hyphen.

foreground–Running under direct control of the terminal; the terminal cannot be used for anything else until a foreground job finishes or is halted.

formatting–Arranging text or data into a suitable visual form.

global–Having extended or general scope. For example, a global substitution of one word for another in a file affects all occurrences of the word.

hardware–The mechanical and electrical components of a computer system.

history–A UNIX facility that maintains a numbered list of previous commands and provides a shorthand notation letting you repeat or modify previous commands.

home directory–The directory assigned to you by the system manager; usually the same as your login directory. Additional directories that you create would stem from your home directory.

housekeeping–Keeping track of what files are where, of who is doing what, and the like.

INGRES–A UNIX-based relational data management system.

input–Information fed to a command, a program, a terminal, a person, etc.

interactive–Allowing the computer and the user to carry on a dialogue.

interpreter–A master program that translates a high-level computer language (such as BASIC) into machine language, a line at a time. Interactive languages use interpreters instead of compilers.

interrupt—To break off a command or other process and, thus, terminating it; a signal that accomplishes this.

job number—An identification number assigned to a job by the C Shell. Unlike the process ID, this number is local to the terminal.

kill—To terminate a process before it reaches its natural conclusion.

learn—A computer-aided instruction program provided with UNIX.

line editor—An editor that works on a line as the basic unit. In general, the user identifies the line she wants changed and, then, indicates the change desired.

link—An entry in a directory file that links a user-assigned name for a file to the systems identification number for that file; a name you give to a file.

loading—Putting the machine-language instructions of a program into memory.

local—Having limited scope; the opposite of global.

login—The process of gaining access to the computer system to begin a session.

login directory—The directory you are placed in when you login; usually your home directory.

login name—The name by which the computer system knows you.

logout—The process of signing off the system.

machine-collating sequence—An extended alphabetical sequence that encompasses uppercase letters, lowercase letters, numerals, punctuation marks, and the various other characters recognized by the system.

machine language—The basic set of instructions understood by a given computer. These instructions are represented internally by means of a binary code.

macro—A compound instruction put together from simpler instructions.

mail—A computer system facility that allows the sending and holding of messages via the computer.

map—To assign a new interpretation to a terminal key. For example, in **vi**, one can map, say, the [@] key to represent the sequence [o] [esc] [j].

metacharacter—A character having a special meaning to UNIX. For example, the UNIX shell interprets the **?** character to stand for any single character.

microprocessor—The essential electronics of a computer miniaturized to a single chip.

modem—Short for MOdulator-DEModulator; a device for connecting a terminal or printer to a computer via a telephone line.

multitasking—Allowing more than one user to access the same program at the same time.

multiuser—Permitting more than one user to use the system at the same time.

network—The linking up of several computers.

null character—An invisible character whose internal code is 0 and which occupies no space if printed; not to be confused with a blank, which is invisible but occupies a space.

object file—A file containing machine-language code.

on-line—Connected to the system and in operation.

operating system—A master program that handles the varied tasks involved in running a computer system, including the user-computer interface.

option—A variation on or modification to a command, usually requested by use of a flag.

optional argument—An argument accepted but not required by a command.

output—Information produced by a command, program, etc., and sent elsewhere; for example, to the terminal, to a file, or to a line printer.

overwrite—To write on an existing file, eliminating what previously was there.

owner—The person who created a file.

page—To advance text on the screen by one screenful (or page) at a time.

password—A secret word, chosen by you, with which you reassure the computer system that you are who you claim to be.

pathname—A name for a file or directory specifying the location of the file or directory in the directory system.

peripheral input-output—Input and output devices attached to a computer; e.g., terminals, printers, and tape drives.

permission—The yes-or-no specification of what can be done to a file. A file has read permission, write permission, and execute permission.

pipe—To make the output of one command or program into the input of another. Also, the UNIX operator (|) that accomplishes this.

pipeline—The program linkage established by performing one or more pipes.

process—A particular computer activity or job.

process ID—A unique, system-wide, identification number assigned to a process.

process status—The current state of the process: running, stopped, waiting, etc.

program—A sequence of instructions telling a computer how to perform a task. A program can be in machine language or it can be in a higher-level language that is then translated into machine language.

prompt—A character or character string sent from a computer system to a terminal to indicate to the user that the system is ready to accept input. Typical prompts are $ and %.

protection—Safeguarding a file from accidental erasure or from the unwanted inspection of others. Protection can be accomplished, for example, by using **chmod** to deny others the right to read a file.

recursive—In reference to a directory system, the application to a directory, to all its offshoots, to all their offshoots, etc. In reference to a computer program, the describing of a program that calls itself.

redirection—The channeling of output to a file or device instead of to the standard output; the channeling of input from a file or device instead of from the standard input.

regular expression—A pattern representing a class of character strings. **Grep,** for example, recognizes the regular expression **h.t** to mean any three-character string beginning with **h** and ending with **t.**

root directory—The base directory from which all other directories stem, directly or indirectly.

scope—The range over which an action or definition applies.

scroll—To shift text up or down one or more lines on the screen.

search and replace—In editing, an operation that finds one or more occurrences of a word or pattern and replaces it with another.

shell—A UNIX program that handles the interaction between user and system.

shell script—A file containing a sequence of shell commands. It can be used as input to the shell or be declared an executable file.

smart terminal—A terminal possessing some computing power of its own.

software—The programs used on a computing system.

special character—A character with special meaning beyond its literal one; a metacharacter.

standard input—Short for standard input device. The device from which a program or system normally takes its input; usually a terminal.

standard output—Short for standard output device. The device to which a program or system normally sends its output; usually a terminal.

stopped job—A job that has been halted temporarily by the user and which can be resumed at his command.

string—A sequence of characters.

subdirectory—A directory branching off from another directory.

time sharing—The allocation of computer resources among several users.

tools—Compact, well-designed programs designed to do a specific task well. Several tools can be linked together to perform more complex tasks.

user—A person using the computer system.

visual editor—An editor that shows a screenful of text at a time and allows the user to move a cursor to any part of the screen and effect changes there.

wild-card—A metacharacter used to represent a range of ordinary characters. Examples include the shell's use of * and ?.

word processing—The use of editors and other computer programs to prepare, alter, check, and format text.

working directory—The directory in which your commands take place, given that no other directory is specified.

write—1. To place text in a file. 2. To use the **write** command to communicate with other users.

F   A Summary of UNIX Abbreviations

Shell Abbreviations for Files and Directories

The following three abbreviations can be used in representing the names of files and directories.

?	Represents (or "matches") any single character.
*	Matches any number of characters (including none)
[ ]	Matches any *one* character from the list included between the brackets; a hyphen (-) can be used to indicate a range.

Examples:

Abbreviation	Some matches	No match
l?t	lit lot lst	lt lout
l*t	lot lout latent lt	lots allot
l[aou]t	lat lot	lout
l[3-6]	l3 l5	l2 l33
l[3-5][7-9]?	l38q l472	l27n l38

The following three symbolisms can be used in identifying directories.

.	Your current working directory.
..	Parent directory to your current working directory.
~	Your home directory; if followed by a login name, the home directory of that person. {BSD}

Examples:

Abbreviation	Meaning
cp ~boozy/recipe .	Copy the file **recipe** from **boozy**'s home directory into your current working directory.
cd ..	Change directories to the parent directory of your current working directory.
cp hormones ~	Copy the file **hormones** into your home directory.

Abbreviations Used by *grep*, *ed*, *edit*, and *ex*

These abbreviations are used in search patterns.

	Matches any single character. (Works the same as the shell abbreviation ?.)
[ ]	Matches any *one* character found in the list between the brackets; a hyphen (-) can be used to indicate a range of characters.
^	Matches beginning of line; i.e., the following pattern must begin the line.
$	Matches end of line; i.e., the preceding pattern must end the line.

Examples:

Abbreviation	Matching line	Nonmatching line
car.o	a carton of milk	carts of fish eyes
car[gt]	a cargo of gold	a tub of carp
^car[gt]	cartoon of frog	a fine cartoon
car.o$	a fresh cargo	fresh cargos

Abbreviations Used by the C-Shell History Function

The exclamation mark (!) alerts the C shell that a history reference is about to be made.

References to Complete Events

In the following, "n" stands for a numeral and "c" for a character string.

!n	The nth event
!-n	The event number which is n less than the current event number.
!c	The most recent event beginning with the string c.
!?c?	The most recent event containing the string c.

Examples:

!12	Run the twelfth event on the history list.
!-2	Run the event that is two before the preceding one.
!ca	Run the most recent command that began with "ca".
!?cow?!	Run the most recent command that contains the pattern "cow".

References to Words Within an Event:

:n	The $(n+1)$th word in the event. (Thus, **:0** is the first word, generally the name of the command, and **:1** is the second word, usually the first argument of the command.)
:^ or ^	The second word (first argument); the same as **:1**.
:$ or $	The last word in the event.
:* or *	All the words subsequent to **:0**; generally the complete argument list of the command.

These forms are used by appending them to an event reference.

Examples:

!32:3	The third argument of the thirty-second command on the history list.
!4$	The final argument of the fourth command on the history list.
cat !5* cat	The arguments of the fifth command.

Some Additional Conventions:

!!	The immediately previous event (the same as **!-1**).
!	The same as **!!**, except this form must be followed by a word identifier.

Examples: (Suppose that the last history entry is **ls /usr**):

!!/bin	means **ls /usr/bin**.
cd !$	means **cd /usr/bin**.

Shell-Script Abbreviations

These are abbreviations used by the shell.

$0	The name of the shell script.
$n	The nth argument of the shell script.
$*	The complete argument list of the shell script.

Suppose the following command has been given, where **freem** is a shell script:

freem click clack clock

Then, within the script,

$0   represents **freem**.
$2   represents **clack**.
$*   represents **click clack clock**.

A WK **Abbreviations**

Here are some more abbreviations.

$n	The nth field of a record (by default, a record is a line).
$0	The entire record.
NF	The number of fields in the current record.
NR	The ordinal number of the current record.
FILENAME	The name of the current input file.

Examples:

{print $3}	Print the third field.
{print $3/NR >> FILENAME}	Divide the contents of the third field by current line number and write the result at end of the current file.

G   UNIX Command Reference

How To Use This Summary:

1. This summary is best used as a quick reference for commands you have already used.
2. Type **boldface** text as shown.
3. Substitute your filenames for file, file2, etc.
4. Repeatable arguments are followed by ellipses (. . .).
5. Arguments in brackets [ ] are optional. Do not type in the brackets.
6. The number in parentheses ( ) following the entry refers to the page number of the command summary in the text.

Starting Up

LOGIN–sign on. (38)
PASSWD–change login password. (41)

Manipulating Files and Directories

CAT–concatenate and print. (87)
    cat [-n,-s,-v] file. . .
Options:
      -n   Numbers lines starting at 1.
      -s   Eliminates multiple, consecutive, blank lines.
      -v   Prints invisible characters.
Example:
    cat file2 displays **file2** on terminal.

CD, CHDIR–change directory. (177)
    cd
    cd directoryname
Example:
    cd /user/reggie/foods/carbo places you in the **usr/reggie/foods/carbo** directory.

CHMOD–change modes or permissions on files. (266)
    chmod ugo, + −, rwx file. . . or directory. . .

Who:

u	Login owner (user).
g	Group.
o	Other users.

Op-codes:

+	Add permission.
−	Remove permission.

Permissions:

r	Read.
w	Write.
x	Execute.

Example:

chmod o-rwx private removes read, write, and execute permissions for others from the file called **private.**

CP–make copy of files. (183)

    cp [-i] file1 file2

    cp [-i] file . . . (file, file . . . , directory)

Option:

    -i   Protects existing files.

Example:

cp flim flam makes a copy of the file **flim** and calls it **flam.**

LN–make file links. (191)

    ln file . . . file . . . or file . . . directoryname

Example:

ln hist /usr/francie links the file **hist** to the /usr/francie directory.

LPR, LPQ, and **LPRM**–use the line printer. (247)

    lpr file . . .

    lpq

    lprm file . . .

Options:

These vary from system to system.

Example:

lpr some stuff sends the files **some** and **stuff** to the printer.

lpq checks the line printer queue.

lprm data3 removes the file **data3** from printer queue.

LS–list contents of directory. (85)

    ls [-**a,c,l,m,r ,s,F,R,**+ others] directory...

Options:

-a	List all entries.
-c	List by time of file creation.
-l	List in long format.
-m	List in a stream output.
-r	Reverses the order of the listing.
-s	Gives the size in blocks.
-F	Marks directories with a "/" and executable programs with a "*".
-R	List recursively any subdirectories.

Example:

    ls -c will list contents of current directory in order of time of creation.

MKDIR–makes a new directory. (176)

    mkdir directoryname

Example:

    mkdir Chapter4 creates a new subdirectory called **chapter4** in the present directory.

MORE–views long files one screenful at a time. (88)

    more file...

Options:

    See on-line manual for many options.

MV–move or rename files. (186)

    mv [-i] filename1 filename2 or filename1 directoryname

Option:

-i	Protects existing files.

Example:

    mv gappy happy changes the name of the file **gappy** to **happy.**

RM–remove files. (180)

    rm [-**i,-r**] file...

Options:

-i	Protects existing files.
-r	Deletes a directory and every file or directory in it. (Be careful!)

Example:

    rm Rodgers removes the file **Rodgers.**

RMDIR–remove directories. (179)
    rmdir directory. . .
  Example:
    rmdir budget65 removes directory **budget65** if it does not contain any files.

REDIRECTION OPERATORS–<, >, >> (250)
  Example:
    cat listA listB >> **listC** appends the files **listA** and **listB** to the file **listC**.

PIPES– | (255)
  Example:
    cat listA listB | lpr joins two files and "pipes" the result to the line printer.

Communication

BIFF–notification of mail upon arrival. (268)
    biff [y,n]
  Example:
    biff y causes you to be notified the moment mail arrives.

FINGER–provides information about users. (53)
    finger [-m,-l,-s] name
  Options:
    -m   Search only login names.
    -l   Display long form.
    -s   Display short form.
  Example:
    finger -s John finds all users with login name of "John."

MAIL–receiving mail. (64)
    mail
  Commands:

1,2,3. . .	Reads message number 1 each time you push 1, etc.
p	Prints the first message.
d2	Deletes message number 2.
s3 filename	Appends message number 3 to filename.
q	Quits mail.

Other commands may exist on some systems

MAIL—sending mail. (63)
    mail loginname(s)
  Examples:
    mail dick bob
    (text of message here)
    [control–d]

MESG—permit or deny messages from write. (268)
    mesg [-y,-n]
  Example:
    mesg n prevents people from using **write** to interrupt you.

WRITE—write to another user. (67)
    write loginname

Housekeeping Utilities

CAL—provides a calendar. (49)
    cal [month] year
  Example:
    cal 05 1942 is the calendar for May 1942.

CALENDAR—a reminder service. (278)
    You create a file in your home directory called **calendar.** UNIX sends
    you reminders by mail.
  Example:
    Your **calendar** file might look like:
      Buy goose March 19
      call gus mar. 20 at 3 pm
      3/23 Report due

DATE—gives date and time. (47)

LOCK—reserves your terminal. (272)

PWD—prints working directory. (171)

UPTIME—checks system status. (273)

W—who is on the system and what they are doing. (273)
    w
    w [-h,-s] user

Options:

-h   Suppresses the heading.

-s   Short form.

Example:

w -hs Katie lists the user, Katie, idle time, and job name.

WHO—Who is on the system. (51)

who [am I]

Example:

who   Tells who is on the system.

On-Line Help

LEARN—computer-assisted lessons. (71)

Type **learn** to start these lessons.

MAN—find manual information by keywords. (70)

man [-k] [keyword]

Option:

-k   Produces a one-line summary.

Example:

man cat displays the on-line manual explanation of **cat.**

Text Processing and Formatting

ED—line-oriented text editor. (123)

ed file

NROFF—advanced typesetting. (338)

See Chapter 12 for details.

PR—prints partially formatted file. (249)

pr [-n,-m,-t] file. . .

Options:

-n   Arranges text into n columns.

-m   Prints all files in multiple columns.

-t   Suppresses heading on each page.

Example:

pr myths prints file **myths** on the terminal.

VI–the screen-oriented text editor. (163)
    vi file

Information Handling

AWK–pattern scanning and processing language. (342)
    See Chapter 12 and the AWK manual.

CMP–compares two files. (240)
    cmp filename1 filename2
  Example:
    cmp Janice Susan finds and prints by byte and line number the
    first difference between the two files.

COMM–finds lines common to two sorted files. (241)
    comm [-1,-2,-3] file1 file2
  Options:
    -1   Don't print the first column.
    -2   Don't print the second column.
    -3   Don't print the third column.
  Example:
    comm listA listB prints three columns. First, lines only in **listA**, secondly,
    lines only in file **listB,** and thirdly, lines in both files.

DICTION–will print wordy sentences. (341)
    diction file. . .

DIFF–finds the difference between two files or directories. (241)
    diff [-b,-e,-r] file1 file2 or directory1 directory2
  Options:
    -b   Ignores trailing blanks.
    -e   Output in the form of **ed** commands.
    -r   Apply to directories recursively.
  Example:
    diff giftlist1 giftlist2 shows how to make **giftlist1** like **giftlist2.**

FIND–finds designated files and acts upon them. (328)
    find pathname searchcriteria action(s)

Search Criteria:

-name filename	Files named "filename."
-size n	Files of size n blocks.
-links n	Files with n links.
-atime n	Files accessed n days ago.
-mtime n	Files modified n days ago.
-newer filename	Files modified more recently than the file "filename."

(Note "n" without a sign means exactly n, " + n" means greater than n, "-n" means less than n.)

Actions:

-print	Prints the pathname of the found files.
-exec command \;	Executes the given command upon finding a file; { } represents the found file.
-ok command \;	Same as **-exec,** except your approval is requested before each execution; reply with a **y.**

Example:

find /usr/bob -mtime -10 -print finds all files in usr/bob directory that have been modified within 10 days and prints pathnames.

GREP—search a file for a pattern. (323)

grep [-n,-i,-c,-w] pattern file. . .

Options:

-n	Precedes each matching line with its line number.
-i	Ignores the case of letters.
-c	Prints only a count of matching lines.
-w	Matches only complete words with the pattern.

Example:

grep -iw hop bugs searches the file **bugs** for the words "hop", "HOP", "Hop", etc.

HEAD—looks at the head of a file. (234)

head [-n] file. . .

Option:

-n	Print "n" lines.

Example:

head -15 hunter prints the first 15 lines of the file **hunter.**

SORT sorts and merges files. (237, 334)

   sort [b,-d,-f,-n ,-o,-r] file. . .

Options:

-b	Ignore initial blanks.
-d	"Dictionary" order.
-f	Ignore upper and lowercase letters.
-n	Sort numbers by value.
-o filename	Outputs to file called filename.
-r	Sort in reverse order.

Example:

   sort -fr -o sortbag grabbag sorts the file **grabbag** in reverse order, ignoring upper and lowercase letters. Results stored in **sortbag.**

SPELL—find spelling errors. (336)

   spell file. . .

TAIL—gives the last part of a file. (235)

   tail [-n] file

Options:

   -n   Start "n" lines from the end.

Example:

   tail -20 gate prints the last 20 lines of the file **gate.**

UNIQ-remove duplicated lines from file. (243)

   uniq [-u,-d,-c] inputfile [outputfile]

Options:

-u	Prints only lines with no duplicates.
-d	Prints one copy of lines with duplicates.
-c	Prints number of times line is repeated.

Example:

   uniq -d ioulist urgent scans the file **ioulist** for lines that appear more than once. One copy of each line placed in the file **urgent.**

WC—word count. (233)

   wc [-l,-w,-c,-p] file. . .

Options:

-l	Counts lines.
-w	Counts words.
-c	Counts characters.
-p	Counts pages (66 lines).

Example:

wc -w Essay counts the number of words in file **Essay.**

Running Jobs and Programs

AT—execute commands at a later time. (278)
 at time [day] [file]
Example:
  at 23 cmdlist runs the commands in the file **cmdlist** at 23 hours
(11:00 p.m.).

CC (215)
 cc [**-c,-o**] file...
Options:
  -c   Creates object file suppressing loading.
  -o filename Uses filename for file **a.out.**
Example:
  cc payroll.c compiles **payroll.c** file, with the executable program
   placed in **a.out** file

F77—compile FORTRAN programs. (218)
 f77 [**-c,-o**] file...
Options:
  -c   Creates object code file suppressing loading.
  -o filename Uses filename for **a.out.**
Example:
  f77 payroll.f compiles **payroll.f** file, with the executable code placed
   in **a.out** file

JOBS will list stopped and background jobs. (307)
 jobs [**-l**]
Option:
  -l Gives long listing that includes process identification number (PID)

KILL will terminate jobs. (308)
 kill [**-9**] job number or process ID
Option:
  -9 This is a sure kill.
Example:
  kill %3 or **kill 3492** kills Job[3] or PID #3492.

PC—compiles Pascal programs. (219)
 pc [**-c,-o**] file...

Options:

    -c   Creates object code file suppressing loading.

    -o filename   Uses filename for **a.out.**

Example:

    pc payroll.p compiles **payroll.p** file, with the executable code placed in **a.out** file

PS—the Process Status Report. (308)

    ps [a]

Options:

    a   Displays **ps** information for all terminals.

TEE—split output. (258)

    tee [-i,-a] file

Options:

    -i   Ignores interrupts.

    -a   Sends output to the end of named file.

Example:

    ls -l /usr | tee -a clutter produces the long listing of the **/usr** directory on the terminal and also appends it to the end of the file **clutter.**

TIME—will time a command. (277)

    time commandname

Example:

    time cc woo.c runs the command **cc woo.c** and prints execution time when finished.

Adjusting Your Environment

ALIAS will list aliases or make aliases. (300)

    alias

    alias abbreviation command

    unalias abbreviation

Example:

    alias list ls makes **list** equivalent to **ls**.

HISTORY prints a list of last commands given and provides abbreviations for running commands. (294)

Examples:
!! will repeat the previous command.
!5 will run event No. 5 on the history list.

.LOGIN or **.PROFILE** is your personal startup file. (279)

Graphics

GRAPH will draw a graph. (349)
    graph filename | **plot**
See Chapter 12 or the on-line manual for more details.

PLOT2D will draw a graph. (349)
    plot2d filename
See Chapter 12 or the on-line manual for more details.

H   *ed/vi* Command Reference

The *ed* Line Editor—a Quick Summary

The command for editing the file "filename" is

ed filename

If no such file exists yet, it will be created when this command is given.

Modes (pages 100 & 110)

Command Mode:	Lets you use any of the commands described in the following section.
To Enter:	You are placed in the Command Mode when you invoke **ed**. To enter the Command Mode from the Text Mode, begin a new line with a period (.) and hit the [return] key.
Text Mode:	Lets you use the keyboard to enter text.
To Enter:	Use an **a**, **i**, or **c** command.

Commands (page 104)

In general, commands consist of an address and an instruction. The address identifies the lines to be affected.

Addresses (page 105)

In the following, "n" and "k" are integers.

n	The nth line.
n,k	Lines n through k.
.	The current line.
$	The last (i.e., final) line.
+n	n lines after the current line.
−n	n lines before the current line.
$-n,$	The last n+1 lines.

Instructions (page 117)

For clarity, we will include simple forms of addresses with the instructions. Instructions shown with an address range will also accept a single address. Instructions operate on the current line if no other address is given.

n,kp	Print lines n through k.
na	Append (text is added after line n).
ni	Insert (text is inserted before line n).
n,kd	Delete lines n through k.
n,kc	Change lines n through k to new text.
n,kmj	Move lines n through k to after line j.
n,ktj	Place a copy of lines n-k after line j.
s/patl/pat2/	Replaces the first occurrence of "pat2" with "pat1" on the current line.

Searches (pages 108 & 121)

/pattern/   Causes **ed** to search for the next line containing a pattern.

A search pattern can be used in place of an address in a command. For example:

/slop/d	Delete the next line that contains "slop."
/dog/s/dog/hog/	Find the next line containing "dog" and replace the first occurrence of "dog" on that line with "hog."
/dog/s//hog/	Short form of the preceding command.

The Global Parameter *g* (page 121)

The **g** parameter, when following an **s** command, makes the substitution affect all occurrences of "pat1" in a line. When preceding an **s** command, it makes the command affect all lines. Both uses can be made in the same command:

g/house/s//home/g	Substitutes "home" for "house" everywhere in the file.

Saving Text and Quitting the Editor (pages 100 & 111)

Editing work is done in a temporary buffer and must be "written" into a file to save it.

w	Writes the current text into a permanent file.
q	Quits the editor, ignoring all changes since previous **w.**
wq	Write and quit.
q!	Emphatic form of quit.
n, kw file2	Writes lines n through k into another file.

The *vi* Screen Editor—A Quick Summary

The command for editing the file "filename" is

vi filename

If no such file exists yet, it will be created when this command is given.

Modes (page 132 & 135)

Command Mode:	Lets you use the commands described in the following section.
To Enter:	You are placed in the Command Mode when you invoke **vi.** To enter the Command Mode from the Text Mode, hit the [esc] key.
Text Mode:	Lets you use the keyboard to enter text.
To Enter:	Any of the following commands will put you in the Text Mode: **a**, **i**, **o**, **O**, **R**, and **c**.

Using *ed*-Like Commands (page 161)

While in the Command Mode, type a colon and follow it with the desired **ed**-like command; for example:

:g/dog/s//mango/g

or

:14,42w newfile

You are returned to the regular Command Mode after the **ed**-like command is executed.

401

Cursor Movement Commands (pages 134 & 145)

Vi commands take place at the cursor location. These commands help you to place the cursor where you want it to be in the text. The cursor will not move beyond the bounds of the existing text.

j	Move the cursor down one line.
k	Move the cursor up one line.
h	Move the cursor left one space.
l	Move the cursor right one space.
[control–d]	Move the screen down a half page.
[control–u]	Move the screen up a half page.
nG	Move the cursor to the nth line of file.

Text Entering Commands (page 135)

a	Appends text after cursor position.
i	Inserts text before cursor position.
o	Opens a new line below cursor position.
O	Opens a new line above cursor position.

Text Deletion Commands (page 139)

x	Deletes character under cursor.
dw	Deletes from cursor to beginning of next word.
dd	Deletes line containing cursor.
d)	Deletes rest of sentence.
d}	Deletes rest of paragraph.

These commands can be preceded by an integer to indicate the number of characters, words, etc., to be affected.

Text Alteration Commands (page 139)

All but the **r** command needs to be terminated with an [esc] after the new text is entered.

r	Replace character under cursor with next character typed.
R	Write over old text, beginning at cursor position.
cw	Change word (beginning at cursor) to new text.
c)	Change sentence (starting at cursor) to new text.

Search Commands (page 150)

/pattern	Search for next occurrence of "pattern".
?pattern	Search for preceding occurrence of "pattern".
n	Repeat the last search command given.

Text Moving Commands (also see Text Deletion Commands) (page 151)

yy	Yank a copy of a line, place it in a buffer.
p	Put after the cursor the last item yanked or deleted.
P	Put before the cursor the last item yanked or deleted.
"cY	Yank a copy of a line, place it in buffer c, where c is any letter from a to z.
"cp	Put after the cursor the contents of buffer c.

Saving Text and Quitting the Editor (page 143)

Editing work takes place in a temporary work area and must be saved by "writing" it into a permanent file.

:w	Write the current text into the permanent file.
:q	Quit, ignoring changes since last **w**.
:q!	Emphatic form of quit, use when **:q** fails.
:wq	Write and quit.
ZZ	Write and quit.
:n,kw file2	Write lines n–k into another file.
:n,kw >> file2	Append lines n–k to another file.

I   Entering and Exiting the UNIX Shell

One of the major problems facing beginning UNIX users is how to go from the shell to various utilities and how to get back to the shell again. Here are some examples:

IN	*OUT*
ed filename . . . . . . ED EDITOR . . . . wq or q
learn . . . . LEARN . . . . bye
mail . . . . MAIL–RECEIVE . . . . EOF
mail username . . . . MAIL–SEND . . . . EOF
more filename . . . . MORE . . . . interrupt key
man Command . . . ON-LINE MANUAL . . . . interrupt key
[control–z] . . . . TO SUSPEND A JOB . . . . fg
[control–s] . . . . TERMINAL OUTPUT . . . . [control–q]
login . . . . UNIX SHELL . . . . EOF or logout
vi filename . . . . . . VI EDITOR . . . . :wq or :ZZ or :q!

Use the following keys for:

Interrupt: The "interrupt" signal stops most processes. On most systems, the signal is sent by typing [control–c]. Other common choices are the [del] or [rub] keys.

EOF: The "End-Of-File" character is usually transmitted by typing [control–d].

In order to check which characters are used to control your terminal input and output, type in the UNIX command:

    stty all

You should be given a list of characters presently used to:

1. Erase character.
2. Erase line.
3. End of file.
4. Control terminal output.
5. Erase word.
6. Interrupt jobs.
7. Suspend jobs.
8. Other things.

These control characters can be changed as described in Chapter 10.

Index

TO THE READER

Sams Computer books cover Fundamentals — Programming — Interfacing — Technology written to meet the needs of computer engineers, professionals, scientists, technicians, students, educators, business owners, personal computerists and home hobbyists.

Our Tradition is to meet your needs and in so doing we invite you to tell us what your needs and interests are by completing the following:

1. I need books on the following topics:

_____
_____
_____
_____
_____
_____
_____
_____
_____

2. I have the following Sams titles:

_____
_____
_____
_____
_____
_____
_____
_____
_____

3. My occupation is:

_____ Scientist, Engineer	_____ D P Professional
_____ Personal computerist	_____ Business owner
_____ Technician, Serviceman	_____ Computer store owner
_____ Educator	_____ Home hobbyist
_____ Student	Other _____
	_____

Name (print)_____

Address_____

City _____ State _____ Zip _____

Mail to: **Howard W. Sams & Co., Inc.**
Marketing Dept. #CBS1/80
4300 W. 62nd St., P.O. Box 7092
Indianapolis, Indiana 46206

22028

Need Other Books in the Sams/Waite Primer Series?

UNIX® PRIMER PLUS
This newest of the Sams/Waite Primers presents the elements of UNIX clearly, simply, and accurately, for ready understanding by anyone in any field who needs to learn, use, or work with UNIX in some way. Fully illustrated. Includes two handy, removable summary cards. By Mitchell Waite, Donald Martin, and Stephen Prata.
Ask for No. 22028 . . . .$19.95

CP/M® PRIMER (2nd Edition)
Completely updated to give you the know-how you need to begin using and working with new or old CP/M versions immediately, in *any* application. Includes CP/M terminology, operation, capabilities, internal structure, and more, plus a convenient, tear-out reference card listing CP/M commands. By Mitchell Waite and Stephen Murtha.
Ask for No. 22170 . . . .$16.95

SOUL OF CP/M®: HOW TO USE THE HIDDEN POWER OF YOUR CP/M SYSTEM
Teaches you how to use and modify CP/M's internal features, including how to modify BIOS, use CP/M system calls in your own programs, and more! Excellent if you've read *CP/M PRIMER* or are otherwise familiar with CP/M. By Mitchell Waite and Robert Lafore.
Ask for No. 22030 . . . .$18.95

CP/M® BIBLE: THE AUTHORITATIVE REFERENCE GUIDE TO CP/M
Highly detailed, all-version CP/M reference manual that gives you instant, one-stop access to all CP/M keywords, commands, utilities, conventions, and more. A must if you use any version of CP/M. By Mitchell Waite and John Angermeyer.
Ask for No. 22015 . . . .$19.95

BASIC PROGRAMMING PRIMER (2nd Edition)
Improved, expanded edition, now usable with the IBM PC and similar computers. Features new advanced BASIC coverage, game-program listings and self-tests with answers! Highly useful, user-friendly, how-to-program material for beginners and more advanced users alike. By Mitchell Waite and Michael Pardee.
Ask for No. 22014 . . . .$17.95

PASCAL PRIMER
You'll generate powerful programs in UCSD® Pascal as this Sams powerhouse guides you through Pascal program structure, procedures, variables, decision-making statements, and numeric functions. A remarkable book that also contains eight appendixes. By Mitchell Waite and David Fox.
Ask for No. 21793 . . . .$17.95

COMPUTER GRAPHICS PRIMER
Almost every page of this Sams best-seller has a color drawing, a photograph, a picture, or a schematic that helps you learn graphics programming quickly and easily—including computer animation! Examples can be easily adapted to any computer running a version of Microsoft BASIC. By Mitchell Waite.
Ask for No. 21650 . . . .$14.95

MICROCOMPUTER PRIMER (2nd Edition)
A little more technical than the other Primers to better cover basic computer concepts, the electronics behind the logic, what happens inside the computer as a program runs, and a little about languages and operating systems. Excellent introductory material. By Mitchell Waite and Michael Pardee.
Ask for No. 21653 . . . .$14.50

YOUR OWN COMPUTER (2nd Edition)
Shows how you can go about choosing and buying a computer for your own uses. Explores applications, buzzwords, programs, hardware, and peripherals. Compares 30 different models of personal and small-business computers. By Mitchell Waite and Michael Pardee.
Ask for No. 21860 . . . .$8.95

Apple II, Apple II+, and Apple IIe are registered trademarks of Apple Computers, Inc. ● CP/M is a registered trademark of Digital Research, Inc. ● UCSD is a trademark of UC Regents, San Diego campus ● UNIX is a trademark of Bell Laboratories, Inc.

SAMS BOOK & SOFTWARE ORDER CARD

Catalog No.	Qty.	Price	Total	Catalog No.	Qty.	Price	Total

☐ Check   ☐ Money Order

☐ MasterCard   ☐ Visa

Subtotal _____

Add local tax where applicable

Add Handling Charge   2.00

Total Amount Enclosed _____

Account Number _____ Expires _____

Name (print _____

Signature _____

Address _____

City _____ State _____ Zip _____

Offer good in USA only. Prices subject to change without notice. Full payment must accompany your order. | X0438 |

Call 1-800-428-3696 for the name of your nearest Sams retailer or distributor (residents in IN, AK, HI call 317-298-5566).

If your retailer or distributor doesn't stock the Sams publication you need, you can order it through him or directly from us. Orders placed directly with us are subject to a $2.00 additional handling charge per order.

PHONE ORDERS

Depending on where you live, call either number listed above and charge your Sams publication to your VISA or MASTERCARD.

MAIL ORDERS

Use the order form below, or if it's missing, send your order on a plain piece of paper.

(1) Include your name, street or RD address, city, state, and zip.

(2) Tell us the titles of the books you need, the product numbers (see other side of this card) and the quantity of each one you'd like.

(3) Add up the total cost for the books, add your state's sales tax if applicable, and then add $2.00 for handling.

(4) Include your check or money order for the full amount due, or

(5) Charge it to your VISA or MASTER CARD. To charge it, list your account number and the card expiration date. Shipping charges will be added to credit card orders.

(6) Mail your order to:
Howard W. Sams & Co., Inc.
Dept. No. X0438
4300 West 62nd St., P.O. Box 7092
Indianapolis, Indiana 46206

In Canada, contact Lenbrook Electronics, Markham, Ontario L3R 1H2

Prices subject to change without notice. All books available from Sams distributors, bookstores, and computer stores. Offer good in U.S. only. Note: Distributor, computer store and dealer inquiries are welcome.

See other side for list of Sams/Waite Primers and their prices.

Place Stamp Here

HOWARD W. SAMS & CO., INC.

**4300 WEST 62ND STREET   P.O.BOX 7092
INDIANAPOLIS, INDIANA 46206**